LEO DAMORE

THE CAPE COD YEARS OF
JOHN FITZGERALD KENNEDY

FOUR WALLS EIGHT WINDOWS
New York / London

Copyright © 1967, 1993 by Leo Damore

Published by
FOUR WALLS EIGHT WINDOWS
P.O. Box 548, Village Station
New York, N.Y. 10014

First printing June 1993

All rights reserved.
No part of this book may be reproduced, stored in a retrieval system,
or transmitted in any form, by any means, including mechanical,
electronic, photocopying, recording, or otherwise, without the prior
written permission of the publisher.

Library of Congress Cataloging-in-Publication Data

The Cape Cod Years of John Fitzgerald Kennedy
by Leo Damore
p. ; cm.
ISBN 0-941423-81-6
$12.95
1. Kennedy, John F. (John Fitzgerald), 1917-1963—
Homes and haunts—Massachusetts—Cape Cod.
2. Cape Cod (Mass.)
3. Presidents—United States—Biography. 1. Title.
E842.D3   1993
973.922'092—dc20
[B]   93-20153
CIP

AUTHOR'S PREFACE TO THE NEW EDITION

Cape Cod has always meant something special to the Kennedys—in particular, young Jack. At Hyannis Port the Kennedy family gathered in summer for an annual reunion where, more than in any other place, the clan tradition began and flourished. Here were spent carefree days rigging a sailboat, running the wind racing the *Victura* on sparkling harbor waters where later the *Marlin* cruised for three Presidential summers. These were golden days that began a unique relationship between a youth destined to be President, and a quiet piece of New England he loved as boy and man.

Hyannis Port is quieter now than it was when John Kennedy was President. On Irving Avenue, where he once leaned across the rose bushes to greet well-wishers as a candidate, and where he awaited election returns, the President's house stands empty. "President Kennedy giving his acceptance speech at the Armory in Hyannis constitutes undoubtedly the most significant and dramatic historic event ever to occur on Cape Cod," proclaimed the Town of Barnstable Annual Report for 1960. "Nothing to approach it is likely to happen again."

This year marks the 30th anniversary of John Kennedy's assassination. It seems a most appropriate time to remember, not the tragedy of his death, but the glorious years of his life lived and shared on Cape Cod.

Although a memorial stone wall, rotunda and reflecting pool stands in his memory in Hyannis, the real monument John Kennedy left behind is the Cape Cod National Seashore Park, created by legislation he sponsored as a testament to his love for this place.

The Cape Cod Jack Kennedy loved still endures—if one can overlook the congestion of summer traffic, and an invasion of condominiums and shopping malls. The same sea-washed sunlight still bleaches to weathered grey the cedar shingles of "tidy and shipshape" cottages; and long stretches of abandoned beaches can yet be found, along with the stillness of salt marshes and bog. It is an eternal landscape as enduring as the spirit of John Kennedy this book invokes, not as elegy but in celebration of a time, a place, and a president.

Old Saybrook, CT
March 1993

AUTHOR'S NOTE

If a man's roots can exist on a seasonal basis, then it can be said that John F. Kennedy's existed on Cape Cod—first at his father's house at Hyannis Port, and later at his own house on Irving Avenue.

Jack Kennedy considered himself a Cape Codder, although he did not need to be reminded that his identification with the Cape was not acknowledged by all. Most Cape Codders quickly dismiss Hyannis Port as being too precious and specialized a part-time summer colony to be ever taken seriously in an account of one's heritage. And Hyannis Port itself placed arbitrary designations of its own in order to separate those who "belonged" from those who did not. Jack Kennedy liked to tell of the time his father attended a meeting of Hyannis Port's Civic Association in 1951 and, after listening attentively to the discussion, had been finally recognized by the chairman:

> "My father had spoken only about 30 seconds when a lady who had been a resident for at least 70 years stood up. She interrupted to tell the chairman she had not come to listen to that 'Johnny-come-lately' make a speech, then she stomped out. Of course, we had only lived in Hyannis Port for 25 years."

John F. Kennedy passed almost 40 summers at Hyannis Port, but by 1963 it was growing evident that his seasonal days as a part-time Cape Codder were drawing to an end.

Virtually evicted from his own unprepossessing house on Irving Avenue by his clamoring constituents and the demands of security in such close quarters, Kennedy twice sought the refuge of rented houses on close-by Squaw Island.

Increasingly cut off from the village where, in years past, he had recouped his energies with casual ease, Kennedy could not help but be dismayed by the spectacle of his neighbors joined in public protest against his summer residency. In more ways than one Hyannis Port was too small to contain a President of the United States. And while it wasn't very dignified for a Chief Executive to have to apologize for his continued presence, Kennedy's impeccable manners did not fail him: He often personally telephoned Hyannis Port Golf

Club's pro Tom Niblet to ask if "it was all right to play a few rounds."

By the fall of 1963 arrangements had been made to transfer the summer White House to a Newport estate adjacent to Hammersmith Farm. Despite public assurances that Kennedy would resume his Cape Cod excursions the following June, no place of residence had been specifically set aside for his use during the anticipated summer of 1964.

But there was not to be a presidential summer of 1964 at Hyannis Port or Newport.

On July 8, 1966, a $60,000 memorial to John F. Kennedy was dedicated in a corner of Hyannis' Veterans Park overlooking a spacious but uninteresting view of Lewis Bay. The memorial consisted of a large wall of native fieldstone split down the middle by a panel of green Vermont marble on which had been affixed a bronze medallion of John F. Kennedy's profile looking westward toward Hyannis Port. Even before the memorial was officially dedicated its circular pool, with a lighted bubbler resembling Arlington's eternal flame, was turned into a "wishing well" by well-meaning pilgrims. More than $2,000 had been flung into the pool by the end of 1966.

It is in its off-season, however, that Hyannis Port affords a singular tribute to John F. Kennedy—an inadvertent memorial:

With the coming of a late afternoon's dusk, floodlights brilliantly illuminating John F. Kennedy's house on Irving Avenue are turned on and a guard hired to protect the property from vandals or souvenir seekers takes his place to supervise the former summer White House until dawn. It seems particularly fitting that in Hyannis Port's off-season, John F. Kennedy's light still shines.

This book should not in any way be regarded as a work written by one with an "insider's" view. Nor is it an "authorized" work, written under the aegis of the Kennedy family.

Many of the close to 200 individuals consulted in connection with this book requested that they remain anonymous. I acknowledge the large debt I owe them collectively.

I wish particularly to express my appreciation to "Pete" Williams, editor of the Barnstable *Patriot* for the invaluable assistance he gave me during my earliest researches. He, along with Dick Haskins and Barbara Williams, among others at the *Patriot's* offices, made the several weeks I spent with them among my pleasantest experiences while at work on this book.

I appreciated also the courtesy with which I was received by J. Richard Early, editor of the New Bedford *Standard-Times*, and his associates James Besse, Milton Silvia and librarian Maurice Lauzon. (Milton Cole, managing editor of the Cape Cod *Standard-Times* granted me uninterrupted use of that newspaper's library.)

I wish to thank Selectman E. Thomas Murphy and former Chairman of Selectmen Victor Adamas, as well as Robert O'Neil and Mr. and Mrs. Larry Newman of Hyannis Port; Fred Caouette, Alfred A. Dumont, Jeanne Clement, Tommy Rodericks, James Woodward, George W. Walsh, Sophia and Nicholas Joakim, Gordon Caldwell, Zilpha Anderson, Germon Reavis and Robert Owens of Hyannis; and John Linehan, Wilbert Crosby, Jr. and Chester Crosby of Osterville.

Also, the Rev. Kenneth Warren of Barnstable and Rev. Edward C. Duffy of New Bedford; and Mr. and Mrs. Walter Stevenson of Falmouth.

A valuable contribution was made to this book by Mrs. Ann Laird of Lexington and Mrs. Rosamund Fuller of Wianno; Sgt. John Kates, NCO in charge of Otis Base Hospital public relations, and former Sgt. John German (retired) of the Sippican *Sentinel*, Mattapoisett; Ida Mae Anderson of Cotuit's Public Library, Wes Stidstone, of radio station WOCB in West Yarmouth, Otto K. Hoffman of West Barnstable; Dorris Weber and Alice W. Peak of Barnstable, and Robert "Red" Ryan of Cummaquid.

I owe a particular debt to those photographers and collectors who allowed pictures to be borrowed for use in this book: "Pete" Williams, George Walsh and Harold Cobb of Hyannis, Larry Newman of Hyannis Port, Donald Doane of Brewster, Chick Craig of East Dennis, Ken Ilg and Charles Spooner of Falmouth and Julius Lazarus of New York. (Bradford Brayton of Falmouth processed many of the photographs reproduced in this book.)

I owe, as well, a personal debt of gratitude, accumulated during the time this book was being researched and written, to Eleanor Malchman Smith of Falmouth.

And I wish to thank my wife, who was of incalculable help in arranging interviews during which I was the beneficiary of her skilled telephone diplomacy (persuading often unenthusiastic Cape Codders to agree to talk with me), notwithstanding that she was otherwise occupied with her own busy schedule and two excessively active children.

There would not have been a book but for Shirley Fisher of McIntosh and Otis, Inc. And fortunate, indeed, is the author whose manuscript has the benefit of such intelligence and care as has been given to mine by its Publisher.

Falmouth, Massachusetts

To Patricia
and Jean
and Jennifer Kuen
wonderful hosts

For
Nicholas

Best wishes

Leo Damore

nov. 18, 1993

CONTENTS

Prelude

HYANNIS PORT

It was a wilderness once, lusher, more verdant than now. A place where nature had exercised all her prerogatives, where bearberry carpeted the hillside and moor with a springy mat of waxen leaves and wild lupin and eglantine blossomed in untended masses under the juniper, holly and birch.

Even the dunes were green. Pale beach grass grew more than two feet tall beside the goldenrod and spurge; and lichens crept over rock and spent seaweed down to the water's edge.

In summer the top of Sunset Hill was occupied, not by the neo-Gothic gargoyles of St. Andrew's-by-the-Sea [1] (Episcopal), where God is worshipped only "in season," but by a colony of wigwams tended by the squaws of the Cummaquids—Hyannis Port's first summer residents—a small, docile tribe of Mattakeset Indians, whose domain centered in the village of Mattakeese on Cape Cod's north shore.

By custom owners of lands to the south, the sachems of the Cummaquids traditionally passed summers at Hyannis Port, journeying the four miles of narrow, crooked foot trails that cut through

1

forests overgrown with horse brier and dogwood and linked the north shore with the warmer waters of the southern sea.

Here on Sunset Hill, where a meandering creek provided fresh water close to their encampment—and where golfers now ply the well-tended greens of the Hyannis Port golf club—the Indians enjoyed a vast, unblemished view of the meadowlands and marshes below. Beyond the dark, irregular contour of Squaw Island, thick with giant white cedars and seething with shore birds, the ocean spread out majestically toward the horizon while the natural harbor swept around in an uneven arc. There the sachems and their entourages bathed in the warm shore waters, where sanderlings fed at the edge of the surf, and fished the harbor and abundant fresh water ponds close by. Deer, partridge and great quantities of waterfowl provided food and good sport in the surrounding forest and marsh not far from the ocean's edge.

Hyannis Port provided the Cummaquid with a veritable summer paradise, but it was not unlike their "home place" at Mattakeese, where, after the summer journey, the Indians enjoyed a degree of comfort and affluence that went far to mitigate their savage nature.

The naturally gregarious Indians lived in close settlements: "Behind the screen of pines and oaks were clearings dotted with Indian dwellings connected by well-worn paths with other groups of villages . . . no chance camping places but fixed abodes inhabited by generations of natives." * The wigwam was set aside, in preference for round, arbor-like huts made of young saplings bent over, with both ends stuck into the ground, then covered inside and out with thick mattings of sedge and bulrush and decorated with hart's horn and porcupine quills.

The Indians were experienced agriculturalists; they had long cultivated the cleared, fertile fields beyond the great salt marshes, scratching at the earth with sharpened clam shells and, when necessary, spreading herring for fertilizer. A plenitude of rain increased the harvest of beans and pumpkins, as well as of the Indian staple, corn,' which was stored for winter safekeeping in baskets under four feet of mounded sand.

The Indians need not have relied only on the fruits of their squaw's labors in the fields to provide them with sustenance, however, for the waters of the ocean yielded up bountiful harvests of herring, mackerel

* Henry C. Kittredge, *Cape Cod—Its People and Their History* (Cambridge: Houghton Mifflin Company, 1930).

and cod. Often a blackfish or drift whale, misjudging the tide, would be beached on the harbor flats. The tribe held its lobster, oyster and clam feasts on a long finger of duneland across the harbor, which is now called "Sandy Neck." Wild geese, duck and snipe populated the adjacent marshes, and the surrounding forests' tangle hid wild plums, huckleberries, walnuts and strawberries, as well as a profusion of wild flowers. Dill, samphire, wild mustard, mushrooms, yellow gentian, and the bark of the sassafras tree provided not only a rude pharmacopoeia but the beginning of a native cuisine as well.

It is said that the Indians took the first ship they saw for a walking island, "the masts to be trees, the sails white clouds and the discharge of ordnance lightning and thunder; but this thunder being over and this moving island steadied with an anchor they manned their canoes to go and pick strawberries there." * But by the time Bartholomew Gosnold arrived on May 14, 1603, the Indians were sufficiently accustomed to visiting ships to welcome him offshore in a shallop of European origin, in which one Indian was dressed in European clothing evidently salvaged from some shipwreck on the coast.

Coming to anchor near a great quantity of codfish, Gosnold was inspired to call the place "Cape Cod," a name disapproved of by King James, who changed it, not unsurprisingly, to "Cape James." ("Cape Cod," Cotton Mather said later, "is a name which it will never lose till shoals of codfish be seen swimming on its highest hills.")

Gosnold's relations with the Indians were most cordial. A feast of broiled fish with mustard and corn cakes was prepared in his honor, and he was impressed, not only by the Indians' genuine friendliness and hospitality, but also by the beauty and bounty of the landscape. Returning to England, Gosnold tirelessly advocated the colonization of Cape Cod.

A plague in 1617 greatly depopulated Indian settlements on Cape Cod, soon to be so quickly outnumbered by the swelling tide of colonization signaled by the *Mayflower's* departure from Plymouth on September 16, 1620. The Pilgrims paused for only a brief time on the Cape. It was long enough, however, to sign the Mayflower Compact, in Provincetown's harbor on November 11. The signatories submitted themselves voluntarily to a government, entrusting all power to the majority.

While needed repairs were made to the *Mayflower*, an exploring

* Frederick Freeman, The History of Cape Cod, Annals of the Thirteen Towns of Barnstable, Volume 1 (Boston: W. H. Piper and Company, 1869), p. 103.

party was sent inland to find fresh water. Coming upon an Indian graveyard, the colonists ransacked the sepulchers, taking whatever trinkets and mementos of native craftsmanship that appealed to them. And, discovering a store of Indian corn at Truro, they stole as much of it as they could carry. Later they exchanged musket fire for arrows during the so-called "first encounter" at Eastham and returned to the *Mayflower*, "delivering our corn into store to be kept for seed, purposing to make satisfaction should we meet with any of the inhabitants of that place." *

The Indians did receive satisfaction in small measure at the hands of the colonists conveniently located across Cape Cod Bay at Plymouth. The frequent contacts established with the natives were of great benefit to the white settlers, particularly when it became necessary to draw upon Indian granaries to stave off starvation.

In 1621 nine sachems of Cape Cod subscribed to an instrument of submission to King James. The first mention of the famed Mattakeset sachem, Iyanough of Cummaquid, is made in colonial records in connection with the search for the wandering colonist, 18-year-old John Billington. Landing at Cummaquid harbor, the search party sent out from Plymouth was brought to Iyanough, "a man very personable, gentle, courteous and fair-conditioned—about twenty-six years of age—indeed, not a savage, save in his attire." **

Using his good offices, Iyanough located the boy, safe with the Nausets at Eastham, who delivered him up without incident. A festival of singing and dancing celebrated the return to Mattakeese, and, before the search party's departure, Iyanough personally filled the colonists' rundlets with fresh water and, at the last, took a bracelet from his own neck and placed it on the leader of the party to signify his friendship.

But relations between Indians and colonists were not destined to remain so cordial. Seizing the pretext of a rumored incipient Indian rebellion, Miles Standish of the Plymouth Colony killed four Indians at Weymouth, and another Pilgrim party murdered two others. News of the massacre sent Iyanough and many Cape Cod Indians into hiding in a swamp, where few survived a "pestilence."

Cape Cod was annexed by the Plymouth Colony in 1630, but already a trickle of colonization had begun, purchases of land from

* Freeman, *op. cit.*, p. 74.
** Freeman, *op. cit.*, pp. 96–97.

the Indians having been recorded as early as 1623. By 1639 enough of a settlement had been established so that Mattakeese had become Barnstable,³ acquiring its new name even before it became officially a town on September 3, 1639.

When John Lathrop shepherded his flock from Scituate in October of 1639, swelling the population of white settlers to more than two hundred, a dozen thatched-roof houses were already in evidence in Barnstable. The newcomers, attracted by a harbor flourishing with fish at high tide and at low tide covered with clam flats, were most particularly impressed by the magnificent stretch of salt marsh—"Hay Grounds," as they were called—which offered unlimited free pasturage for the profitable raising of cattle and sheep, which brought high prices in the colonies.

The church wielded enormous power at first, abetted by the General Court, which in 1651 decreed that, "if any lazy, slothful, or profane persons in any of the towns neglect to attend public worship they shall pay for each offence ten shillings or be publicly whipped."

Excommunication for "carnall carriages" and "too much jeering" were commonplace, and men were set in the stocks "for ribaldry." Citizenship was limited to church members. Discipline was a simple matter, as long as the church was supported by the local magistracy, but, as the electorate became more independent, the pastor's difficulties increased. Although the settlers were devoted churchmen, they were prone to differ on interpretation of the Bible, although all accepted it as the word of God. "Lethargy and contention" were said to be diseases of colonial times.

Most of the colonists had not come to America for freedom of worship alone.⁴ All wished to improve their worldly condition as well, and ownership of land provided the strongest lure for men from a country where the landlord was ubiquitous and where for centuries kings and aristocrats had claimed the deer-filled forests as their private hunting preserves.

Beginning in 1641, Barnstable expanded its land purchases to accommodate a burgeoning population, with new settlers arriving from Saugus, Weymouth and even the Plymouth Colony itself. Common lands were divided and distributed by lot, a problem that "divided the wise and perplexed the good."

The prices paid for vast tracts of land were minimal: four coats, two axes, brass kettles, a broad hoe or a day's ploughing. The colonials

5

paid whatever they could pay, and the Indians accepted it. The Indians cared little for land ownership, as long as they retained the right to hunt and fish over it and to hold small plots for their own corn.

Although at first the Indians lived amicably side by side with their new neighbors, marveling at the plow's "magic" and the windmill's efficiency, they soon began to feel the burden of white men's law. By 1673 Indians were worked for debt, drunken ones fined and publicly whipped and indigent ones bound out to labor and compelled to pay fourfold for theft.

The sachem Nepoyetum succeeded Iyanough in Mattakeese during the land purchases on the north shore; on the south shore a second Iyanough (but spelled "Yanno"), most likely Iyanough's son, in 1646 conveyed lands encompassing what is now Hyannis, Hyannis Port, Craigville and Centerville. The deed, dated July 19, 1664, was negotiated by Thomas Hinckley, later to be elected governor. "Consideration" paid was £20 and two small pairs of breeches.

In 1666 Nicholas Davis built a warehouse and trading station in Hyannis on Lewis Bay, persuading Yanno to make him a gift of the land. The town fathers, however, exacted 10 shillings from him toward what the town had already paid Yanno two years before for all his land. Davis, the first white settler on the southern sea did a good, if lonely, business shipping oysters pickled in brine and packed in kegs to New York and colonial ports on Long Island Sound, in exchange for goods.

By the end of the century a dozen families who preferred oystering to agriculture had moved across-Cape, and settlement of the south shore began in earnest when the division of common lands in 1697 precipitated a large-scale migration from the north. Despite the enormous problems and bitter controversy such distribution aroused, final division of all Barnstable common lands was completed by 1703. Encouraged by Barnstable's example, the rest of Cape Cod divided its common lands during the succeeding twelve years. By 1715 such property had gone out of existence.

Cape Codders were not sailors or fishermen by inclination or heredity; they were farmers and herdsmen until well past 1700. Few ventured on the sea without acute consciousness of its perils; enough had perished in the bay on packet trips to Boston because of rough seas, poor ship construction or bad seamanship to remind the prudent man in the field that he was better off where he was.

But farming held no challenge or appeal for younger generations born with the familiar sound of the sea in their ears. To them the watery playground of their childhood was a natural place, as familiar as the salt-tanged air they breathed. At first, tentative trips out into Cape Cod Bay and Nantucket Sound to hand-line for cod proved not only agreeable diversion but good business as well. As more and more men began to follow the sea rather than the dull oxen in the field— and return to shore safe and sound and with good profits in hand as well—the old fears dwindled away. As shipbuilding flourished, agriculture lost ground, and, as much of the forest disappeared, the productivity of the land decreased proportionately.

When Plymouth, never much of a seafaring town, decided to farm out its fishing rights, young men of Cape Cod were ready to go. But the rise of a fishing industry was seriously hampered by the American Revolution, which forced every fisherman, West Indian trader and whaleman ashore and kept him there for the war's duration.

The British established a naval base in Provincetown's harbor and cruised both sides of Cape Cod's unprotected shore line unmolested, doing little actual damage but keeping residents in a constant state of anxious expectation. "There is scarcely a day that the enemy is not within gunshot of some part of our coast," an observer noted, "and they very often anchor in our harbors."

Although no major skirmish was fought on Cape Cod soil, the battle lines were nonetheless drawn among the citizenry in every community: The Tories remained loyal to England and the King; the Patriots were on the side of the Revolution. Constant requisitions— for men and supplies, particularly beef—reduced bands of home guardsmen to a minimum, and by 1782 Cape Codders were on such short rations themselves that they could no longer send more supplies to aid the Revolutionary Army.

When the war ended and the seas were again open, Cape Codders found themselves with sloops and schooners that had warped and shrunk beyond repair during the seven-year hiatus on the beach. Indifferent to a possible resurgence of agriculture, the Cape instead set about rebuilding its fishing fleet with financial support from Boston investors.

The postwar rise of a fishing industry brought with it the need for salt. Soon the south shore was covered with wharves, shipyards and salt works redolent of hemp and drying salt cod. In 1802 Lot Crocker came over from Barnstable village—or "high Barnstable"—to build

7

the first salt works on a broad flatland west of Squaw Island in Hyannis Port. Lot Hinckley followed, bringing his salt works with him in sections and reconstructing it along South Hyannis harbor adjacent to Hyannis Port. Others spread out on the plains below Sunset Hill, and salt works were still in existence in Hyannis Port as late as 1856.

In 1830 the *Nantucket Inquirer* gave an account of an excursion aboard the steamer *Marco Bozzaris*, which carried more than two hundred passengers across the Sound in three hours, stopping briefly at Hyannis Port. The village of Hyannis Port was described in glowing terms. Only a dozen houses existed, and, although only two of them were large and elegant, the others nevertheless struck the sightseers as exhibiting "much neatness and looked like abodes of contentment and competence."

"Abodes of contentment" they were, indeed: neat shingles bleached gray by salt spray and wind, frames in the familiar steep-roofed Cape Cod style, each with its own garden of larkspur and hollyhock and the inevitable scarlet rambler roses leaning over the pickets. Inside each, on the crane over the firedogs, hung pothooks, hangers, skillets, skewers and a spit. A large turkey wing leaned against the brickwork to sweep the hearth clean, and from the deep brick oven came brown bread and baked beans every Saturday night. On Fast Day—proclaimed by the governor—all the villagers went to meeting and ate salt codfish and dried-apple pie. And, while children played leapfrog or "I Spy," sailed decoy ducks and gathered white huckleberries, the big girls made tape trimming or tatting as they waited for beaux on the side piazzas. The Boston *Weekly Journal* and *Christian Register* were read by lamps lit by lard oil and camphene.

In 1849 Thoreau made the first of four journeys to Cape Cod. His articles later published in *Putnam's Weekly* extolled the unspoiled seascapes that he had seen and drew attention to an area that up to that time had been isolated and much neglected.

Dark days were presaged when, after the Civil War, maritime fortunes on Cape Cod rapidly began to decline, hastened by the railroad's approach to Sandwich in 1840, replacing the stagecoach and packet. By 1873 the rails had progressed to Hyannis, creating an avenue of communications as well as transportation with the rest of the commonwealth and bringing better supplies of food and goods— and, most important of all, quantities of vacationers—to Cape Cod for the first time.

By 1871 the Hyannis Land Company had been formed; it acquired some forty parcels of land, including most of Hyannis Port—an area of approximately one thousand acres—for around $100,000. The spring and summer of 1872 witnessed the staking out of streets, the plotting of lots and the publication of an elaborate prospectus. The only hotel in the village, renamed "Iyanough House," was used as headquarters, and it was from there that large parties from Boston, Springfield and Worcester were sent out in carriages to choose their lots along the seashore. During its first year, the company erected more than a dozen cottages, and the new colony was well launched. The Hyannis *Patriot* celebrated the event by proclaiming: "The dream of many is realized. Hyannis is to be a place of summer resort for the crowded denizens of the city."

By 1873 natives could scarcely recognize Hyannis Port because of its "beautiful, neatly laid-out avenues, a new three-story mansard roof hotel [Hallett House] and fairy-like cottages" with piazzas, lookout towers and lantern cupolas. Hyannis Port had also suffered the fate of many latter-day real-estate developments: A photograph taken in 1873 shows scarcely a tree, and mention is made of Hyannis Port's "barren hills."

The first building boom lasted until 1879, when the Hyannis Land Company went bankrupt and its holdings were broken up. After a lapse in activity in the 1880s, another boom filled the village with houses, and by the 1890s Hyannis Port had achieved its cachet of swank. A modest Cape Cod house halfway up Sunset Hill fetched $1,000 for a season's rental. The harbor was thick with sailing yachts, the clean sand beaches thronged with bathers and croquet was played on the pine needles. Tall windmills for pumping water sprouted on the landscape, with the letters "IXL," the manufacturer's initials, prominently displayed on the blades of the wheels.

In 1908 forty stockholders subscribed $25,000, the original and only capital to establish Hyannis Port's golf club; they purchased the site of the former Marchant estate from a Pittsburgh syndicate that had controlled much of the property for speculative purposes.

While Hyannis Port blossomed, development of the rest of Cape Cod lagged far behind. "It seemed like the last outpost of civilization in those days. The roads were terrible, of course, it wasn't until after the turn of the century they surfaced over the sand and started oiling them—they used to have poles alongside Main Street in Hyannis to guide the horse and buggies, the streets were so rutted."

9

On November 13, 1872, a deed had been drawn in Barnstable Court, in which Frederick Scudder of Barnstable "in consideration of two hundred and fifty dollars" sold "a certain piece or parcel of lands situated at Hyannis Port" to Eliza F. Prince.

In May 1903, the property now known as the "Prince Cottage" was conveyed to Emily E. Whelden, who, the following August, "in consideration of one dollar and other goods and valuable considerations" sold the land "together with the cottage" to Beulah A.B. Malcolm of Nutley, New Jersey.

Also in 1903 the "Prince Cottage" was resold by Beulah Malcolm to Colonel J. L. Hallett and moved to a lot adjoining his house. Contracts were placed with L. Frank Paine for a new cottage to be built upon the original site. By January 1904 work was progressing on the new Malcolm cottage, despite the bitter cold and an acute shortage of carpenters. By July the Malcolms were occupying their new cottage. Additional land adjacent to the property was purchased from Elisha G. Scudder of St. Louis in 1907. In the spring of 1926, the Malcolm cottage was rented for the first time to Joseph Patrick Kennedy of Boston, his beautiful wife and their seven children.

Part One

SUMMERS AT HYANNIS PORT
1926–1944

One

*. . . social affairs are now in full swing and the
season has been launched with a bang. Things are
running along swimmingly and everybody is
happy. No troubles, no nothin', except to make
whoopee and pursue dalliance.—"Hyannis Port
Society Notes" in the Hyannis* Patriot, *July 11,
1929*

A new "boosterism" was infecting Cape Cod in the 1920s; many
strident voices were raised to proclaim the glittering prospects for
future development. In the fall of 1924, one editorialist lamented:

> "Cape Cod, somehow, has been missed by the professional promotors.
> Some day there will come a realization of the opportunities which the
> region presents for the large real estate operator and then will begin a
> boom that will mean the building up of the Cape through lavish ex-
> penditures to cater to the whims and fancies of those who seek rest and
> recreation and who demand all that goes to make modern pleasure
> seekers happy.

Eyes turned enviously southward; many felt that Florida's land
boom[1] had set Cape Cod's development as a summer resort back
twenty years. *The Cape Cod Magazine* predicted, "A few professional
developers such as have been successful elsewhere, could transform
Cape Cod into a second Florida within two or three years time,"
adding that Cape Cod afforded even better natural facilities then did
Florida, as well as a "locale and a climate attractive to thousands who
only need the proper kind of inducement."

"We hope that the Cape has within its people the spirit that has
made other localities grow," another booster added a year later, "the
spirit that has built our Miami, our Los Angeles and our Atlantic

13

City, none of which have any better reason for their growth and popularity than has Cape Cod."

"The proper kind of inducement" apparently had not been found to persuade President Calvin Coolidge to spend his summer vacation on Cape Cod in 1926, despite the invitation tendered by two native fishermen, who appeared at the White House appropriately costumed and bearing gifts of Cotuit oysters and Chatham quahogs. Sponsored by "real estate interests," the invitation failed to produce more than a photograph taken on the White House lawn, "which gave Cape realtors the publicity they desired."

Boosters on Cape Cod were only too aware of the importance of publicity. In 1926 Craigville was being touted as the "fourth best bathing beach in the world," and the Chamber of Commerce was distributing seals carrying an outline of Cape Cod on a blue ground, with the slogans "Come to Cape Cod" and "We Face Four Seas." People were urged to place seals on the backs of letters and parcels in order better to advertise the attractions of Cape Cod.

By 1926 it was growing apparent that some had, indeed, listened to the boosters' siren call. Promoters and real-estate speculators were swarming over Cape Cod—to the vocal consternation of older businessmen in Hyannis—with a great variety of ventures, ranging from the manufacture of imitation pearls from "essence" of fish scales to the development of Grand Island, across Cotuit harbor, as an exclusive summer colony to be called "Oyster Harbors."

The Queen's Buyway—"A unique summer shopping center without an equal in America"—a deliberately picturesque plaza of some 26 summer shops that included a lighthouse and a windmill in its design was ready for occupancy in Hyannis' West End. And in an adjacent soigné French Tudor-style business block, O. H. Wetherill played the $10,000 Hook and Hastings orchestral organ at the new Hyannis Theater while John Gilbert silently ravished Greta Garbo in *Flesh and the Devil*. (When, however, notice was given that selectmen had issued a permit allowing the theater to show films on Sunday, the ensuing furor among those "who believed in protecting the Sabbath" forced withdrawal of the permit.)

Some Cape Codders, unhappy at the prospect of seeing Cape Cod turned into another Miami, Los Angeles or Atlantic City, hoped that the summer people and tourists would eventually go the way of the salt works and the packet coasters and turned their backs on the boom to cultivate the cranberry crop. Others found the prevailing euphoria difficult to resist. Business *was* booming. The impact of the automobile had far surpassed the earlier impact of the railroad. Selectmen were meeting for the first time to discuss serious new traffic and parking problems, for the number of Oaklands, Reo Flying Clouds and Graham-Paiges crowding the highways to Cape Cod was increasing every year. The report, in August 1926, that two men, working in shifts, had counted 16,258 motor vehicles passing the intersection of Barnstable Road, Main Street and Ocean Street in thirteen hours—breaking all previous records—could do nothing but buoy the spirits of those who were coming more and more to depend on a summer economy. And no one loved statistics more than those who manned the boosters' omnipresent propaganda mills.

But another form of free enterprise was occupying some people in 1926: Cape Cod during Prohibition was a peninsula literally surrounded by alcohol. Fishermen, sailing to rendezvous in waters beyond territorial limits, found liquor an incontestably more profitable catch than lobster or whiting. A well-financed syndicate out of Boston took over an imposing Victorian summer mansion on the South Hyannis shore—a widow's walk provided the ideal place to flash a beacon to offshore boats. The enterprising moonlighter in his dory rowed supplies of liquor from larger boats stationed outside the harbor to some well-protected cove and found the large profits in bootlegging well worth the risks.

Liquor was frequently cached in unoccupied summer houses—although the owners sometimes happened down to the Cape unexpectedly early. Occasionally cases of bootleg liquor hurriedly dumped overboard at the approach of the Coast Guard were washed up on the beach at high tide—and were immediately impounded by dry enforcement officers.

In June 1926 a novel sight could be witnessed in Horace P. Baxter's field near the Hyannis–West Yarmouth line: the largest meeting of the Ku Klux Klan * ever held on Cape Cod. Estimates placed the crowd at six thousand and a band furnished appropriate musical background while two hundred new members were initiated.

More wholesome pastimes were avilable, however, to summer

---

* The Klan rose to some influence on Cape Cod immediately after the Civil War, when it is alleged that a cross was burned on the top of Sunset Hill in Hyannis Port during a rally. Many prominent local men had associations with the Klan during its later heydey in the 1920s and 1930s, but soon afterward the organization dropped out of sight and entirely ceased to exist. There is, at present, no Klan activity on Cape Cod.

pleasure seekers. Joe Rines' Sun Kist Orioles played for "well supervised" dancing every Wednesday and Saturday night beginning the last Saturday in June at Mill Hill's Sun Kist Gardens. The Bournehurst, on the banks of the Cape Cod Canal, provided more opulent settings for Paul Whiteman, Vincent Lopez and the B. F. Goodrich Silvertown Orchestra, featuring the Silvertown Masked Tenor. Dancers could watch, from the ballroom's lanterned terrace as the New York boat steamed through the canal's narrow channel.

Strawberry festivals, clambakes and quilting pageants vied with such imported attractions as the softball game between the House of David Team and a team of Hyannis All-Stars and the annual visit of Downie Brothers' Big Three Ring Animal Circus, Museum and Menagerie. Cape Cod's summer repertory theaters presented well-known Broadway stars, and one could follow the adventures of Rin Tin Tin, the Dog Hero, or admire Gloria Swanson's *sang froid* in *Madame Sans Gêne* at the Idlehour, Hyannis' year-round movie theater.

Vacationists arriving daily at the Hyannis depot in the East End encountered a still-charming New England village, where arching elm and maple branch dappled Main Street with patches of sunlight. A public library was ensconced in a former sea captain's house, and many private homes were still in existence beyond the year-round business center. A boundary of trees and woodland—a natural park that eventually would give way to progress in the form of a shopping plaza—separated the West End's exclusive summer shops, many of them branches of smart Boston, New York and Palm Beach stores, from the town's center.

Turning off Main Street and proceeding south on Sea Street—later to be inaccurately described as "Depression-proof"—a long row of summer rooming houses displayed their "Vacancy" signs until one reached the edge of the harbor and an area once called "South Hyannis," a separate small colony of large summer houses facing Nantucket Sound.

There the road veered westward as it met the flatlands bordering the harbor. Where the vista of space and sea opened out from the sandy beach and a small causeway crossed over a narrow pocket of marsh that had crept inland, the atmosphere abruptly changed. Quiet settled. The roadside was empty of pedestrians, and the sour-spicey smell of the sea contributed to an air of expectancy.

16

One entered Hyannis Port at the next left turn, before the road took a sharp right curve to face the jutting pier and the glittering waters of the harbor laced with the feathery sails of boats. One had the feeling there of absolute order and of a prim seemliness beneath the village's proper air of tidy gaiety that contrasted markedly with the slap-dash pace of booming Hyannis, a mere two miles away.

The windmills were gone and with them any mementos of the salt works, the shipyards and the village's long maritime past. Few natives were left; they had been replaced by considerable colonies from Pittsburgh, Cleveland, Chicago and St. Louis—and one family that traveled from Biloxi, Mississippi, by private railroad car.

Eschewing simple Cape Cod architecture, Hyannis Port had rapidly filled up with elaborate summer houses, usually large and frequently homely places that made up in size what they lacked in style. Most had been built during the height of Hyannis Port's own building boom during and after the turn of the century, when such great eastern resorts as Newport, Bar Harbor and Southampton were turning away "the Pittsburgh steeler, the big butter and egg man, the mining man and oil man," who, according to Cleveland Amory in *The Last Resorts*, "were taken to task for their *lèse majesté*."

Many who failed to qualify at those resorts sought refuge elsewhere; and many found it in Hyannis Port. Perfectly situated on the Atlantic Coast midway between Bar Harbor and Newport (and close to either in the event that later reconsideration should open closed salon doors), Hyannis Port was accessible by railroad. Its waterside facilities were every bit as good as Newport's, and the weather—when a nor'easter wasn't blowing or a damp fog settling in from Nantucket Sound—was incomparable. Most of all, new people were welcome. Cape Codders were not prone to give themselves social airs and graces, reserving petty snobberies for themselves. The aspiring midwestern matron's gaucheries were tolerated. Money alone was enough to impress.

Encouraged by their example, others followed, and by 1926 Hyannis Port was already being referred to as "the leading summer resort on Cape Cod." Very little land was available for building, and most latecomers had to content themselves with buying older houses and then spending almost equal amounts to renovate them.

Gardeners, fretting over the thin, sandy soil, had made the once-barren hills bloom again, and even the former estate of H. T. Dunn,

17

President of Fisk Rubber Company, was professionally maintained, although the driveway, surrounded by lawns, shrubbery and well-tended flower beds, led nowhere. All buildings had been destroyed by fire years before.

Chauffeurs slowly traveled the narrow avenues in Packards, Cadillacs and Cunninghams, bringing their limousines each evening to Eldredge's or Phinney's garages, which stood side by side at the village periphery, for overnight storage. Many house lots were too narrow to accommodate the later addition of garages, and automobiles had to be put under cover, for their varnish finishes would turn off-white if habitually left out in the salt air.

The old Hallett House was gone—burned to the ground in 1907— but a new hotel, The Gables, had risen. Wealthy transients were put up in a style Gideon Hallett could never have matched.

Cora Lumbert's general store—open only in the summer and located in an inconspicuously converted cottage—sold "anything from a toothpick to a McCormick Harvester"; it was tolerated as a piece of necessary local color and fondly regarded as an institution.

Two summer churches served their sunburned parishioners: Union Chapel, of simple white clapboard erected in 1890 by summer residents of various faiths, and, at the top of Sunset Hill, commanding a magnificent view of Nantucket Sound from its tower, the much more pretentious and fashionable St. Andrew's-by-the-Sea, built of dun-colored knobbed stone. Catholics made the trip into Hyannis to attend mass at St. Francis Xavier on South Street.

A superb eighteen-hole golf course stretched from the rolling hillside down to the marsh flats between the bluffs and the sea. A small public beach—East Beach—was used only by those residents who were not members of the private West Beach Club, mostly servants and menials and a few "townies" from South Hyannis, who wandered over to the village pier at the foot of Irving Avenue to flirt with young Irish servant girls on their traditional Thursdays off.

Few tourists ever ventured into this obviously private and prohibited preserve of the rich, where the tennis frocks, printed voiles, linen knickers and white flannels worn by residents were more redolent of the Victorian era than the unconventional "Roaring Twenties." Flaming youth was at a disadvantage in the Hyannis Port of 1926, well outnumbered by the more conservative middle-aged population addicted to fan-tan, the new craze for bridge, Ping-Pong and evenings spent playing records on a Victor arthophonic machine, pumping Q.R.S. piano rolls or listening to the most popular programs on elaborately carved "Temple" console radios.

On June 10, 1926, the Hyannis *Patriot* noted that "Mr. and Mrs. John P. Kennedy (Rose Fitzgerald) of Boston have taken the Malcolm cottage at the Port for the season"; obviously confusing Joseph P. Kennedy with his father-in-law John F. "Honey Fitz" Fitzgerald, former Mayor of Boston.[2]

Cape Cod had not been Joseph P. Kennedy's first choice as a summer refuge. The Fitzgeralds and the Kennedys had spent one summer together at Old Orchard Beach in Maine and later had summered at Nantasket Beach, not far from Boston; Joseph, Jr., had been born in Hull, a small resort town on the south shore. In 1922 the Kennedys took a large gray frame house overlooking the rocky beach at Cohasset, where many of Boston's most patrician families summered.

Hostile to any newcomers but reserving its most particular scorn for Irish newcomers, Cohasset brutally snubbed the Kennedys. The beautiful daughter of "Honey Fitz," although considered "high Irish," was looked down upon by the matrons of Cohasset. "And who was Joe Kennedy[3] but the son of Pat, the barkeeper?" When Kennedy applied for membership in Cohasset's country club, he was blackballed.

Joseph P. Kennedy was no stranger to Cape Cod by 1926—those summer policemen stationed at Four Corners in Centerville as early as 1924 still vividly remember him waving from the back of his chauffeured Rolls-Royce on his way to Craigville Beach. He made a shrewd choice in Hyannis Port. Despite its cozy air of gentility, it was a resort of well-off businessmen who were, like himself, still in the process of amassing their fortunes.

Unlike Cohasset, with its pure bred Boston Brahmin homogeneity, Hyannis Port was a summer village of many disparate elements that did not mix. Geography seemed to be the prime determinant of social acceptance: The Pittsburgh residents tended to band together, and the St. Louis and Chicago groups followed suit. Members of a small Boston-area colony—including the Falveys and the Prendergasts, the Port's first Irish Catholic residents, who had arrived before the turn of the century—must have felt like orphans in their own back yard; they kept pretty much to themselves.

Hyannis Port's reaction to an invasion of Kennedys in 1926 was understandably divided. Although the village failed to welcome them with open arms, at least it did not withhold its approval either—that would come later. The department-store owner from Pittsburgh might sniff at the Kennedys as "moneyed Irish from Boston," but that's as far as it went. Most of those comfortably established at Hyannis Port in 1926 were but a generation removed from *persona non grata* status at more sumptuous eastern resorts and were more prone to exercise the prudence of those who live in glass houses than to echo J. P. Morgan's edict from Bar Harbor: "You can do business with anyone, but you can only sail a boat with a gentleman."

Joseph P. Kennedy in 1926 was a young man of 37, moving so swiftly in his quest for a second million that Hyannis Port scarcely had a good look at him during the first three summers his family spent in the village. Tall, red-haired, freckled, with a trim, athletic figure, he masked his good looks with prim dark-rimmed spectacles that gave him the misleading appearance of a disapproving schoolmaster.

The Malcolm cottage, which Kennedy was to rent for three successive years, was a rambling white clapboard house of undistinguished design with green shutters located at the end of a lane on a bluff two and a half acres of lawn away from a private beach and Nantucket Sound.

"Bill Danforth had bought a place in Centerville and he told me Kennedy was interested in buying a house," James "See Me First" Woodward said. A lean, good-looking go-getter in the forefront of local boosterism, Woodward had moved to Cape Cod in 1926 during a prolonged Brockton shoe strike.

Kennedy greeted him on the wide veranda of the rented house overlooking Hyannis Port's harbor. "The first thing he asked me if I wanted a drink. He didn't touch a drop himself, I knew that, but he was a regular guy.[4] No big-shot airs about him. We got to talking about property. He knew how the Cape was booming. He asked me what I had listed and I mentioned several houses."

"I can buy *this* place for $25,000," Kennedy said with a gesture that took in the veranda, the wide spread of lawns and the magnificent view of the Sound. Although he expressed surprise at the price of such obviously valuable shore property, Woodward said nothing further until Kennedy added, "I was just interested to see if you could do any better."

"I don't think I can do any better," Woodward said. "And I don't think *you* can do any better."

A year later Kennedy purchased the estate. The deed does not specify the price paid, but it is not unlikely that he got the house for the figure mentioned.

Almost at once remodeling began. L. Frank Paine, the Boston architect who had designed and built the original house in 1903, was put in charge of building an addition that would approximately double the house's size to fourteen rooms and nine baths and provide a children's playroom in the form of a theater in the basement.

Work on the house began in January, and a day later the new owners left for a European tour, Kennedy's first vacation in almost three years. Seriously underweight, he was finished with Hollywood except for tenuous connections with Gloria Swanson's independent film company and Pathé. Returning to Hyannis Port six weeks later to find the house nearly ready for occupancy, Kennedy hastily revised his plans for the children's theater to include what was to be the first private installation of talking-picture apparatus in New England at a cost of approximately $15,000.

As if the first private motion-picture sound theater in New England weren't enough to focus the glare of attention on the newcomers, the appearance of Gloria Swanson herself, a weekend guest at the Kennedy house, set staid Hyannis Port on its ear. In August 1929 Gloria Swanson arrived, every inch the film star. Her entrance would have done justice to her most flamboyant film roles: Miss Swanson and her party landed *on* the harbor near the breakwater not far from Kennedy's summer house, in a Sikorsky amphibious aircraft. Hyannis Port residents gaped from the beach as Miss Swanson—petite, chic, flawlessly coifed and a member of the aristocracy since her marriage to the Marquis de la Falaise de la Coudraye—deplaned, waving.

Her later appearances on the beach (although she did not bathe) and at the nearby Craigville beach-club dining room caused further excitement among her astonished and dazzled fans. Later she even managed to visit the "clubhouse" of an informal girls' club that Kathleen ("Kick") Kennedy shared with playmates, where she scrawled her autograph on the wall.

"We were all thrilled, of course," one eyewitness said. "Her name stayed on that garage wall for years."

But summers at the Port rarely held out such exotic excitements. The high point of an ordinary day was reached after dinner, when it seemed that the whole village collected at the post office for the evening's mail delivery at about 7:30. A special policeman was stationed at the corner to control the traffic of automobiles, children, maids, chauffeurs, bicycles and dogs that converged on the narrow corner post-office building.

"I remember running through people's yards," one resident has said of a Hyannis Port childhood, "and being called at through the open window of our dining room and wanting to get up from the table without even finishing dinner, actually *willing* to skip dessert to go with the crowd gathering at the post office."

Before its first Hyannis Port summer in 1926, the Kennedy family had grown to seven children, with the birth of Robert the previous November, and the newly rented house fairly reverberated with the shouts, skirmishes, comings and goings of Joseph, Jr., John, Rosemary, Kathleen, Eunice and Patricia, then a toddler of two. (Jean joined them in 1928, and Edward, named for Eddie Moore, Joseph P. Kennedy's confidential secretary and a close family friend, completed the family in February 1932.)

The household revolved entirely about Rose Kennedy, a beautiful, dark-haired and self-possessed young matron in her thirties, who had completely shouldered the responsibility for raising the children during her husband's frequently protracted absences. Ever since the Brookline days of her early married life, he had dedicated himself to the pursuit of his fortune. As the daughter of Honey Fitz, Rose was well prepared by the example of her mother, who was often left alone while her husband prowled the hustings looking for votes.

Strong-willed and self-sufficient, Rose Kennedy had no difficulty coping. The influence she exerted on her children was noticeable even in the inflections in their voices. "When Jack spoke, I would hear his mother's voice," a friend said. And Eunice would recall that "mother was always a strong influence on Jack, especially since Daddy had to be away a lot."

Jack would refer to his mother in later years as the "glue" that held the Kennedys together during the time his father worked in Hollywood, the years "we saw him only for short stretches." It was Rose who encouraged Jack's early interest in books; she would "talk about history, too," although, according to her son, "I wouldn't say that she was interested in public affairs."

Affectionate and wholly devoted to her children, Rose Kennedy was nonetheless a strict disciplinarian in her own soft-spoken way. "I used to have a ruler around and paddled them occasionally because when they're young that's all they understand."

The children's allowances were kept small as a means of discipline; Rose impressed on her children the value of nickels and dimes and constantly preached thrift as a way of life, so that they were never conscious of wealth. It was more in a prankster's spirit than from necessity, however, that Kennedy children tried to gain admission to the Idlehour for 10 cents, claiming that they were all under twelve. By 1929 trust funds of a million dollars for each child had already been established by Joseph P. Kennedy. In 1936 and 1949 two additional funds brought the total to more than 10 million for each of his children.

Each morning without fail Rose attended early mass at St. Francis Xavier on South Street in Hyannis, where she was a daily communicant. A devout Catholic, deeply committed to her faith, she returned to breakfast with her oldest children and frequently drilled them in catechism. The children were expected to know not only the liturgy of the mass but also the significance of each of the priest's vestments and, on the occasions when they accompanied her, the meanings of the sermons that had been preached.

"I wanted them to form a habit of making God and religion a part of their daily lives, not something to be reserved for Sunday." (In later years, Robert Kennedy would frequently step over the railing at St. Francis Xavier and act as altar boy in place of a summer truant, serving the mass without error in either ritual or responses.)

Separated by age, the youngest were tended by a nurse and strictly forbidden to ride their bicycles off the property. A governess supervised the older children, who were expected to be in the house when the lights went on at dusk. All had to be in their places at the dining table five minutes before mealtimes.

Activities usually centered at the West Beach club, where Rose soon adopted the local custom of identifying children by individually colored bathing caps and swimsuits in order to facilitate quick census-taking at the crowded beach. The club was also the scene of the annual Labor Day weekend water carnival and swimming meets, in which the Kennedy children were always entered "in different age categories so we didn't have to swim against each other" and exhorted by their father to win. "The thing he always kept telling us was that coming in second was just no good," Eunice recalled.

Other summer pleasures were as simple as packing a picnic hamper for all the Kennedy children and as many others in the neighborhood as could be squeezed into the blue Rolls-Royce touring car and driving to Wequaquet Lake, then a sparsely settled sylvan hideaway where a good beach provided the novelty of fresh-water bathing beside the ocean.

Only occasionally in those years did Joseph P. Kennedy appear behind the wheel of a 1928 Chevrolet—the only automobile he was known to drive himself—to take his children to Craigville Beach, where rented lockers were available. More often than not, though, the children, too impatient to change, came already dressed in swimsuits in order to swarm out of the automobile and plunge directly into the waves.

In later years, the older Kennedys attended few public functions without being accompanied by at least one of their children. And even those who expressed the most vehement feelings against Joseph P. Kennedy envied and admired his extraordinary involvement with his children. "Most fathers in those days simply weren't that interested in what their children did," a Hyannis Port resident said. "But Joe Kennedy knew what his kids were up to all the time."

The fierce family loyalty so carefully cultivated by Joseph P. Kennedy and inculcated rigorously into the younger children by his oldest son and namesake was received with less than admiration. "The Kennedys tried to crash Hyannis Port, and when they were rebuffed they banded together against everyone else," was the likeliest explanation for the phenomenon in the minds of many of Joseph P. Kennedy's summer neighbors.

"No matter what anyone else had done, the Kennedy children always praised each other's accomplishments to the skies," one childhood playmate recalled. "While it was amusing and touching for a time, it got to be rather tiresome after a while."

Those who granted the Kennedy children a well-deserved popularity—the lawns surrounding Joseph P. Kennedy's large house were frequently crowded with playmates—conceded that they "weren't snotty and stuck on themselves like a lot of other rich summer kids";

others felt like "sparring partners" and "just somebody for the Kennedys to play against."

That there would "be hell to pay if they didn't win every race" could be verified by anyone on the civic association's pier at the end of a sailing event to witness the graceless way in which Kennedys lost.

Mutterings that the Kennedys "cheated" in order to win as often as they did by using nonregulation-size sails or other trickery were too frequently given credence, despite the fact that races were strictly supervised by committee boats like *Bookie*, which had been contracted to manage races for the Wianno yacht club; it not only designated the course each race was to take but also acted as water policeman to maintain rules.*

There were carefully supervised invasions of Hyannis to scout Woolworth's on Main Street and, before home movies were available in their own basement, to sit wriggling through the uproar of a children's Saturday matinee at the Idlehour. Afterward everyone would line up for double dips of homemade ice cream at the Cape Cod Creamery on Sea Street.

The first of what would be a series of Kennedy sailboats appeared in 1927 and was promptly christened by Joe, Jr., and Jack *Rose Elizabeth* for their mother. The two brothers bent every effort to master the vessel, to learn to sail it properly and, above all, to win races—a preoccupation that was to dominate many of their summers at Hyannis Port.

No record was kept of *Rose Elizabeth*'s class or in what series of races it participated, but the Kennedy brothers did, in fact, win a sailboat race in 1927. Afterward, while looking at magazines on the veranda of their father's house, their attention was drawn to an overturned boat in the harbor. Rushing back to their own boat, the boys sailed out into the open sea again and managed, after some difficulty, to pull an exhausted man, who was clinging to the bottom of his overturned boat, into *Rose Elizabeth* and bring him to shore.

Prodded no doubt by the boys' doting grandfather Honey Fitz, the

* The Kennedys customarily crewed their own boats during the time when as many as 35 boats of the Wianne, Osterville and Hyannis Port fleet hired professional crews. A crewman frequently earned up to $75 for two races a week. During the mid-1930s it was not unusual to see the "skippers" of such boats hit the decks wearing afternoon wash-silk frocks; they would sit on canvas camp chairs, white gloves on the tillers, "sailing" to victory, for the rules allowed professionals to do everything but touch the tiller.

Boston *Post* referred to the incident as a "daring rescue" and to the boys—apprentice seamen at best—as "champions." Nonetheless it gave early indications of initiative and self-reliance: Joe, Jr., was only twelve and Jack only ten at the time.

As the children grew older and school and other activities separated them, the house at Hyannis Port became the scene of family reunions and the place where Joseph P. Kennedy would seek to shape his children.

A deeply emotional man who did not "want his love for his children to overwhelm them," he seemed on the surface to be gruff, dour and difficult to please. Lectures on the necessity of striving for excellence in every endeavor were reinforced by the example of his own accomplishments. Not a knowledgeable sailor himself, he nonetheless followed the boats his children raced, taking note of anyone who carelessly fouled a mark or appeared to be giving less than his whole effort to winning. Afterward the culprit would be certain to receive a blistering tongue-lashing in front of the other children and be sent from the dinner table in disgrace to eat in the kitchen. But all would be forgiven once the recalcitrant confessed his mistake and promised to try harder the next time.

Sharing with Rose the conviction that, if the older children were well brought up and given particular attention, the younger ones would naturally follow their lead, Kennedy selected his oldest son, Joseph, Jr., as the model for the other children.

Sturdily built, with a shock of thick straight hair, lively blue eyes and a square face, Joe, Jr., was rugged and fearless, full of restless energy, "a very wholesome boy without being goodie-goodie about it." He is remembered from Sunday-school days in Brookline as a "hell-raiser" and the kind of boy who "couldn't pass a hat without squashing it in or leave an unprotected shin unkicked. He was cracked on the head by the Sisters with a catechism book so often it was a wonder the top of his head wasn't flatter than a pancake."

Joe, Jr., took his role as family exemplar very seriously, spending long, patient hours with his younger brothers and sisters on the broad green lawns at Hyannis Port teaching them to ride a bicycle, throw a football and play tennis. (In later years it was Joe who coined the phrase "the Kennedy clan.")

Though he was a hero to the younger children, Joe was more often than not a thorn in the side of his brother Jack. Physically opposite from his brother, tall for his age, slender and wiry, with a small, open face, snub nose and hair that tended to bleach in the sun and resist combing, Jack refused the role of disciple at the feet of a domineering brother-paragon whom he was expected to obey and emulate.

"He had a pugnacious personality," Jack said of his brother in later years. "Later on it smoothed out, but it was a problem in my boyhood." Determined to resist the total submersion of his own personality, Jack soon realized that determination alone was no substitute for muscle when Joe, forced to implement his authority, settled their differences and tests of will by pinning Jack, without too much difficulty, to the ground.

Yet Jack later wrote with typical generosity: "I think if the Kennedy children amount to anything now or ever amount to anything it will be due more to Joe's behavior and constant example than to any other factor."

It is remarkable that in the volume of reminiscences [5] Jack edited after his brother's death he could look back on those years without the slightest trace of bitterness, only halfheartedly listing Joe's "defects" as a hot temper [6] and (perhaps moved by his own experience) "an intolerance for the slower pace of lesser men."

There must have been many times when the Cape Cod sun seemed virtually clouded over by the overbearing presence of his older brother, for whatever qualities Jack possessed tended to pale next to his brother's, and almost all the years of his boyhood and adolescence were lived in the shadow of Joe's superior accomplishments.

Jack, the most self-absorbed of the Kennedy children, later spoke of Hyannis Port, "where no two summers were ever quite the same," and remembered the year he was twelve as "the first time I *met* Bobby Kennedy. Of course, I had known him for three and a half years; after all he was my brother." But Joe had suffered no such oversight in recognizing his younger brother's identity, and when Bobby was old enough it was Joe who saw to it that he could catch a football and sail a boat.

Jack was frailer in health than he would ever admit; the summer days of his boyhood were often spent recuperating from various illnesses in a bedroom, surrounded by a collection of friends who "made so much noise a governess would finally have to ask us to leave." Jack was given no quarter and asked none from his brother Joe; and, though the situation between them remained stalemated for some

27

years, life at Hyannis Port was not merely a struggle between model and laggard pupil. Once, abandoning all caution, Jack ate his own piece of chocolate-cream pie, then snatched up Joe's piece and, cramming it all in his mouth, fled from the dining-room table with Joe in hot pursuit and the rest of the family following. Jack was about to dive off the breakwater fully clothed when Joe, convulsed by the sight of "Big Jack's" terrified face smeared with whipped cream, relented.

In September 1929 the older Kennedys left for a European tour. Jack and his brothers and sisters attended a dinner party in honor of the fortieth wedding anniversary of their grandparents, ex-Mayor and Mrs. John F. Fitzgerald, which was held at their rented summer house in West Hyannis Port. After the dinner a motion picture was shown in the private theater at the Kennedy house.

Honey Fitz took that occasion to complain that Cape Cod was not advertising its attractions enough. "The right kind of publicity," he said, "could bring the whole country here."

But in the summer of 1929 it seemed that the whole country was on Cape Cod already. The annual report of the Chamber of Commerce was lyrical, predicting that the season would unquestionably hit all-time record highs. Traffic on Hyannis' Main Street was congested with the latest models of Essex, Dodge and Nash. The most sumptuous new houses in Oyster Harbors were selling fastest.

From his veranda Joseph P. Kennedy could have looked eastward across the harbor to the gay awnings and the long twinkling streamers of colored lights illuminating the deck and top mast of the former barkentine *Fairhaven*, which had been brought to Hyannis' railroad wharf early in the spring, remodeled into an elegant new night club and christened "La Goleta." It was one of many new business ventures that had opened that season.

A new collection of smart shops had filled the Queen's Buyway to overflowing, and long waiting lists were reported for space in other business blocks rapidly being built to meet the unprecedented demand. Many Cape Codders were playing the stock market on margin in 1929, availing themselves of the new facilities at the Queen's Buyway branch of the stock brokerage house of E. M. Hambling and Company of Boston. "You wouldn't see the front page of a newspaper in a lot of houses in Hyannis because everybody had it turned to the financial section for the latest stock prices." Even recent arrivals from Portugal and Finland, urged to attend Americanization classes at Barnstable High School three nights a week and barely able to sign their own names, were coining money from the market.

Tourist dollars poured into cash registers faster than anything the Cape had ever seen before, and the rich flow of gold looked as if it would never end. It would.

On Tuesday, October 29, 1929, it ended with a crash.

Two

What effect the national economic crisis would have on the coming tourist season was of most concern to Cape Codders in the spring of 1930, as they anxiously looked toward the arrival of the summer people—if, indeed, there were going to be summer people anymore.

The habit of "boosting"—as inevitable as the equinox on Cape Cod in March—was difficult to submerge entirely, even under such trying circumstances. The usual published forecast of a bigger season than ever reported not only that demand for summer houses was greater than in the previous year but also that many more higher-priced homes had already been taken for the summer. The announcement, however well-intended to build morale, was greeted for once with stony skepticism. One observer was moved to note that the houses were being snapped up by "ex-millionaires afraid of height who think it'll be easier to drown themselves."

Some would gibe at misfortune, but others faced the prospect of a disastrous summer with growing apprehension. Suffering habitually from unemployment * in the off-season, Cape Codders had come to depend almost entirely on tourism and the winter building boom to see them through the year. The shock of the market's collapse and the uncertainty that followed hardly provided an encouraging atmosphere for further real-estate speculation. Home-building came to a dead stop, as builders concentrated on unloading, if they could, their inventories of unsold property.

Without its tourist summer, Cape Cod was bound for hard times. The fishing industry had diminished to such an extent that it could

* During the celebration of his golden jubilee in the priesthood in May 1938, Reverend Mortimer Downing, pastor of St. Francis Xavier Church brought a roar of appreciative laughter from a large audience in the Barnstable High School auditorium when, speaking of Cape Codders in winter, he said: "I was once asked about the occupations of the people of the Cape. I said: 'They have nothing to do, and they do it.' "

be said still to flourish only in Provincetown. Agriculture had dwindled sharply through the years: The cranberry industry, with its limited harvest season, provided only minor, short-term job opportunities; there was a little truck farming (asparagus- and strawberry-growing) but nothing that could counterbalance the loss of tourist dollars.

By mid-June, when summer rooming houses on Sea Street began to fill up again, the Hyannis Board of Trade was sufficiently emboldened to proclaim the area "Depression-proof," excerising the first bit of cautious optimism for the season ahead.

"Cape Codder" trains arriving in July crowded with New Yorkers offered encouraging testimony that the Cape had not entirely lost its power to entice summer visitors to its shores; and, though the streets appeared less crowded than in former years, the Chamber of Commerce's annual end-of-season report made the best of what could only have been a middling season. It reasoned that, although approximately the same numbers of people had visited Cape Cod, they had spent less money, and it predicted a better summer the next year.

But the next year was not better; nor was the summer after. As the years advanced further into the 1930s, Cape Cod lost, rather than gained, further ground each summer. Once proud of its insularity and able to boast with some truth that anyone setting foot on its sandy soil moved "blessedly out of the roaring 20th century back into the tranquil 18th," Cape Cod was abruptly gathered into the mainstream of economic malaise that gripped the rest of the country.

There were no corner apple selling and no suicides. There were only "a strange quietness," a gathering sense of hopelessness and a perceptible tightening of belts. Whatever hardships were ahead, however, most Cape Codders were prepared to face them on Cape Cod. Few left to seek to improve their chances elsewhere.

"In many ways we were luckier than city folks," an observer recalled. "Nobody here was exactly used to easy living. Cape people were thrifty by nature *and* necessity. Short rations in winter was nothing new—it was the boom years in the twenties that had been the exception."

The oil lamps, still kept handy in many a wealthy Cape Cod attic for use when hurricanes and electrical storms shut off power, were for others the standard lighting appliance. Electrification—only extended the full length of the Cape in 1928—had never arrived at all in some

31

Cape homes, where wiping chimneys clear and trimming wicks had been always part of the morning's domestic routine.[1] The privy was still part of the landscape and central heating a luxury few could afford.

Fillet of gull's breast, once a common meat dish, could, under straitened Depression circumstances, fill that role again, and "all you needed was a bucket and a shovel to go dig up a mess of clams."

As the Depression wasn't going to go away, Cape Codders were prepared to make the best of it.

Summer theaters thrived, and Bette Davis, a charming young actress, was repeating her broadway success in the comedy *Broken Dishes* at the Cape Playhouse in Dennis.

Best & Company and Milgrim, both well-known New York shops, opened branches in the Queen's Buyway. Although few year-rounders could afford cotton afternoon frocks marked $39.95, it was encouraging to see such things advertised, an indication that at least *someone* on Cape Cod was expected to be able to buy them.

The Depression failed to change the face of Hyannis Port. In no way did it appear to affect the idyllic summer way of life there. It was apparent that many of Joseph P. Kennedy's neighbors had also had the farsightedness to rescue significant portions of their fortunes from the wreckage of the stock-market crash.

The Hyannis Port Civic Association went about its business of neighborhood improvement, building a plank walk on the pier and seeing to it that the harbor was dredged so that pleasure boats could come conveniently closer to shore.

And the Association also secured police protection for both day and night—evidence that others were sharing Kennedy's mood of growing uneasiness. Kennedy saw the future in the blackest possible way. In *I'm for Roosevelt*, published in 1936, he would write:

> I am not ashamed to record that in those days I felt and said I would be willing to part with half of what I had if I could be sure of keeping under law and order, the other half. Then it seemed that I should be able to hold nothing for the protection of my family.

If his father was deeply distressed for the future of the country, Jack Kennedy was unaware of it. The utter changelessness of Hyannis Port probably explains a letter he wrote to his father during his first year at Canterbury School; he requested magazines and newspapers "because I did not know about the Market Slump until a long time after."

Sailing and swimming—and trying hard to beat his brother at tennis and golf—still occupied the better part of his summer days. Late one evening that summer Jack, accompanied by his older brother, appeared at the door of E. Thomas Murphy, in later years the first Democrat to be elected a selectman in the town of Barnstable.[2] "It was around 11 o'clock and we were getting ready to go to bed when there was a knock at the door. I recognized Jack and Joe, of course," Murphy has said. "Everybody in town knew the Kennedy kids."

Apologizing for the lateness of the hour, the brothers stated their mission. They were on a treasure hunt. In order to win they had to find one more item: a derby hat. Remembering from conversations with their grandfather Honey Fitz that Murphy's father[3] had been one of the few on Cape Cod to support Al Smith during the 1928 election, the boys wondered if he owned a derby.

"Indeed he did," Murphy said. "I gave them my father's derby and they promised to return it the next day. They were both good-looking, nicely-spoken boys, but I think what impressed my father and me more than anything else was how cleverly they had used their heads, working out the location of what must have been, at that time, just about the only derby in Hyannis."

Recovered from the emergency appendectomy that had abruptly ended his year at Canterbury, a select Catholic preparatory school in New Milford, Connecticut, Jack was again placed in his brother's shadow, as he reluctantly followed Joe to Choate in the fall of 1931.

In August 1931 Jack was once more a spectator while his brother basked in the spotlight. During the era when aviation accomplishments had first so excited the American imagination, realtor James A. Woodward had prevailed upon aviator Russell Boardman to name his plane *Cape Cod* before one of the many trans-Atlantic flights that had followed Lindbergh's. The plane landed at Istanbul—having successfully crossed the Atlantic and the Continent of Europe for a total of 5,500 miles in 49 hours and 20 minutes from take off in New York. It was the fourteenth successful flight and the longest nonstop flight up to that time. Arrangements for a welcome celebration for Boardman and John Polando, who had accompanied him on the

33

flight, were hurriedly made on Cape Cod. Subscriptions for a gala banquet were sold for $15 apiece, and a total of $6,000 was raised in less than two weeks to pay celebration expenses.

Joseph P. Kennedy offered the use of his Rolls Royce for the reception of the aviators, and Joe, Jr., was at the wheel when *Cape Cod*, a yellow Bellanca, landed at Hyannis Airport to the cheers of some two thousand spectators. While Jack and other members of the family watched, Joe, Jr., led a parade of about sixty decorated floats, automobiles and six bands and drum corps along Main Street, to the acclaim of the biggest crowd Hyannis had seen since the crash.

The banquet that evening at The Coffee House on Sea Street, where the locally raised ducks were said to have been "the toughest birds ever laid on a platter," was nonetheless a rousing success, inspiring Sherman Adams, then Vice-President of Bellanca Airplane Company, to lead three cheers for the aviators.

Although Joseph P. Kennedy had subscribed to the reception, he reportedly did not attend the banquet. His father-in-law, Honey Fitz did, however, and, following a speech in which he compared the fliers to the Pilgrim fathers, the irrepressible 69-year-old stood on a chair to lead those in attendance in the singing of "Sweet Adeline," thus ending the banquet. Afterward, fireworks at the airport attracted a crowd of ten thousand.

By 1932 Joseph P. Kennedy had joined forces with those promoting Franklin D. Roosevelt's candidacy for the Democratic presidential nomination. A contribution of $7,500 to the preconvention campaign placed Kennedy in opposition to Honey Fitz, who, like most Massachusetts Democrats, threw his support to Al Smith. Kennedy's alignment with the Roosevelt forces allied him, at the same time, with James Michael Curley, his father-in-law's bitterest enemy [4] from the gaudy battlefields of Boston politics.

But of much greater importance than looming presidential elections, to a young man who would later admit that he "wasn't much interested in politics," was the arrival in 1932 of the Wianno Senior one-design knockabout,[5] which Jack Kennedy was to name *Victura*. Although he shared the boat with his brother Joe, who did most of the sailing on it at first, *Victura* was the boat he preferred above all others, the boat he scored his greatest sailing successes with and later the boat most identified with him.

With *Victura* and the later proliferation of Kennedy boats came the first in a series of hired "skippers," usually mature men skilled in the arts of seamanship and hired to take full charge of the Kennedy children's sailing activities and to supervise the maintenance of all boats.

James A. ("Jimmie") MacClean, a graduate of the Coast Guard Academy, had served with the Merchant Marine and knew the waters of Hyannis Port well. Soon the slender, mild-mannered man in his late twenties was a familiar sight escorting the Kennedy children in their group invasions of Hyannis. They usually wore their oldest shorts and dungarees and were frequently barefoot as they sat unselfconsciously on Main Street curbstones to wait for a car to be sent from Hyannis Port to pick them up.

Frequently their destination was the Rexall Drugstore—formerly Megathlin's—the first and largest pharmacy in Hyannis. Megathlin's, located in the East End a block from the depot, was a popular stopping place for the Kennedy children; it offered discounted prices on Wyeth's Sulphur, Bude's Pepto Mangan and Boriclor Tooth Paste, as well as a resplendently fretworked soda fountain complete with wire chairs, white-tile mosaic floors and ornate apothecary urns filled with colored water.

"The Kennedys had a charge account with us. The kids would come in a lot with Jimmie for ice cream cones. I remember one day in particular because one of the girls had a dog in her arms. In those days we used to have a big tomcat who loved to sit in the window and soak up the sun. As soon as they came in this day, the dog made a beeline for our cat. There wasn't any real damage done, but the whole window display was wrecked. The Kennedy kids—being kids—got a big laugh out of it." The dog—a scrappy fox terrier with a penchant for fighting bigger dogs—was equally prone to destructiveness in Hyannis Port, particularly with assistance from Jack.

One afternoon, as she was preparing to take *Tenovus* out in rough water, Eunice gave her wristwatch to the "skipper," who promptly put it on his wrist for safekeeping. When the terrier started a fight on the pier with another dog, MacClean scooped both dogs up in his arms with the idea of throwing them both into the water, when Jack, who was standing alongside, pushed the "skipper," the two dogs and Eunice's wristwatch all into the water, to the amusement of the spectators. Barely suppressing a grin, Jack explained the "accident": He'd been "trying to help."

A year later Jack and Joe, Jr., were sailing a new boat—*Flash*, later followed by *Flash II*; both were international star-class boats and were kept in winter storage at the Chester A. Crosby Yard in Osterville. The Kennedy brothers, frequent visitors to the yard, "loved to putter around their boats." Keen to win races and full of enthusiasm for sailing, they worked long hard hours getting their boats ready for each summer's racing.

By 1933 a new "skipper" had taken over. A tall, strapping man with reddish-blonde hair, 35-year-old John ("Eric") Ericson was forceful, loud and coarse, with a colorfully explicit Norwegian-accented vocabulary frequently heard shouting orders to the boys. Manning the power boat *Davilis*, which was used to tow sailboats to and from Wianno for races, he was profane and boisterous, in marked contrast to mild-mannered, quiet-spoken Jimmie MacClean.

Known as a heavy drinker—once during an Edgartown regatta it had taken almost the entire village police force to quell him—Eric always insisted that a bit of beer be added to the paint used to undercoat the bottom of the boats, in order to give them added "buoyancy." The boys were never sure whether he was serious or joking.

Although Ericson was "not the skipper *Rose* Kennedy would have hired," Joseph P. Kennedy, who insisted on nonparochial schools for his sons, so that they would have an early opportunity to compete with a greater variety of boys, was not above seizing any chance that presented itself to educate his sons in the more earthy and various ways of the world. And John Ericson—direct, uninhibited, ingenuous and fiercely fond of the boys—was no one Joe, Jr., or Jack would ever be likely to encounter at Choate and Harvard.

The summer of 1933 had begun propitiously for Joe, Jr. He received the Harvard Trophy as the Choate student who best combined scholarship with good sportsmanship and entered Harvard in the fall.

Jack meanwhile, uninterested in reflected glory, had to be satisfied with the lesser accomplishments of being a cheerleader, winning a pie-eating contest and enjoying a growing reputation, according to his roommate, as the boy who "was reading more books and magazines and current-events publications than anyone else," virtually anything he could put his hands on but school books.

In a letter to Kennedy's parents, Jack's housefather at Choate complained that he "studies at the last minute, keeps appointments late, has little sense of the material values and can seldom locate his possessions."

Although Jack squirmed under the barrage of censure from his father * and admitted his shortcomings, he seemed to be doing little but worrying about his studies until his senior year, when he and his roommate LeMoyne Billings had "definitely decided to stop fooling around."

"I really do realize how important it is that I get a good job done this year, if I want to go to England," Jack wrote to his father. "I really feel, now that I think it over that I have been bluffing myself about how much real work I have been doing."

His father applauded the "forthrightness and directness that you are usually lacking" and commended his improved penmanship, but there was really little change. Maids at Hyannis Port still complained about Jack's room: the wet towels in a heap on the floor, the tangle of ties in one corner, the bureau drawers turned over and emptied in the middle of the bed in a hurried search for some wanted item. Joe, Jr., availed himself of the services of the Belmore Tutoring Studios in Hyannis during the summer to improve his studies; Jack procrastinated and sailed boats.

In 1933 the NRA eagle had made its debut in Hyannis at S. Burman's Ladies and Gentlemen's Wearing Apparel. (In September, Jack was present as Honey Fitz made a Sunday-afternoon speech under the auspices of the local NRA committee at a mass meeting at Hallett's Field. A band accompanied while he sang "Sweet Adeline.")

Barnstable voted overwhelmingly to license the sale of wine and malt beverages during a special election, and the Casa Madrid opened its doors, offering a stunning contrast to the austerity of the rest of Cape Cod in the 1930s, struggling as it was to survive the very depths of the Depression.

A private club that advised its members that "sweaters and knick-

* In view of his reputation, it seems that Joseph P. Kennedy exercised enormous patience with his son Jack, reminded possibly that he himself had flunked out of Boston Latin School for low grades during his final year and had wanted to quit school and go to work. A teacher, visiting his parents had convinced them that he should try again, repeat the year and earn his diploma, commenting: "He can make something of himself if he has the right education."

37

ers would not be tolerated" and entirely enclosed its lavish Spanish-style building in a wrought-iron and stucco wall, Casa Madrid offered evidence that the spirit of the "Roaring Twenties" hadn't entirely died with the crash. A luxuriously appointed "playground for the rich," the club provided a seaplane that members could rent at "reasonable rates," as well as speedboats, squash and handball courts and gymnasium facilities. It also offered the facilities of a not-too-well-concealed gambling casino and was early and often in trouble with the police.[6]

In 1933, the Hyannis *Patriot* announced:

> Cape Cod is vitally interested in President Roosevelt as it can claim him as one of their own since he can trace his ancestry back to the *Mayflower*, he having no less than 11 ancestors on that famous vessel. Six of the 41 persons who signed the Mayflower Compact were his ancestors . . .

Whether or not Cape Cod claimed Roosevelt as "one of their own," it surely wanted nothing whatever to do with him when election time rolled around. A Democrat was a Democrat to Cape Codders, no matter how impeccably Republican his lineage.

In July 1934 Joseph P. Kennedy was appointed chairman[7] of the newly created Federal Securities and Exchange Commission. Hyannis Port, a place where Roosevelt's name was anathema, was aghast to find a bona fide New Dealer in its midst. "Of course we were shocked!" a resident said. "We never dreamed a man in his position would ever go to *work* for Roosevelt."

Kennedy had never sought popularity in Hyannis Port, but the appointment was hardly calculated to improve relations with his neighbors. Considered standoffish and abrupt at the golf club, where he played his game and left without the usual locker-room camaraderie with other members, Kennedy had little enough time to spend at Hyannis Port, and he preferred to spend it with his family. He was always ready to contribute to any worthwhile community cause, and he later came to be hailed as "the greatest booster Hyannis Port ever had," one of the first millionaires to take a financial interest in community affairs.

The year 1935 marked a change in Jack Kennedy. He had enjoyed a respite from fraternal domination during the previous summer, when Joe, Jr., had toured the Soviet Union with socialist Professor Harold J.

Laski and his wife before spending a term at the London School of Economics. Jack had enjoyed the taste of being head boy, if only temporarily, and had taken a larger interest in his younger brothers and sisters. Although he had won few sailing races, 1934 had been a pleasantly noncompetitive summer.

Now, a year later, Jack was six feet tall, wiry, fully recovered from a severe case of pneumonia and gayer, more outgoing, than he'd ever been. Although he was graduated from Choate 64th in a class of 112—a graduation snapshot shows scuffed saddle shoes sticking out beneath his ill-fitting graduation robe—his classmates had nonetheless elected him "the senior most likely to succeed."

The honor gave him a terrific lift; although it wasn't the Harvard Trophy by any means, it did represent recognition of himself entirely separate from his older brother.

Jack had discovered girls while at Choate, and he was popular and sought after at weekly dances at the Wianno club. The summer was filled with frequently peremptory telegrams summoning LeMoyne Billings, his roommate at Choate, to parties at Hyannis Port.

That same summer there was a new "skipper," who offered a striking contrast to boisterous, hard-drinking John Ericson. A tall, thin, strict, native Cape Codder, the newcomer was used to catering to the milder whims of a seasonal gentry at Osterville, which attracted a more staid, genteel breed of summer aristocracy. In comparison, the Kennedys seemed "raw and crude." The relationship was to last— with one long interruption during the years of Joseph P. Kennedy's ambassadorship—a total of three stormy years, providing the most direct confrontation between the Kennedys and a Cape Codder determined "not to let them get away with anything." Neither enjoyed it very much.

First, a second-hand power boat said to be in perfect working order after a complete overhaul was turned over to the new skipper, who at once pointed out that screws on the boat's engine had rusted over their tops, indicating that the vessel had not been touched in many years. When the boat was put into the water, it promptly began to sink.

With the vessel tied up at Hyannis Port's pier to prevent it from being swamped, Joseph P. Kennedy—who had already earned a local reputation as "opinionated," "hard as nails" and "an impossible man to work for"—refused to admit that he had made a bad bargain. He

39

insisted that the boat could still be made seaworthy. The new skipper managed to get the craft afloat for the short tow to Crosby's at Osterville for repairs, but the vessel sank at the entrance to the boatyard.

Among the Kennedy children placed under his direct jurisdiction —as skipper he was "boss of the kids"—he regarded Joe, Jr., as "the only one in that bunch you could talk to." He frowned upon the deportment of young ladies brought down from Boston to share uproarious sails aboard the Kennedy fleet of boats. Nor did he approve of the children's habit of stepping from their boats and flinging off articles of clothing as they progressed down the pier, in the expectation that someone else would pick up after them.

One mid-1930 Edgartown regatta, degenerating as such events customarily did into an aftermath of drinking and rowdiness—a release from the tensions of the day's hotly contested sailboat races —provided more serious difficulties. One particular victory celebration hosted by the two oldest Kennedy brothers at an Edgartown hotel came to an abrupt end when damage prompted the management to alert police. Both Joe, Jr., and Jack were taken to the village's small, cramped jail. When called to go bail for the boys, the "skipper" flatly refused, instructing the boys that they could "stay where you are" in order "to teach you a lesson." No charges were pressed. The brothers, both under 21, were released the following morning.

Always touchy in direct business relations with summer people, some Cape Codders spoke in sharp disapproval of the Kennedys, who, in their view, "never said thank you" and regarded an employee as "just a machine to work." Natives complained as well of low wages and "always having to ask for my money." Western Union messengers who delivered telegrams to the Kennedy house were warned in advance not to expect large tips.

One Cape Cod matron, an expert seamstress and then a resident of Hyannis' Chase Street, was frequently called upon not only to perform alterations on the Kennedy girls' skirts but also to repair torn boat sails as well. On one occasion, when Jack left the sails down on the Victura after a morning's practice run before an afternoon race, the frequently gusty harbor winds badly tore one of them. According to the seamstress, "It was a big job. The sail was virtually in ribbons— they really needed a new one—but because of the race I dropped everything to get the job done on time."

When the sail was finished, she awaited the arrival of the Kennedy, chauffeur, customarily sent to retrieve mended articles, "who never brought more than a dollar at a time to pay for anything." When his knock came, the seamstress was ready for him. "That'll be seven dollars," she said.

The chauffeur admitted that he had not been given money to pay for the sail's repair. "No money," the woman said firmly, her fingers still stinging from the thick, rough canvas, "no sails."

Furious, the chauffeur argued in vain that the race was to begin shortly, but the woman could not be budged. The chauffeur returned to Hyannis Port to fetch the cash and delivered the sail in time to win that afternoon's race, but, according to the seamstress, "it was the last sail that was ever brought to me again." *

"Cape Codders had been used to taking advantage of summer people for years," a Hyannis Port resident said in defense of his neighbors. "If the Kennedys expected value for their wages, you couldn't blame them. A lot of us pay inflated prices for indifferently performed services and just keep quiet about it. It's just considered part of the price you have to pay for coming to Cape Cod summers."

While his father worked hard to correct market abuses that had earlier helped him to reap a fortune, Jack was using all his powers of persuasion during many "discussions" in a campaign to follow his friends at Choate to Princeton, rather than his brother Joe to Harvard. At Harvard Joe was already repeating his Choate successes, with accomplishments that ranged from making the football and soccer teams to election to the student council.

---

* Years later the same battle was still being waged: Drawing up to a gasoline station on Hyannis' South Street in 1961, the driver of a nearly-out-of-gas automobile containing a group of Kennedy Compound children and a governess asked that the tank be filled up. Recognizing the occupants and aware of the Kennedy penchant for not carrying money, the proprietor challenged the driver, "Who's going to pay for it?"

"We're Kennedys," came the chorused answer, in lieu of cash. Unmoved, the proprietor was unwilling to charge for the fill-up and submit a bill. A telephone call brought a chauffeur from the compound with a container of gasoline sufficient to get the car back to Hyannis Port.

Many local businessmen, however, vied for Kennedy trade. All it took was one telephoned summons to a fashionable summer ladies' shoe shop in Hyannis' West End to propel the shopkeeper into a battered Ford station wagon with boxes of shoes to be left at a security checkpoint for the convenience of a Kennedy Compound customer. Days later, those shoes not found satisfactory would be returned to the shop by a maid.

In the fall, however, Jack's arguments had proved unavailing. If he wasn't going to go to Harvard, then he wasn't going to go to Princeton either.

In September Joseph P. Kennedy and his wife left New York for Europe to place two of their children in school. Kathleen was to study at the Sacred Heart Convent in Paris, and Jack was to follow in his brother's footsteps and study economics with Professor Harold J. Laski at the London School of Economics.

Only when Jack's term in London was abruptly cut short by an acute case of jaundice requiring hospitalization did Joseph P. Kennedy relent. On his son's return to the United States, he was allowed to register at Princeton on October 12, after the freshman class had begun. The jaundice flared up again, and Jack withdrew on December 12; he was sent to Arizona to recuperate.

Joseph P. Kennedy completed the manuscript of his campaign book, *I'm for Roosevelt*, in June. He was reading galley proofs on his veranda overlooking Nantucket Sound when the Hyannis *Patriot* for Thursday, July 23, 1936, arrived, with the following story:

Is Not Afraid

Joseph P. Kennedy announces that he calmly awaits the appearance of his book on the New Deal, well knowing it will make enemies for him among his moneyed friends. He says it contains an unbiased opinion of what the New Deal has accomplished.

Mr. Kennedy is a summer resident of Hyannis Port and was for the first 18 months of its existence Chairman of the Federal Securities and Exchange Commission.

I'm for Roosevelt was published in August by Reynal and Hitchcock, and it infuriated many of Kennedy's neighbors. "My father hit the ceiling," a former resident remembered. "He'd built his own company himself and earned every dollar honestly. He felt that the stock market speculators—'the get-rick-quick-boys,' he used to call them—who had managed the stock pools and driven up prices, then deserted the market to make millions had been responsible for the crash in the first place. Now, one of them had written a book about how wonderful everything was going to be if government regulated business."

Although his father agreed that there should be some regulation, "the idea of it coming from someone like Kennedy was just too much to take."

Several months after the book was published, Joseph P. Kennedy proudly and defiantly displayed a framed note of appreciation, so that any visitor could not help but notice it on the living-room wall of his Hyannis Port house. "Dear Joe," the note read. "*I'm for Kennedy! The book is grand. I am delighted with it . . .*"

It was signed by Franklin Delano Roosevelt.

During an electrical storm in July a lightning bolt struck the *Victura*, splitting the tip of the mast and boring a hole through the hull. After quick repairs at Crosby's in Osterville, *Victura* was winning races again—and winning them with Jack at the tiller.

The summer of 1936 was a memorable one. Fully recovered from his two attacks of jaundice and resigned to entering Harvard in the fall, Jack and two other members skippered the Hyannis Port yacht club boat to victory over Wianno in the first team races for the Darlington Trophy; with his brother Joe as coskipper, *Flash II* tied for the lead in the competition to choose representatives for the Atlantic Coast star-class championship. By the end of 1936 Jack had collected two firsts in the July and August racing series and had won the long-distance race and championship with *Flash II*. Jack was not the only Kennedy winning races that summer. Eunice, skippering *Tenovus*, was frequently a winner in the Wianno Junior class, with the other girls as crew. Though the starting point might be well out in the harbor, Eunice's voice could frequently be heard on shore just before the boats started racing: "All right now! Everyone say a 'Hail Mary!' "

After a long lonely winter of frustration and illness, Hyannis Port provided a happy contrast, a place where Jack could stand in the hallway and shout, "Hi, I'm home and going for a sail—who wants to crew?" And afterward he could work on the canvas sails spread out on the lawn to dry and help his brothers and sisters to improve their tennis and golf. When the weather was too bad to sail, hotly contested games of Monopoly and Twenty Questions were played on the big veranda, and on Friday nights more than 25 young people would watch first-run movies in the basement.

While Jack Kennedy was concentrating on winning yacht races in Hyannis Port in 1936, another young man was making his first appearance on Cape Cod. The congressman from Beverly, Massachussetts, Henry Cabot Lodge, Jr., was hoping to move up to the

43

Senate. He had already been nominated by the recent Republican state convention to succeed U.S. Senator Marcus A. Coolidge, and he had been invited to address a meeting of the Cape Cod Men and Women's Republican Club in Hyannis that July.

Observers didn't rate his chances very high against so proven a vote-getter as the famed "Purple Shamrock," James Michael Curley, who had been elected governor in 1934. Nonetheless the tall, handsome candidate presented to Hyannis supporters a "frank and open countenance and a winning smile."

It is not likely that Jack Kennedy was among the audience of two hundred at Masonic Hall in September 1936 to hear Lodge's speech, but it is quite possible that he and other members of his family attended the large Democratic rally held at the Barnstable High School auditorium, where a standing-room-only crowd of more than five hundred heard James Michael Curley's rebuttal. Curley was never a popular figure on Cape Cod—he had polled only 2,665 votes to 8,560 for his Republican opponent in the gubernatorial election of 1934. The evident star attraction and the reason for the size of the audience was Jimmy Roosevelt,[9] the President's personable son, who shared the platform and spoke first. He began:

> I have been here several times before, most as a summer visitor, and I have sailed my boat into Hyannis Port. I even ran on the mud getting into Hyannis Port, so I feel quite at home here. All I can hope is I won't run on the mud tonight.

Roosevelt went on with a smile:

> I was told before I came to Cape Cod that the meetings here would be small; that there were only something like 50 registered Democrats in this town, so I decided most of this audience must be Republicans. It does you and the American people a world of credit, this being willing to listen to both sides.

Then Curley was introduced. Answering alleged charges that he owned a palatial mansion in Oyster Harbors—"near the Du Ponts"—Curley explained that he had merely rented a cottage for a month or so to be allowed to live near the seventh green. "I was living, my friends, in the most beautiful and most healthful spot in the entire world—Cape Cod near Hyannis." Then, after the applause subsided, Curley added, "It's about as near Heaven as I ever expect to get."

Curley then asked the question, "What brought the new people to seashore and city in New England?"

Well a few years ago I got all six New England governors together in a hotel and got them to promise to raise $100,000 each to advertise our resources. In 1934 we found $400 million in tourist business coming here; in 1935, $550 million and this year of 1936, $750 million. There were a lot of vacant business places and homes down here on Cape Cod before I started this plan, and now come down to Cape Cod and try to hire a $2 room for $5!

Referring to his opponent as "bright, young Mr. Lodge, who always reminds me of that old nursery rhyme, 'Little Boy Blue,' " Curley closed with a long inventory of the millions in Federal money he had brought to Massachusetts.

Applause for Curley's speech was little better than perfunctory. Even though tourism had, indeed picked up, Curley's sly reference to overcharging for rooms—an extraordinary lapse in tact—wouldn't win him any more votes. Cape Cod went overwhelmingly for Henry Cabot Lodge in November, helping elect him to the Senate. And Cape Cod, abloom with sunflower buttons in support of Kansas Governor Alf Landon, joined Vermont and Maine in remaining steadfastly Republican in the face of the biggest landslide in the country's history, giving Landon 11,338 votes to Roosevelt's 4,763.

By September 1937, there were published rumors that Kennedy would replace Secretary of the Treasury Morgenthau after his own term as Maritime Commissioner had expired. Then the Kennedys scattered: Joe, Jr., and Jack to Harvard; Kathleen to Sacred Heart Convent in Noroton, Connecticut; Eunice to Sacred Heart Convent in New York, and Rosemary for her second year at Residence School in New York. The youngest children returned with their parents to Bronxville, New York.[10]

Before the Hyannis Port house was closed for the season, Joseph P. Kennedy was able to get in a few rounds of golf with William O. Douglas, the new chairman of the Securities and Exchange Commission. (Kennedy resigned as chairman of the SEC in September 1935.) In November Marguerite ("Missy") LeHand, secretary to President Roosevelt, and Betsy Roosevelt were guests of the Kennedys at their winter villa in Palm Beach, "La Querida."

The climax of a hectic year came shortly afterward:

The news of the appointment of Joseph P. Kennedy of Boston as Ambassador to the Court of St. James is as gratifying to the people of Cape Cod as to all the other parts of the country which are hailing this selection as one of the achievements of the Roosevelt Administration.

So began an editorial published in the Hyannis *Patriot* on Thursday, December 16, 1937. It went on:

As everybody knows, our new Ambassador has done efficient service to the Administration at Washington and has made the Maritime Commission, of which he is chairman, of such outstanding importance that the only objection we have seen to this new appointment is that his services were still needed in the Commission. This, in itself, is proof of his worth as is also the splendid work done as Chairman of the SEC.

The Boston *Herald* says editorially: "Joseph P. Kennedy, whom President Roosevelt is to name as Ambassador to the Court of St. James has done well at everything he has undertaken. He has been highly successful as a banker, a businessman, a reorganizer and a federal administrator."

While Mr. Kennedy has always been a devoted follower of President Roosevelt, and is believed to have been a restraining influence and, as such, valued at the White House, outspoken frankness is said to be one reason why his views were sought by the President who, by the way, is believed to have made the appointment on his own initiative.

Mr. Kennedy has a record of accomplishment, is definitely American and as a scholar and public speaker, with wide acquaintance with leaders in business and government affairs, is unusually well-qualified for this post which just now presents problems of special importance.

Three

An excited crowd had gathered at the Wianno club's pier in Osterville waiting for the low heavy fog to lift and the starting event of a three-day racing schedule sponsored by the Intercollegiate Yacht Racing Association and held on Cape Cod for the first time. Boats from ten leading Eastern colleges and universities * were already bobbing in the choppy shore waters ready to take part in competition for the prized MacMillan Cup.

The races got under way at 11:00 a.m. For Jack Kennedy it was like coming home for he had sailed the waters of Nantucket Sound since he was ten years old; now, near the end of his sophomore year, he would race on them again as part of a Harvard crew.

"We finished third today," Jack told a reporter on the evening after the first day's racing. "But it was close and we're hoping for the best."

The house at Hyannis Port was virtually closed up. "They opened only enough rooms for Jack and me," Ambassador Joseph P. Kennedy said before disclaiming reports that Jack's "illness" could prevent him from attending Joe Jr.'s commencement exercises at Harvard the next day.

Prior to his arrival at Hyannis Port the Ambassador had admitted no expectation of an honorary degree to be forthcoming from Harvard, telling Boston reporters, "There's going to be one honor degree in the family," referring to his eldest son, due to receive a Bachelor of Arts *cum laude*.

Arriving in New York aboard the *Queen Mary* Joseph P. Kennedy had disclaimed any intention of seeking the Democratic presidential nomination in 1940. Such a move would be, in his view, "a breach of faith" against Roosevelt.

Due to return to England aboard the *Normandie* accompanied by

* Those competing were Brown, Cornell, Dartmouth, Harvard, M.I.T., University of Pennsylvania, Princeton, Trinity, Williams and Yale.

his two sons toward the end of June Ambassador Kennedy confessed, "I'd like to be in London for the Fourth of July."

"The Americans over there always have a banquet," he went on, "and this year I'm supposed to preside with Anthony Eden as speaker."

It was easy to understand Kennedy's eagerness to return to England in 1938. The British were delighted with their ambassador, dubbing him "Jolly Joe" and in a sly reference to the size of his attractive and often-photographed family he was hailed as "the father of his country" and "the nine-child envoy." Kennedy responded with an ebullient and good-humored side of his nature that had seldom been visible in the United States, where he was usually represented as a dour, tough, get-things-done executive of ruthless efficiency or as a mystery man operating in the doubtful corridors of Wall Street and Hollywood.

"Obviously," Rose Kennedy remembered later, "we had superior entry to nearly everything. If we went to the races we watched from the owners' boxes. We all had tea with the Queen. The children got a great deal out of it."

Joseph P. Kennedy spent the following morning completing a voluminous report to be presented to President Roosevelt during their conference. In the afternoon, Kennedy arrived in Wianno in time to see his son Jack skipper a Harvard boat to second place in the final race of the day, putting Harvard on top with a total of 79½ points to Williams' 78¼. Then, blaming the pressure of his duties for having prevented his appearance at Harvard's commencement, Kennedy left early that evening for Washington.

On the final day of the races, Joe, Jr., joined his brother at Wianno. Together they gave a demonstration of well-practiced seamanship, winning two seconds in the morning races and a second and a third in the final afternoon events to defeat rival Yale, the defending champion. They won the prized trophy (nosing out Dartmouth 115½ to 112) and the right to "sip the victor's nectar" from the MacMillan Cup.

That night at the presentation banquet at Oyster Harbors Club, the difference between the two brothers was especially noticeable. In public Jack seemed reserved, almost self-effacing, with people he didn't know.

"Jack looked like a nice enough kid; but it was Joe you noticed and remembered. He had a very magnetic personality. He seemed to know everybody at the banquet, and everybody seemed to know him."

After the intercollegiate yacht racing at Wianno, Jack and Joe, Jr., lingered at Hyannis Port, seizing a last opportunity to sail their boats before leaving for England with their father. Both boys owned automobiles in advanced stages of dilapidation. Jack's was a maroon phaeton with dented fenders and a crushed radiator grill; the hood of Joe's vintage tan Ford roadster was held firmly in place by a stout rope. The cars had, however, provided adequate transportation to bring the boys to both the Hyannis and Center—formerly Idlehour —movie theaters in Hyannis.

Joe, Jr., had merely smiled when asked by the *Patriot* if he was proud of his father's accomplishments. The paper reported "we'll miss the Kennedys," noting at the same time that "both boys can take with modesty the fame of their well-known father and still wear the same sized hat."

Although they were on fairly good terms at Harvard during their undergraduate days, the brothers led separate lives, enjoyed friends and interests of their own, yet frequently saw each other to exchange family news and occasionally went to a movie or saw a musical trying out in Boston. A "C" student and member of the *Crimson*'s editorial board, considered "reasonably inconspicuous" by his classmates, Jack was still aware of being outdone by his brother.

Joe, in robust good health, seemed to have an endless supply of energy, which enabled him to make Pi Eta and Hasty Pudding, as well as both the football and soccer teams, serve three years on the student council, manage the business end of the yearbook, serve as chairman of Class Day activities and still find time, as chairman of the house committee, to select Bunny Berigan's orchestra for a Winthrop House dance. On top of that he kept his grades high enough to be graduated with honors. Jack, on the other hand, in a vain effort to succeed in athletics, had allowed his studies to slip during his first two years at Harvard. And illness continued to plague him. When his father sailed for England to assume his ambassadorship in February 1938, Jack was in Harvard's infirmary with flu, the same illness that was later to prevent him from making the swimming

49

team chosen to meet Yale. Earlier, a practice scrimmage as a 149-pound member of Harvard's junior varsity football team caused a spinal injury that would bring him pain for the rest of his life.

In May 1938 Jack became a millionaire; his coming of age brought to him the initial benefits of a trust fund established for him by his father in 1929. It seemed to make very little difference as far as pocket money was concerned, for in a 1939 letter to his father in London, Jack wrote: "Was wondering what my allowance would be? Could you let me known as I want to arrange my budget."

Forfeiting the $1,000 reward his father profferred to those of his children who neither smoked nor drank before the age of 21, Jack admitted that he had sipped a little beer while at Harvard.

Jack returned to the United States aboard the *Bremen*, going directly to Hyannis Port in September before beginning his junior year at Harvard.

It had been an extraordinary summer for Jack and one he would later recall in *Why England Slept:* "You had the feeling of an era ending, and everyone had a very good time at the end."

But Chamberlain was not prepared to fight a war because of a "quarrel in a far away country between people of whom we know nothing." In September Chamberlain sacrificed Czechoslovakia to Hitler at Munich, in exchange for "peace in our time."

Fully in sympathy with Chamberlain's actions, Ambassador Kennedy drew close to the British Prime Minister. Their friendship grew out of shared feelings that another world war must be avoided at all costs. At Roosevelt's request Kennedy deleted the following phrase from the text of a prepared speech delivered in Aberdeen, Scotland: "I can't for the life of me understand why anybody would want to go to war to save the Czechs."

Later that September a severe hurricane struck Cape Cod, and a high tide spilled over the Ocean Street bulkhead. Flooding was reported in Hyannis Port, where a large crowd had gathered at the harbor. Most of the boats of the summer fleet were still at their moorings when the storm arose; many of the smaller knockabouts were overturned, and others had dragged their moorings and been cast on the beach. The storm had severely damaged the Hyannis Port Civic Association's pier and had completely wiped out that of the Wianno club.

Jack returned to Hyannis Port for Armistice Day to survey the wreckage left in the wake of the hurricane. He brought as his guest Count Alexis de Pourttes of Switzerland, a classmate at Harvard.

His brother Joe was by then serving his father as secretary at the London embassy. Kathleen was at the University of London majoring in languages, and Rosemary, Eunice, Patricia and Jean were enrolled at the Convent of the Sacred Heart at Roehampton. Jack himself would later go to London to work in his father's embassy; the experience in government service, he confessed, could significantly influence his choice of career.

By the summer of 1939 Cape Cod plans had been completed for the tercentenary celebration that would mark the three hundredth anniversary of the Town of Barnstable. No mere tourist "promotion," the celebration reflected native Cape Codders' genuine absorption with their own past.

Fully recovered from the hardships of the Depression, and usually content to let the summer people have Cape Cod pretty much their own way during the "season," the year-rounders proudly reasserted their domination with a celebration that began on a warm Fourth of July, lasted the whole summer through and was climaxed by the first revival of the Old Barnstable Fair since 1930.

Hyannis bustled with special events, exhibits, tours of historic homes opened for the tercentenary, colonial costume balls (dress was specified semiformal or colonial) and the publication of an historical volume.*

A parade sponsored by the American Legion and the tercentenary committee launched the celebration while an estimated eight thousand watched; it was followed by a band contest at the Barnstable High School athletic field. A historical pageant recreated the first settlement of Barnstable in the free verse typical of the genre. The marking of historic sites vied with clambakes, band concerts, special "forefathers" services at churches and other special events.

The centennial of baseball coincided with Hyannis Week activities and was celebrated by a game between a picked team of "Old Timers" and a team of "All-Stars" from the Cape Cod League. Fittingly, the "Old Timers" won.

The matrons' club of the Federated Church in Hyannis sponsored a tercentenary street fair that included a doll-carriage parade, a pet

* *Barnstable: Three Centuries of a Cape Cod Town*, edited by Donald N. Trayser (Hyannis: F. P. and B. P. Goss, 1939).

51

show and various booths exhibiting antiques and handicrafts. In the evening there was street dancing while the fair continued. And a tercentenary regatta was held under the auspices of the Hyannis yacht club, attracting more than 48 boats from Hyannis Port, Wianno, Cotuit, Bass River and Oyster Harbors—the largest fleet ever to race on Lewis Bay.

In mid-celebration, Honey Fitz, who was spending the summer at his son-in-law's house in Hyannis Port,[1] could be heard faintly above the tumult of tercentenary activities. He had not been asked to take part in the celebration; however, his address to the Hyannis Rotary Club on the railroad situation was fiery enough to attract attention in Boston newspapers as well as in the local press.

Pointing out that the New Haven planned to abandon in September the Old Colony Line linking Cape Cod with Boston, Honey Fitz described the situation as "incredible." In an attempt the previous day to go to Boston to see the "Old Timers" game at Fenway Park, he had missed the 10:30 train and had then discovered that he couldn't get another until 6:00 that night.

"Think of that!" the ex-Mayor of Boston said. "You can't get out of this garden spot of the world between 10 and 6 in the daytime by train or bus. And no one seems to be aroused down here about it!"

Adding, somewhat threateningly, that he had already spoken with a representative of the Interstate Commerce Commission in Washington about the situation, he concluded his speech by leading Hyannis Rotarians in singing "Sweet Adeline."

The tercentenary dominated the summer of 1939 on Cape Cod, and one event dominated the tercentenary: the arrival from Liverpool on the liner *Laconia* of Mayor Charles F. Dart and his wife of Barnstaple, England. After being received by a delegation of tercentenary-committee members in Governor Leverett W. Saltonstall's office in Boston and escorted to Cape Cod, the Mayor and his wife were taken to the Oyster Harbors Club for a two-week stay.

Mayor Dart made a strong and affecting impression on Cape Codders at the first public ceremony that he and his wife attended in their official capacity: a reception by the committee at Barnstable High School auditorium, which was attended by more than five hundred people.

During his first public address, Mayor Dart spoke glowingly of the former United States Ambassador to Great Britain, Robert Worth

Bingham. No mention was made throughout Mayor Dart's visit of the current ambassador, Joseph P. Kennedy, a curious lapse considering that Kennedy owned a house in the town of Barnstable—as the selectmen or members of the tercentenary committee undoubtedly pointed out. But Kennedy's popularity in England was already on the decline, particularly after the speech he delivered in October 1938 at the Navy League's Trafalgar Day dinner. It seemed inappropriate only three weeks after Munich to preach peaceful coexistence with the dictatorship of Nazi Germany. Kennedy's admonition, "After all we have to live together in the same world whether we like it or not," had created a furor of criticism on both sides of the Atlantic.[2]

Mayor Dart painted a vivid picture for his Cape Cod audience of England at the brink of war, at the same time making it "quite plain to all that we desire not war, but peace" and explaining that England had "no jealousy of German greatness, nor wish to injure her or block her legitimate interests or power."

"We do not wish to fight her, either with arms or with hostile arrangements of trade, if she is willing to associate herself with us and with other peace-loving nations of the world in covenants of justice, law and fair dealing." Frequently interrupted by applause from what appeared to be a strongly pro-British audience, he concluded a speech in which he sought "to help toward that close union of English-speaking peoples which I think is the best possible guarantee for peace and prosperity."

Then he presented the people of the town of Barnstable with the Steeple Cup, an exact replica of a fifteenth-century cup "which is amongst our civic silver, and one greatly prized by Englishmen whenever they see it"; six engravings of old Barnstaple's Guild Hall and of the quay from which "brave pioneers left the pleasant countryside of Devonshire to come to America"; a small silver bowl from the Association of Barumites in London, and an illuminated scroll conveying municipal greetings of good will.

The tercentenary committee in its turn presented the Mayor with an illuminated scroll in which expressions of good will were preserved in book form, bound in covers of blue morocco leather with silk bindings; messages of friendship were set forth in illuminated hand lettering executed by Cartier's.

Mayor Dart received at the same time a certificate of appointment as deputy sheriff—"a unique distinction . . . being the first foreign

53

citizen ever to be appointed to this position of public trust in the county of Barnstable"—and a deputy sheriff's badge. The mayor's wife received, among other gifts, a necklace of "Cape Cod pearls" made from essence of fish scales.

On the morning of Saturday, August 25, a light drizzle threatened continuing poor weather, but by noon the skies had cleared, and more than eight hundred men and women sat under a large tent erected at the southeast turn of the racetrack on the fairgrounds for the Tercentenary Banquet and ceremonies at 1:00 P.M.

During the banquet, an unannounced visitor, "Johnnie" of Philip Morris cigarettes—three feet tall and dressed in his familiar red jacket and pillbox hat—went to the head table, shook hands with Mayor Dart, turned to the guests and shouted, "Call for Philip Morris."

Among the distinguished guests were Joseph C. Lincoln, author of many popular books about Cape Cod, and George Lyman Kittredge, Gurney Professor of English at Harvard. The star of the show, however, was Mayor Dart, who said in his farewell address:

> We in our country are fully conscious of all we owe this great country, the United States of America. There is a debt which we owe to you which will be very difficult to repay. I speak now of those brave men, the flower of your country who came across to us in our great difficulty and danger in 1917, who stood side by side, shoulder to shoulder with British soldiers. They gave their lives that we might preserve our liberty which we now enjoy and the only possible way we can repay your great country for those brave men is to say that they did not die in vain.

Thanking the tercentenary committee for its many gifts and for the hospitality of the townspeople, Mayor Dart concluded by wishing those assembled good luck and God's blessings. The audience stood, a band played and those attending joined in singing "God Save the King" and "The Star Spangled Banner."

On September 1, 1939, Germany attacked Poland. England went to war two days later.[3]

A trip through Western Europe, the Soviet Union and the Balkans during the spring and summer of 1939 had given Jack Kennedy fascinating insights into a continent poised for war. When the British liner *Athenia*, with 300 Americans among its 1,400 passengers, was torpedoed by German submarines, Jack was sent to Glasgow with his father's secretary, Eddie Moore, to assist the rescued.

Back at Harvard in October, Jack took extra courses in government and economics in order to make up for his semester's trip abroad. He was "doing better with the gals," he wrote his father; he was taking a friend of Kathleen's to the Princeton game and was "interested to see how it works." As a candidate for a degree with honors, he was required to write an undergraduate thesis.

At the beginning of 1940, a "Kennedy for President" boom sprang up in Massachusetts, and a campaign was launched to elect delegates pledged to him in the March Democratic primary. When he returned to Boston for a checkup at the Lahey Clinic, Joseph P. Kennedy was questioned about the "phony war" in Europe. "All hell will break loose in the spring," Kennedy warned, at the same time announcing that at the termination of his duties as ambassador his political life would be at an end.

"Appreciating as I must the great honor implied in this step," Kennedy said, declining support for those booming his candidacy for the presidential nomination, "I must nevertheless with positiveness state that I am not a candidate."

Throughout the winter and spring of 1940, Jack devoted himself to his thesis,* taking time out only to chair an undergraduate committee that raised $1,200 for Red Cross war relief. He avoided participation in the famous debate raging on Harvard's campus over the issue of United States involvement in the war in Europe; Joe, Jr., in his second year at Harvard Law School, took the lead among those who supported a policy of strict nonintervention.

"Finished my thesis," Jack wrote his father in the spring. "It was only going to run about the average length, 70 pages, but finally ran to 150. Am sending you a copy. It is the third carbon as the other two had to be handed in. I'll be interested to see what you think of it, as it represents more work than I've ever done in my life."

After being awarded a grade of *magna cum laude*, Jack began to think of having his thesis published. "I thought I could work on rewriting it," he wrote his father, "and making it somewhat more complete and more interesting for the average reader—as it stands

---

* Appeasement at Munich: The Inevitable Result of the Slowness of the British Democracy to Change from a Disarmament Policy," published by Wilfred Funk, Inc., in July 1940 under the title, *Why England Slept*. The new title was suggested by Arthur Krock, and the book sold forty thousand copies in the United States and an equal number in England.

now—it is not anywhere polished enough, although the ideas, etc. are O.K."

Although his father was enthusiastic about the idea, he suggested that Jack recheck his material, for "I have found several instances where you have misspelled names and got your dates wrong." Later the Ambassador asked Arthur Krock to recommend an agent; long-time friend Henry Luce was prevailed upon to write a foreword.

Jack's graduation *cum laude* from Harvard was witnessed that summer by Joe, Jr., Kathleen, Rosemary, Eunice and Honey Fitz. His mother was there too and observed later that "Jack seems a little depressed that he let his girl get away. He says she is the only one he really enjoyed going out with and yet he admits that he did not want to get married."

Jack spent the summer attending weekly dances at Hyannis Port and Wianno and participating in a busy schedule of sailing races when he wasn't reading galleys of *Why England Slept.*

In June Mayor Dart of Barnstaple appealed to Cape Codders to provide homes for from fifty to sixty war-threatened English children. A drive to raise $10,000 was promptly launched, and foster parents willing to care for the children for the duration of the war were urged to volunteer at a registry established on the second floor of the town offices on Hyannis' Main Street.

Eventually the plan to evacuate children was entirely suspended, and the money raised by Cape Cod residents was spent instead on a nursery for bombed-out Barnstaple children, officially dedicated a year later by Ambassador and Mrs. John G. Winant.

Involvement in World War II loomed larger—the draft was already being debated in Congress that summer—but, for the Kennedy children, 1940 was a memorable summer, the last they were all to share at Hyannis Port. And, although there were still touch football and softball games on the spacious lawns; hard-fought mixed doubles on the tennis court; sailboat races on *Victura, Tenovus* and *Onemore,* and evenings in the family's basement theater to watch first-run movies, Joe, Jr., had already launched his political career, winning a delegate's seat from Boston's West End district to the Democratic convention at Chicago.[4] Kathleen had joined the staff of the Washington *Times-Herald,* and Jack made his debut as author and budding political philosopher with publication of the well-received *Why*

England Slept in July; it became a Book-of-the-Month Club selection and soon appeared on best-seller lists as well.

Why England Slept was stocked at the News Store in Hyannis Port, which had opened its doors in a new building adjacent to the post office after Cora Lumbert's general store had closed in 1938.

"It sold quite well," Robert O'Neil, then owner-manager of the shop said. "We didn't do anything special to promote it; I guess people were just curious. They'd known Jack ever since he was a little boy running around the 'Port barefoot. Jack would come in now and then, but he never asked how the book was doing."

In August the Hyannis *Patriot* paid tribute to the young author and, after referring to a sequel, "England Awakens," to be published in the September issue of *Current History*, quoted a radio interview in which Jack had declared:

> Politics must not decide our national defense policy. The only solution is for us to realize the sacrifices which all groups must make. We cannot tell people to keep out of our hemisphere unless we are prepared to back our demands to the point of going to war.

When the book was published in England, *The Times Literary Supplement* said of it, "a young man's book, it contains much wisdom for older men."

"You would be surprised how a book that really makes the grade with high class people stands you in good stead for years to come," Jack's father wrote to his son jubilantly in August.

The book brought Jack his first important earned money, about $40,000. He donated the English royalties to the badly bomb-damaged town of Plymouth, and used part of his American royalties to buy himself a new Buick.

A visitor to Hyannis Port in 1940 marveled at the whirlwind of activity: "I was fascinated by them. Jack was autographing copies of *Why England Slept* while Grandfather Fitzgerald was reading to him a political story from a newspaper. Young Joe was telling them something that happened to him in Russia. Mrs. Kennedy was talking on the phone with Cardinal Spellman. A tall and very attractive girl in a sweat shirt and dungarees turned out to be Pat, who was describing how a German Messerschmitt plane had crashed near her father's house outside London. Bobby was trying to get everybody to play charades. The next thing I knew all of us were choosing up sides for touch football and Kathleen was calling the plays in the huddle for the team I was on. There was something doing every minute. The conversation at the dinner table was wonderful, lively and entertaining, ranging from the war and Washington politics to books, sports and show business."

Even the family's black French poodle, Spookie, made headlines that summer when he became lost attempting to follow the car taking a group of Kennedys into Hyannis. Found several miles away from the Kennedy house and turned over to the ASPCA agent in Hyannis, the dog expressed his appreciation, when a chauffeur was sent to the kennels, by performing a favorite trick of "praying"— bringing his paws together and only releasing them with the word, "Amen."

On a late-summer London broadcast, Ambassador Kennedy was quoted as having remarked that loss of sleep from bombings was not so unusual to the father of nine children. But his humor had an empty ring. Alone in London, missing his family and with his frustration mounting as more and more policy was dictated directly from Washington, Kennedy was increasingly out of favor with the English press. Although he admired Britain's "stiff upper lip," he didn't see how she could take much more punishment. With invasion apparently imminent and the ever-present danger of German parachute landings, Kennedy made no secret of his belief that "the defeat of England is unavoidable."

In an unprepared speech given in East Boston at a reunion of parishioners of Our Lady of the Assumption Church, where Joseph P. Kennedy had once been an altar boy, he outspokenly articulated his noninterventionist convictions, stating explicitly, "This is not our war." The speech was acidly attacked in the weekly *Spectator:* "It would seem there are plenty of eminent persons in the United States to give isolationist advice without the Ambassador to the Court of St. James, who knows all our anxieties, all our ordeals, finding it necessary to join himself to that number."

Jack and Joe, Jr., were among those young men registering for the draft in October 1940, when Ambassador Kennedy returned to the United States, bringing with him an air-raid siren, which, he said, he intended to use at Hyannis Port to call the children from their boats at dinner time.

"This country must and will stay out of the war," Kennedy said in a radio speech urging the re-election of President Roosevelt. (The largest vote in the history of Cape Cod in November gave Willkie 12,659 votes to Roosevelt's 5,351.)

The day after Roosevelt's re-election Joseph P. Kennedy resigned his ambassadorship, agreeing to stay on only until a successor could be named; then he flew to the West Coast to visit Jack, who was studying business administration at Stanford University.

By December Camp Edwards in Falmouth was preparing to receive the first conscripts under national Selective Service, and Cape towns were arranging to provide gifts and entertainment for all batteries of the 68th regiment at a huge Christmas party to be held at the camp.

On December 1, after an outspoken interview with Louis Lyons of the Boston *Globe* in which Kennedy claimed, among other things, that "democracy is finished in England," it was publicly announced that his resignation as ambassador was submitted on November 6.

Four

December 7, 1941, dawned cold but sunny on Cape Cod.

The 181st Infantry chapel at Camp Edwards was filled to overflowing. Hyannis' Main Street had been festively decorated for Christmas, and an open house for soldiers and civilians was planned at Masonic Hall from 2:00 P.M. to midnight. Many uniformed young men were being welcomed into Cape Cod homes for Sunday dinner when the first news came of the attack on Pearl Harbor.

Coast guardsmen from the Sandwich station began at once policing the Cape Cod canal to prevent sabotage and, using a picket vessel and a lifeboat, searched all ships approaching the waterway from the east, while the cutter *General Greene* stopped those entering from the west.

Civilian defense-district warning centers in Hyannis, Falmouth and Chatham were tested and went into immediate operation on a 24-hour basis.

There was no indication of any troop movement from Camp Edwards, where twenty thousand men had returned from Carolina maneuvers, but the camp commandant issued a plea to civilians to refrain from telephoning the camp because no war information was available and telephone operators were being swamped with calls.

Cape Codders were lining up by the time recruiting centers opened the following morning. Barnstable Post 206 of the American Legion broadcast an urgent appeal for volunteers to man aircraft observation stations; the waters of Cape Cod Bay and Nantucket Sound were heavily patrolled.

News of the Cape's first fatality of World War II was received when Private First Class Robert S. Brown, 26, of Chatham was reported killed in action at Hickam Field, Hawaii.

Following his resignation as Ambassador to Great Britain, Joseph P. Kennedy had attacked President Roosevelt's Lend-Lease Bill as likely to lead to war and had called for "all aid to Britain consistent with our own defense needs." From his Palm Beach winter home he wired President Roosevelt on December 7: "In this great crisis all Americans are with you. Name the battle front. I'm yours to command." [1]

But the previous summer Kennedy's oldest son had already volunteered his services. On July 10, 1941, Joseph Kennedy, Jr., sailed *Victura* in a senior-class race over an 8:08-mile course at Hyannis Port for the last time before entering the Navy. Having volunteered in June, he left Hyannis Port to begin preliminary training as a navy pilot at Squantum Air Station, abandoning his studies at Harvard Law School, where, as a student leader, he had been "unequivocally opposed" to convoying munitions and other supplies to Great Britain. "My ideas haven't changed. I still don't think we should go into the war," Joe said. "But I thought I ought to be doing something and I'll do whatever they tell me to do."

Asked by reporters how his father felt about his entering the Navy, Joe answered, "My father, especially, approves of what I am doing."

Jack, too, had sought to volunteer. Upon returning from a winter tour of South America after an unsatisfactory semester of graduate courses in business administration at Stanford University, he had planned to enter Yale Law School in the fall. Applying first to army, then to navy, recruiters, Jack was rejected both times because of the back injury he had suffered at Harvard.

During the summer of 1941, Jack lifted weights and followed an intensive regimen of diet, treatment and exercise to build his strength. And, although the old excitement of racing the *Victura* seemed lessened in comparison with greater battles being fought elsewhere, Jack did get his first look at PT boats on Nantucket Sound that summer.

On Joseph P. Kennedy's 53rd birthday, celebrated at a dinner party in Hyannis Port, all his family was present except Joe, Jr., who was in training in Jacksonville, Florida. But very soon Jack left, having finally passed the Navy's fitness tests. He was sent to Washington to work in the intelligence section in the office of the Navy Chief of Staff. At about the same time Rosemary was sent to St. Coletta's School, a Catholic institution for the mentally retarded in Jefferson, Wisconsin.

To an earlier suggestion that Rosemary be sent away to an institution, Kennedy, Sr., had replied: "What can they do for her that her family can't do better? We will keep her at home." But by 1941 she had become increasingly more difficult to handle, more withdrawn and irritable. Informed by doctors that Rosemary would never get better, her parents had to make the long-delayed decision.

Cape Cod was a surprise to returning summer visitors in 1942. The narrow strip of land thrust out to sea had become an armed camp.

Beside huge sprawling Camp Edwards, there was a vastly expanded Coast Guard detachment operating between Sandwich and Provincetown; a naval base at Woods Hole; an antiaircraft training center at Scorton Neck Beach, and two amphibian commando training units at Camp Can-Do-It in sleepy unspoiled Cotuit and in Waquoit, adjacent to Falmouth. Hyannis Airport had been activated as a simulated flattop for the training of Naval Air Corps cadets; later it became an Army Air Corps antisubmarine base.

All cameras were banned from ocean-beach areas by order of the Eastern Defense Command; between sunset and sunrise the public was barred from beaches fronting the ocean. Possession of radio-transmission sets, codes, explosives and firearms was strictly prohibited at all times in these areas, as was the use of binoculars and signaling devices.

Blackouts were held in July, "primarily to acquaint summer residents with regulations." Cape Codders and summer visitors alike were urged to save waste paper, magazines, tinfoil, cardboard, aluminum, everything containing steel—and to conserve electricity, oil, coal, gas and wood. Posters warning, "Loose talk can lose lives" reminded Cape Codders never to repeat idle gossip of a military nature. The Mayflower Restaurant on Main Street in Hyannis added, "Remember Pearl Harbor" to the top of its bill of fare; it was to appear there "every day until Japan was beaten."

Honey Fitz raised his voice to render "Sweet Adeline" during a dance-of-the-week program at Hyannis' new USO Club, where Ping-Pong, dances and community sings were available and female companionship were provided from a roster of more than four hundred registered USO girls. Other local organizations worked closely with the Morale and Recreation Office at Camp Edwards (where in June Kay Kyser and his College of Musical Knowledge offered a two-hour show) to supply further entertainment for servicemen, in the form of clambakes, beach parties, street dances and hospitality in Cape Cod homes.

In June Jack Kennedy returned to Hyannis Port on leave. He had applied for sea duty immediately after Pearl Harbor but had been sent from Washington to a project in the South defending war plants from sabotage. Fearful of spending the war behind a desk, Jack had appealed to his father to use his influence with the Navy Department, particularly with Undersecretary James Forrestal, who had formerly been associated with a Wall Street firm of investment bankers.

Finally Jack was transferred to a Motor Torpedo Boat training station at Melville, Rhode Island (close enough to Hyannis Port for off-duty visits), where he worked hard to master the PTs in practice runs on Naragansett Bay.

Thin but boyishly handsome in his navy uniform, Jack cast it aside on the occasional weekends spent on leave at Hyannis Port and donned dungarees and oilskins to race the *Victura* to third place in a senior-class race in June.

The war appeared finally to be reaching into the seemingly impregnable and remote confines of sedate Hyannis Port; the thirteenth annual water carnival that September at the West Beach Club was "an impromptu affair since the committee had earlier decided to cancel the event this season."

In July the *Cape Cod Standard-Times* reported that

Hyannis Port had tough sledding to find enough boats to even have a race. The Senior and Weather Class yachts were among the missing, but a three boat race was sailed off in the Junior Class. Ross Richards' craft was the victor over the two Kennedy boats [*Tenovus* and *Onemore*] sailed by Pat and Eunice Kennedy.

The first annual Wianno senior-class regatta, originally scheduled for Wianno, was moved to Lewis Bay in Hyannis when it was discovered that the army would undertake firing maneuvers in the former area, closing those waters for three weeks. *Victura*, skippered by Bobby Kennedy, placed thirteenth out of fifteen boats racing.

That summer the facilities of the ultraexclusive Wianno club were extended, from 5:00 to 10:00 P.M. daily, to enlisted men stationed in Osterville, and long, patient lines at the Hyannis and Center Theaters waited to see *This Above All* and *Mrs. Miniver*. As the

Russians retreated toward Stalingrad under heavy German attack and the battle of El Alamein raged in Libya, gas-rationing stickers appeared on automobile windshields, and depot parties at the Hyannis railroad station sent native recruits off to war with tercentenary medals presented by the USO and cigarettes, courtesy of the Hyannis Board of Trade. Send-off chairmen saw to it that Cape Codders bound for military training were given snacks from the Red Cross canteen before boarding the train. It was a summer like no other Cape Cod had ever seen, a summer of Camel caravans, V-Mail, cuffless pants and victory gardens, which came into their first harvest as Hyannis suffered through a "beef famine" in July. It was a summer when year-rounders and summer people alike were encouraged to telephone Hyannis 1-0000 "at any sign of enemy activity on Cape Cod."

Never before had the Cape been so crowded. Every rooming house, inn and summer hotel reported "no vacancy," and overnight cabins were filled with army wives. Local USO and Travelers' Aid Societies were besieged with requests for accommodations, as army families poured onto the Cape along with an accelerated flow of vacationers. Communities near Camp Edwards were faced with the most critical housing problem in their history while the arrival of soldiers' families numbering in the thousands continued unabated; troops arrived on Cape Cod from Florida, Texas and Georgia. When the summer season finally drew to a close, Camp Edwards families rushed to take possession of vacated summer houses.

At his first public appearance since his resignation as ambassador, at naval recruiting exercises in Symphony Hall in Boston late in August 1942, Joseph P. Kennedy declared that it was easy for him to feel a kinship with the mothers and fathers of the recruits because he himself had two sons serving in the Navy. Limiting his remarks to simple and sincere words of patriotism, Kennedy could not have helped thinking, as he looked over the audience of young men who faced him so respectfully hushed, that many of them, like his own sons, might meet death in the months ahead. Afterward one thousand recruits—all residents of eastern Massachusetts—took the service oath.

The elder Kennedy was quiet and subdued, hardly the firebrand he had been declared to be. Reminding his audience that the occasion was not one for giving advice but rather "to derive inspiration from

64

your actions," he termed enlistment in the Navy a "simple act of faith, an act of devotion to your country and [it] arouses in us who are on the home front a deep sense of what we owe to you and what we must do to sustain you."

In September Joseph E. Casey, an ardent supporter of the Roosevelt administration, won the Democratic party's endorsement to oppose Henry Cabot Lodge, defeating John F. ("Honey Fitz") Fitzgerald by more than 27,000 votes.

In November Lodge easily carried Cape Cod; he won re-election by a total majority of 70,000 votes. Barnstable villages also voted "wet" on three controversial liquor questions, despite an active campaign by well-organized temperance forces to ban liquor in areas around army bases.

Early in 1943 Jack Kennedy shipped out from San Francisco for the South Pacific, where by March he was commanding his own PT boat in the Solomons.

By the spring of 1943, Cape Cod's fishing industry had been revitalized to such an extent that record loads of mackerel and whiting were fetching top prices. But a new peril attended the resurgence: There was always the danger of finding live torpedoes in the drag along with flounder and cod. Fishermen were warned by the Coast Guard that "it is very dangerous to allow any object hauled from the bottom to sink or be dumped overboard once it is on the surface as an explosion may occur which will sink or damage your craft."

A mock German village of fifteen buildings, complete in every detail from German signs to flower boxes and birdhouses, was erected by members of the 150th Engineer Combat Battalion from Fort Devens on a range area in Camp Edwards, to prepare soldiers-in-training with actual village-warfare conditions.

By 1943 rationing had been extended to canned and processed foods, meat, fish, butter, fats and oils, coffee, sugar, gasoline, fuel oil and tires. Hyannis shoe stores were crowded with customers rushing to use their coupons before expiration.

News of race riots in Detroit and the Pennsylvania coal miners' back-to-work movements after a strike led by John L. Lewis were largely ignored by Cape Codders, who turned to the weekly "Our Men and Women in the Service" column in the Barnstable *Patriot*. The list of casualties among far-flung Cape Cod members of the armed forces mounted, and gold stars began appearing at six-over-six Cape Cod windows.

In early August eleven-year-old Teddy Kennedy was buying newspapers for Honey Fitz at the News Store in Hyannis Port when he glanced at the Boston *Herald*. Four line drawings on the newspaper's front page depicted the ramming of a PT boat, and an accompanying story described the eventual rescue of most of the crew. "I was dumbfounded," Teddy said. "I hadn't been told anything about it."

Joseph P. Kennedy had been informed that his son Jack was missing four days before but had said nothing to anyone. Years later he recalled his wife rushing toward him, crying: "I just turned on a news broadcast. They say Jack's been saved. Saved from what?"

The former Ambassador turned away. "Oh . . ." he shrugged. "Nothing. It was nothing." Later, he wired Jack, "Thank God for your deliverance!"

On August 19, 1943, the New Bedford section of the Cape Cod *Standard-Times* published the following story under Leif Erickson's byline:

JOHN KENNEDY, CREW RESCUED: WERE BELIEVED LOST AT SEA

U.S. Torpedo Boat Base, New Georgia, Aug. 8 (Delayed) (AP).

Out of the darkness a Japanese destroyer appeared suddenly. It sliced diagonally in two the PT boat skippered by Lieut. (jg) John F. Kennedy, son of former Ambassador in London, Joseph P. Kennedy, a summer resident of Hyannis Port, Massachusetts.

Crews of two other PT boats patrolling close by, saw flaming high octane gasoline spread over the water. They gave up as certainly killed that black morning of Monday, August 2, skipper Kennedy and all his crew. But Lieut. Kennedy, 26, and ten of his men were rescued today from a small coral island deep inside Japanese controlled territory and within range of enemy shore guns.

I was aboard the PT boat making the rescue, a daring and skillful bit of navigation through reef-choked waters off Ferguson Passage (Ferguson Passage is between Gizo and Wanwawa Islands in the New Georgia group).

Two men of Kennedy's crew were lost when the enemy destroyer rammed the boat at a speed estimated by the skipper at 40 knots.

Those who survived with Kennedy were Ensign Leonard Thom, Sandusky, Ohio, executive officer and former Ohio State tackle; Ensign George Henry Robertson "Barney" Ross, Highland Park, Illinois; Machinist's Mate Patrick H. McMahon, Los Angeles; Machinist's Mate

Gerald E. Zinser, Belleville, Illinois; Gunner's Mate Charles Harris, Boston; Radioman John Maguire, Hastings-Upon-Hudson, N. Y.; Machinist's Mate William Johnston, Dorchester, Mass.; Ordnanceman Edmond Mowrer, St. Louis; Torpedoman, Roy L. Starkey, Garden Grove, California; and Seaman 1st Class Raymond Algert, Cleveland, Ohio.

McMahon was burned badly on his face, hands and arms. Although the burns were infected by salt water and exposure, he did not once utter a word of complaint.

"McMahon's a terrific guy," Lieut. Kennedy said. "It was something which really got you seeing old Mac lie there."

"You could see he was suffering such pain that his lips twitched and his hands trembled," Thom added. "You'd watch him and think if you were in his place you'd probably be yelling, 'Why doesn't somebody do something?' But every time you asked Mac how he was doing he'd wrinkle his face and give you a grin."

Zinser suffered burns on both arms. Johnston, a tough little fellow called "Jockey," was sickened by fumes he inhaled. Ross was unhurt but coral infected his arm after he was rolled on a reef by the waves.

All the others came through their experience without injury.

On three nights, Lieut. Kennedy, once a backstroke man on the Harvard swimming team swam out into Ferguson Passage hoping to flag down PT boats going through on patrol. Ross did the same one other night. But they made no contacts.

On the afternoon of the fourth day, two natives found the survivors and carried to the PT base a message Kennedy crudely cut on a green coconut husk.

Chronologically, Kennedy, Thom and crewmen told the story the same way.

"At first I thought it was a PT," Kennedy said. "I think it was going at least 40 knots. As soon as I decided it was a destroyer I turned to make a torpedo run."

But Kennedy, lean and nicknamed "Shafty" by his mates, quickly realized the range was too short for the torpedo to charge and explode.

"The destroyer then turned for us," he said.

"It all happened so fast there wasn't a chance to do a thing. The destroyer hit our starboard forward gun station and sliced right through. I was in the cockpit. I looked up and saw a red glow and streamlined stacks. Our tanks were ripped open and gas was flaming on the water about 20 yards away."

McMahon, Zinser, Harris and Johnston had beeen spilled in the water, some on one side of the destroyer, some on the other. Thom swam out after Johnston. Ross went after Zinser. Kennedy went out to get McMahon who had been at the engine station and was knocked into the water in the midst of flaming gasoline.

"McMahon and I were about an hour getting back to the boat"

(watertight bulkheads kept the bow afloat), Kennedy said. "There was a very strong current."

After getting McMahon aboard Kennedy swam out again to get Harris.

The skipper and his men shouted and called for the two missing men but could get no response.

"We seemed to be drifting toward Kolombangara," Kennedy said. "We figured the Japs would be sure to get us in the morning, but everybody was tired and we slept."

Just before dawn, the current changed to carry the survivors away from the Japanese held coast. At 2 p.m. Kennedy decided to abandon the bow section and try to reach a small island.

Kennedy swam to the island towing McMahon. The others clung to a plank and swam in a group. It took about three hours to make it. The men stayed on this island until Wednesday when all coconuts on the island's two trees had been eaten.

Late that afternoon they swam to a larger island where there were plenty of coconuts.

At night Kennedy put on a lifebelt and swam into Ferguson Passage to try to signal an expected PT boat.

"One night, 'Shafty' had a hell of a time," Thom said. "The current carried him hell-and-gone and he didn't get back to us until noon of the next day."

Two natives found the survivor group Thursday afternoon. On Saturday morning a large canoe loaded with natives brought food and a small kerosene stove and gave the men real food and hot coffee. That night a little after midnight our rescue boat guided by a native pilot went in the twisting passage to make contact with Kennedy on an outer island.

The survivors were given a drink of brandy, some coffee and bread. "Jockey" Johnston, whose lungs had been seared by burning gas, was unable to retain the food he had eaten, but he still had spirit.

"Are we expendable?" he exclaimed. "Brother, if you think I want to go through that again you can kiss my foot."

The PT boat's explosion and the exertions of rescue and survival that followed seriously aggravated Jack's old back injury, causing him considerable pain. A later bout of malaria brought his weight down to 125 pounds, and in December he left his MTB squadron and was reassigned to Miami, Florida, as an instructor in the PT training program. In the late spring of 1944, Jack Kennedy entered Chelsea Naval Hospital, close to his father's East Boston birthplace, for spinal surgery.

That August a prolonged heat wave coincided with the arrival in Hyannis Port of Joe, Jr., on his last furlough before going overseas and achieving his wish to "get to England where there was combat flying." He was joining the first naval squadron to fly B-24s with the British Coastal Command on dangerous patrols over the Bay of Biscay. He sailed the *Victura* again in Hyannis Port waters and also celebrated his return in a more spectacular fashion by borrowing a training plane from the small naval air station at Hyannis Airport to buzz the Port's harbor one crowded summer afternoon, until he was "persuaded" by airport authorities—plagued by a flurry of telephoned complaints—to return the plane to the station.

At 4:00 in the afternoon on September 8, 1943, the pealing of bells and the sounds of whistles and sirens were heard on Cape Cod for five minutes to celebrate the surrender of the Italian army; and the Third War Loan drive was launched on Cape Cod, where Hyannis Port residents were being severely taken to task by civilian-defense officials as dimout violations continued to increase in that village.

In May the London *Times* formally announced the engagement of Kathleen Kennedy to Lord Hartington, a recently defeated candidate for the House of Commons. Friends since 1938, when Kathleen had met Billy Cavendish in court circles during her father's ambassadorship, they were married two days later at a registry office. Both families opposed the match on religious grounds. Joe, Jr.,[2] was the only member of the Kennedy family to attend the wedding, although both the Duke and the Duchess of Devonshire, Lord Hartington's parents, were present and tried hard to smile for photographers after the ceremony. Rose Kennedy, undergoing an annual physical checkup, blamed wartime travel restrictions for having prevented her attendance at her daughter's wedding.

The Hyannis Port house was opened in early June, and Eunice, a student at Radcliffe, joined her parents there. Later Jean, a senior at Rosemont College, and Patricia, attending Sacred Heart Convent in Noroton, Connecticut, arrived, and by July the Kennedy family was almost reunited, with Jack visiting weekends from Chelsea. Only Kathleen and Joe, Jr., who had refused proffered leave and persuaded his crew to remain on duty for D-Day, were missing.

On June 12 John F. Kennedy was awarded the Navy and Marine Corps Medal. The citation that accompanied the award read:

> For extremely heroic conduct as commanding officer of Motor Torpedo Boat 109 following the collision and sinking of that vessel in the Pacific

war area Aug. 1–2, 1943. Unmindful of personal danger, Lieut. Kennedy unhesitatingly braved the hazards of darkness to direct rescue operations, swimming many hours to secure aid and food after he had succeeded in getting his crew ashore. His outstanding courage, endurance and leadership contributed to the saving of several lives and were in keeping with the highest traditions of the U.S. Naval Service.

Commenting on the decoration from Chicago, Joseph P. Kennedy said: "Jack's a pretty good lad. Naturally I'm proud of him. I only wish I could have been with him."

The Navy and Marine Corps Medal was presented to him by Captain Frederick L. Conklin, commanding officer at Chelsea Naval Hospital, where Jack remained a patient throughout the summer of 1944, visiting Hyannis Port only on weekends.

Unable to sail the *Victura* (Bobby had taken command of the boat, placing last in the Wianno senior race event at the annual Edgartown regatta the previous year), Jack had to content himself with sitting in a wicker armchair on the sunny veranda of his father's house looking over the busy harbor, the beginning of a slow convalescence. He was gaunt, painfully thin, with skin still yellow from malaria beneath a heavy tan; the experience of war and pain had left a profound mark on him.

"Jack was like a different person that summer, quieter, more drawn into himself. It was what he'd been through in the Pacific and the pain his back was giving him. He never complained but you could tell it bothered him a lot."

On July 20, 1944, the day before Roosevelt accepted the Democratic nomination for a fourth term, choosing Harry S Truman as his running mate to oppose Thomas E. Dewey and John W. Bricker, Joseph P. Kennedy addressed students at Hyannis State Teachers College. Shortly afterward, he made his last public speaking appearance for many years when he shared the speaker's platform at the annual meeting of the Cape Cod chapter of the American Red Cross, held at the Eagleston Inn on Hyannis' Main Street.

Two weeks later two priests called at the Hyannis Port house. Kennedy emerged from that interview shocked and crushed, his eyes brimming with tears, to inform his children that their oldest brother, Joe, Jr., had been killed in the course of an air strike against German submarine pens on the French coast.

"What can I say?" Kennedy told reporters the next day. "We received word yesterday. All my younger children are here and young

John came down from Chelsea Naval Hospital but had to go right back."

While messages of condolence poured into the Hyannis Port house, the Kennedy family attended a solemn requiem mass conducted by Reverend Thomas J. McClean at St. Francis Xavier Church, where Joe, Jr., had once attended Sunday school and where he had taken holy communion during his last furlough before going overseas.

Several days later, in a simple, unpublicized ceremony, a gold star was placed beside the name "Lieut. Joseph P. Kennedy, Jr." on the honor roll in front of the Barnstable town office building in Hyannis.

The worst hurricane in Hyannis Port's history struck in mid-September. Winds of one hundred miles an hour demolished Union Chapel, hurled the West Beach clubhouse off its foundations and halfway into the street and heavily damaged the roof of the golf club on top of Sunset Hill. The storm ripped porches from summer houses, smashed windows and uprooted trees; flooding from the torrential downpour of wind-driven rain and high tides washed away the Civic Association's pier and the yacht club's building.

Many Hyannis Port residents were evacuated at the height of the storm, including one Pittsburgh family marooned by high water that had quickly engulfed its shorefront home; the family was rescued by a coast-guard commander and a Hyannis Port resident, who plunged through raging surf to lead the family to safety.

Damage to Hyannis Port, to the colony of summer houses at adjacent South Hyannis and to Hyannis itself—as well as to the rest of Cape Cod—was reported to be in the millions.

The hurricane swept Hyannis Port's harbor clear of boats, and many of those that came ashore were smashed to pieces on the beach. The *Victura*, however, escaped serious damage; Jack Kennedy, on leave from Chelsea Naval Hospital, was at the pier site on the night of the hurricane and managed to secure the Wianno senior knockabout on the beach. Later he was stranded on Chase Street in Hyannis, blocked from returning to Hyannis Port by the high waters flooding Sea Street. When a sympathetic resident, noticing him hunched in the front seat of his Buick, offered coffee and a chance "to get out of the storm," Jack politely refused and settled down to wait for the waters to recede.

In the warm stillness that followed the hurricane, Troop C of the

107th National Guard patrolled the heavily damaged Main Street business area in Hyannis, where store fronts had been smashed, windows broken and some shops flooded. Cape Codders were already clearing away the vast amounts of debris left by the storm, assisted by a Negro engineering battalion from Camp Edwards, which was preparing to move from village to village helping natives in cleanup work under the supervision of local tree wardens.

A controversy later flared up over the issue of allowing German prisoners of war quartered at Camp Edwards to help clear away hurricane wreckage. It centered on the assumption that the prisoners would be paid 80 cents an hour for their labor. The furor quieted down when officials of the War Manpower Commission and the War Labor Board decided that the prisoners should receive only one hour's pay per day; the balance would go to the Treasury Department. Only once during their internment was escape attempted by prisoners at Camp Edwards, all members of Rommel's elite Afrika Korps captured in North Africa: Two prisoners were recaptured by coast guardsmen when they tried swimming the Cape Cod canal.

Late on the afternoon after the storm two sisters from nearby Gosnold Street in Hyannis, coming to inspect the hurricane damage and carefully picking their way over deep puddles and the muddied rubble of ruined Iyanough Avenue, noticed two young men casually poking in the debris of broken sailboats and pieces of plank walk that had been flung from the lost pier onto the churned-up sand of Hyannis Port's East Beach.

As the sisters drew closer, one of the young men stepped forward and greeted them with a wide, disarmingly boyish smile. An animated conversation followed, during which the young man introduced his friend as a caption writer for *Life* assigned to cover the hurricane and then introduced himself: "I'm Jack Kennedy," he said. Gesturing quickly, he added, "I live over there."

Wearing a blue baseball cap, an open white shirt, khaki slacks and sneakers, Jack Kennedy looked much younger than his 27 years, despite the slightly yellow pallor remaining from his malaria.

"He looked ill," one of the sisters remembered, "but he certainly didn't *act* it. And he had the most charming smile."

Later Jack stretched out on a cleared space of beach, his hands propped behind his head, his legs drawn up and one ankle resting on his knee, while he chewed ruminatively on a long blade of beach grass. He was obviously attracted to the younger of the two sisters, who had somewhat shyly confessed that her name was "Ann," a very pretty eighteen-year-old telephone-company employee with sparkling blue-green eyes, who was becomingly dressed in a pink raincoat.

"We were just going to get something to eat," Jack said, looking up at her from his prone position. "Would you girls like to join us?"

While the sisters hesitated, Jack, inclining his head, turned to face his friend. "I'm not supposed to be going out because I'm still in mourning," he said, "but I think this'll be all right, don't you?"

The girls were finally persuaded, and Jack helped them into a blue Ford station wagon and drove down Sea Street to the Panama Club, one of the few restaurants that had opened after the storm and a place Jack suggested because, "I think we can go there as we are."

A once-elegant restaurant *cum* night club located in the Queen's Buyway and decorated in red and white velvet, the Panama Club's reputation for swank had been somewhat compromised by its wartime popularity with soldiers from Camp Edwards, who, crowding the bar four deep, frequently gave the place a rowdier air. At a table in the nearly empty dining room, Jack ordered cocktails for himself and his friend (the girls did not drink) and steaks and salad.

The conversation quickly turned from the subject of the hurricane to well-informed and articulate discussions of politics, the progress of the war and magazine writing. "Listening to Jack talk with his friend," Ann said, "I realized he was older and more mature than he looked."

"When the orchestra started playing for dancing, Jack decided to go home and change because he didn't think he was dressed well enough, so we all went back to Hyannis Port with him." The khaki navy uniform he put on was "so rumpled and unpressed-looking it probably had just come out of a suitcase."

The girls were led to the garage, for the station wagon was about to run out of gas, and it was necessary to change automobiles. The garage contained a sleek Cadillac, as well as a black Buick convertible.

"What car should we take?" Jack said.

"Of course, I chose the convertible," Ann said.

"While we were dancing, I remembered reading an article in *The Reader's Digest* about Jack's experience in the war. It had only dawned on me who he was when we had gotten into the car to go back to Hyannis Port. I suppose I wanted to appear as well-informed as he was so I asked him: 'How's your back?' "

"Right now it's not very good," Jack admitted. Would she mind if they went back to their table?

"Of course I didn't mind," Ann said. "He was such a good dancer I had no idea his back was bothering him. If I hadn't mentioned it he probably wouldn't have said anything."

During a break in the dancing Jack Kennedy made it plain that he was thinking beyond the day of his imminent discharge from the Navy and had already made some plans for his future. "Are you girls going to vote for me when I run for Governor?" he asked.

"He was very serious," Ann said. "And he seemed very confident, too, as if he'd definitely made up his mind."

Jack was not in the least offended when the girls answered frankly: "No, we're not. We're Cape Codders," adding unnecessarily, "and we're Republicans."

"We just sat at the table and talked and watched my sister and his friend dance until we all decided to go back to the house again."

Water had seeped into the huge living room of the Hyannis Port house through French doors that led to the large veranda. The rug had been soaked, and many waterlogged books had fallen from the wide bookshelves and were spread out to dry around the room. Additional damage had been done to the basement movie theater.

The living room was chilly and damp. A servant brought hot coffee from the kitchen. "We were all gathered around the grand piano singing while Jack's friend played when Bobby came in with a friend."

After being introduced, Bobby announced that he was going to bed, as he had spent the day studying. As he mounted the staircase, Bobby turned at the landing, looked down at his brother and said, "Aren't you glad to see me?"

"He was obviously deeply hurt and troubled about something," Ann said. "I remember we all stopped what we were doing and Jack sort of smiled and passed it off."

"I'm always glad to see you," Jack said.

"The next night we went to the Center Theater in Hyannis. When the lights came on at intermission a woman in her fifties who was sitting in a front seat turned around and recognizing Jack waved to him."

Excusing himself, Jack went down the aisle, greeting the woman with a hug and kissing her. Returning to his seat, he said: "That's one of my favorite people in the whole world. I just love her." Then, adding, "I'm so glad I'm with you, because it's important to me that I make a good impression on her."

The next day Jack came personally to the house on Gosnold Street in the afternoon to apologize for having to break their evening date. His family was gathering in New York to comfort his sister Kathleen, whose 26-year-old husband, the Marquis of Hartington, had just been reported killed in action in France.

For Jack Kennedy this journey to New York marked the beginning of his assumption of the familial duties expected of the eldest son, duties that had been passed to him at his brother's death. And in assuming those duties, Kennedy inherited as well the goal his brother had earlier set for himself, when he confided to Harold Laski his ambition to become "the first Catholic President of the United States."

Part Two

THE WAY TO THE SUMMER WHITE HOUSE
1946–1960

Five

*"Jim, there's no Democratic vote at Cape Cod
. . . "—Franklin D. Roosevelt to Postmaster-
General James A. Farley on the suggestion of a
commemorative stamp marking Cape Cod's three
hundredth anniversary.*

Long before the first forsythia bloomed, presaging as always the
advent of summer, the Cape Cod Chamber of Commerce was anticipating the first peacetime season in five years. Its newsletter asserted
that inquiries for accommodations received by February 1946 had
doubled those of the previous year.

Although the Chamber seemed to be rushing the season even more
than usual, it had good cause, for by March's end Camp Edwards had
been deactivated as an army base, signaling the end of a populous
military establishment that had, with other wartime installations,
brought Cape Cod to a year-round prosperity it had seldom enjoyed
before—or was likely to again.

That summer more than one thousand celebrants attended the first
annual V-J Day Ball at Barnstable American Legion Post 206, recalling the previous warm August evening when, at just past 7:00 P.M.,
the first news had come over radios from Washington of Japan's surrender and a wildly elated crowd had surged and cavorted into the
streets of Hyannis. They had thrown confetti, torn newspapers and
popcorn and had perpetrated small acts of vandalism in the spirit of
the long night's patriotic rejoicing, though bars and night clubs closed
early at the request of police and military authorities.

The following day's victory parade, hastily put together from the
civilian remnants of marching bands and service and veterans' organizations, was deliriously applauded by spectators massed along Hy-

annis' Main Street. By the celebration's end, however, the revels dedicated to war's victory had given way to the first apprehensions for the prospects a postwar future might hold.

Cape Codders could not be blamed for regretting the foreseeable passing of the huge military investment the government had made on the peninsula, particularly at Camp Edwards. This investment had provided not only jobs for a large number of civilians but also thirty thousand servicemen, who had pumped money and *elan* into the Cape's off-season and—not the least consideration—had provided husbands for a significant portion of Cape Cod's unwed female population.

The once-ubiquitous serviceman gradually disappeared from the streets of Hyannis, although his uniform was temporarily metamorphosed into civilian clothes during the severe shortage of men's clothing that coincided with the large-scale return of discharged veterans.

Eager as they were to return to peace, many Cape Codders viewed with dismay the revival of a prewar "normalcy" that meant almost total dependence once more on a frequently perilous and brief summer economy.

Editorially, at least, Cape Cod was represented as being much the same as ever in 1946: "quiet, sheltered communities basking in a summer sun that sheds its warmth at the same time a friendly breeze cools the air." Intended more to reassure and encourage the return of those seasonal residents deprived of Cape Cod summers during wartime than as a serious assessment of the true situation, this pitch was a forgivable white lie. For natives were all too aware of the enormous problems besetting the Cape, particularly as they were personified by the returning veteran, who was frequently unable to find either a job or a place to live.

The Cape's serious housing shortage was particularly painful in view of the miles of vacant summer homes that provided three-month tenancy to their off-Cape owners; scarceness of materials made government "priorities" offered to veterans for home building meaningless, for none in quantities was available.

The most important single problem facing the Cape, however, was the necessity of returning to a tourist industry during, in the Memorial Day rhetoric typical of the times, "the postwar readjustment period."

"We must pay more attention to important details that we, as hosts, may have overlooked," Cape Codders were told several years later during an event unique in the Cape's history: a three-day "scrambled eggs and curtseying" seminar, calculated "to protect Cape Cod's reputation for hospitality," which exemplified a renascent preoccupation with the tourist industry.

Prompted by growing awareness of the increase in peacetime competition for tourist dollars, the seminars, conducted at the Hyannis Inn under the direction of the Cape Cod Chamber of Commerce in concert with the New England Council's Recreation and Development Committee, stressed the fact that Cape Codders must provide "services the traveling public most desire," if they expected to improve their profits. Hotel, guest-house and cottage-colony owners and managers throughout Barnstable County were held enthralled by lectures on bookkeeping methods ("dollars and sense management," delivered by a researcher from the Federal Reserve Bank in Boston), advertising, "housekeeping science," brochure design and "the care and feeding of guests" (by a spokeswoman for the New England Poultry and Egg Institute).

The seminars put an end, at least officially, to the myth that Cape Codders were basically hostile to vacationers. Although some year-rounders persisted in deceiving themselves, others did not. "The unspoiled Cape is still here, but each summer you have to go farther out the sandy roads to find it. The cities disgorge, the Cape absorbs. Beer cans, half-eaten hot dogs, Dairy Queen cups are the heritage," said the weekly Orleans *Cape Codder* in an editorial later reprinted by the Barnstable *Patriot*.

But what "is not hard to take," the *Cape Codder* said boldly, "is the money which the summer trade brings to Cape Cod . . . the infusion of city dollars that carried the Cape through the quiet economics of the winter."

At the other end of the Cape the Falmouth *Enterprise* was expressing the fear that "standards of living will suffer if ordinary families can no longer depend upon rooming house income for taxes, improvements, luxuries and Florida vacations."

Commenting at the end of the season on evidence that guest houses had not done as well as in seasons past because of competition from burgeoning new motels,[1] it observed that "the privacy and convenience of the motel are hard to come by in private homes opened to

81

the public. . . . The rooming house income is worth fighting for! One way to preserve it is to give bigger value to the room renter and render more service and advertise more. This room rent income is hardly likely to any longer be as easy as putting a sign on the lawn . . ."

There was a time when it had been that easy. The vast and complex trappings of a full-grown industry had been originated by wives of men engaged in more virile, remunerative but dangerous maritime occupations. The wives supplemented domestic incomes by "letting out" spare bedrooms, and the money was considered no more important than the traditional "egg money" that women had always claimed as their own.

A summer boarder was no one for a husband to get "het up" about in the days when the salt works were running and packets and coasters still crowded in at the wharf. Later the more foresighted converted hen houses into austere but serviceable "cottages," furnished with castoffs, for the undemanding early vacationers brought by the railroad to the Cape's primitive but singularly picturesque waterside. But such developments as Hyannis Port's elaborate subdivision "as a place of summer resort" in the 1870s were the product of off-Cape intelligences. Among the natives, the very idea of cupolaed mansions blooming in the place where salt vats once prevailed aroused skepticism and high humor. (They were temporarily proven correct when the Hyannis Land Company, a syndicate organized by Boston and Framingham investors, went bankrupt in 1879.)

By the advent of the railroad and, to a greater extent, of the automobile, a quasi industry—tourism—already existed despite itself, and toward it Cape Codders naturally, if dubiously, turned *faute de mieux* when their maritime fortunes declined. And it was to be this alien stepchild, born of necessity rather than of volition, that would prove the hardiest, longest-lived and most steadfastly generous of all the Cape's occupations, from Colonial cattle raising and agriculture through the rise and fall of its fishing fleets, salt works and offshore whalers and coasters. It survived world wars, hurricanes, Prohibition and the Depression to bloom each spring, renourishing the commercial hopes of Cape Cod's native population for each new summer season.

And never before had Cape Codders looked more hopefully to their tourist occupations than in 1946—and never did more new businesses proliferate and fail. In Provincetown alone 36 eating places opened their doors for business that year, more than enough to accommodate a townful of ravenous vacationers.

Preparations for the season were well advanced when, over Easter weekend, disaster struck: the worst forest fire in Massachusetts history. At its height it threatened to wipe out the town of Mashpee and adjacent Forestdale with flames reaching one hundred feet, sending clouds of menacing smoke into the skies over Sagamore and Buzzards' Bay, which adjoin the canal gateway to Cape Cod. They burned a black swath through some 35,000 acres of brush and woodland before 2,000 volunteers brought the fire under control.

Already uneasy about the season's prospects, Cape Codders were horrified at the publicity that could well discourage tourists from seeking what sounded, from graphic newspaper accounts, like a resort area rendered into a burnt-out wasteland.

The forest fire was one discouraging setback, and the wave of national labor unrest that hampered an already faltering postwar industrial machine was another, a distress signal that could bode discouragement for the season ahead. For the Cape had learned that nothing significant happened around the nation that did not sooner or later have its effects on Cape Cod. The experiences of the 1930s were not quickly to be forgotten; they had provided a severe lesson in economics for natives who had felt immune, by reason of geography, to any national economic emergency. Cape residents had discovered that the summer season was not "Depression-proof."

Although it was not entirely true, as a waggish local cracked, that "if New York eats horseradish, Cape Cod gets heartburn," by 1946 all residents acknowledged that more than the Bourne and Sagamore bridges connected Cape Cod to the rest of the country.

One strike in early summer was a crueler and more direct blow, portending unavoidable potential damage to tourist travel: a railroad stoppage just prior to the season's beginning.

A procession of traffic, freed from gas rationing, poured onto Cape Cod in such record numbers during the Fourth of July weekend as to create the worst traffic problems ever faced and officially inaugurated the long-awaited season. (The following year citizens and summer visitors alike were invited to voice their objections when Main and South Streets in Hyannis were made one-way for the first time in an attempt to alleviate congestion.)

Cape Cod's famed summer theaters reopened: Dennis' Cape Play-house marked its first resumption of summer repertory since 1942 with Gertrude Lawrence in *Pygmalion*.

A good Cape Cod tan could substitute for paint on a lady's legs (nylons were still scarce), and a few extra miles could be coaxed out of prewar automobiles until the long waiting lists for new ones could be satisfied. The most serious and prevalent shortage was the shortage of food.

Grocers reporting good supplies at the beginning of the season found it increasingly difficult to replenish their shelves from off-Cape warehouses, which were customarily supplied by the strikebound railroads. Both Cape Codders and an enormously increased summer population began to feel the pinch.

Despite Economic Stabilizer Chester Bowles' prediction to the contrary, such basic foodstuffs as milk and bread continued in intermittently short supply. A pound of hamburger was frequently cause for celebration, as meat, particularly beef, was extremely scarce, despite skyrocketing prices. (Cape Cod Hospital, in the throes of a campaign to raise $1.25 million to expand already overburdened facilities, was placed in the uncomfortable position of having to solicit funds at the same time that it was "resorting to horsemeat," when poultry and lamb were unavailable for its patients.)

Cape Codders, urged to conserve food, found it difficult enough "scrambling to get food, not to save it." A local housewife's well-publicized grievances echoed an accurate cross section of public opinion: Favored customers, said she, were able to obtain all the food they wanted "because they are wealthy and idle and are able to telephone or leave orders, while others who must work have to spend hours waiting in line for food that often isn't there anymore."

The criticism was the sharpest ever publicly directed at summer colonists—"scrambled eggs and curtseying lessons" notwithstanding—but there was good reason for the strong undercurrent of resentment that had finally boiled to the surface. For the summer colonies were embarked upon the gayest, most frivolous season in years, and enough money could buy anything.

The Wianno club, retrieving its facilities after graciously lending them part-time to armed forces quartered in Osterville during the war, introduced a new dining pavilion under a striped canopy on the broad beach directly facing Nantucket Sound, where members could lunch from an abundant and sumptuously varied buffet presided over by white-clad chefs who did not have to restrict the bill of fare. The ultimate in seashore convenience was provided for bathers, who could dress in their rooms and then take an elevator to the beach. Races in the yacht club's West Bay were resumed, as were round-robin tennis tournaments and weekly Saturday-night dinner dances in the main ballroom. A small adjacent ballroom served for private parties.

The resumption of a peacetime summer season in Hyannis Port was something else again, for it truly was a village "basking in the sun," an editorial writer's dream come true. Except for restyled automobiles and changed resort fashions, it could have been 1926 all over again in Hyannis Port, for all the difference twenty years had made. The narrow streets were as tidy as ever, the lawns and hedges fastidious. Even the busyness at the pier had a proper air about it. Always the most low-keyed and restrained of the Cape's wealthy resorts, Hyannis Port never deliberately flaunted its riches. Whatever ravages had been brought by war and nature had been nicely put to rights.

Materials, priority or not, had somehow been located to rebuild Union Chapel completely after its destruction in the hurricane of 1944, although it served, at best, a three-months congregation. (In 1945 services had been conducted at the indestructible fortress of St. Andrews-by-the-Sea, whose parishioners had offered the use of its facilities during the interim.)

The Civic association had restored its pier, wiped out by the same storm, and had reconstructed the devastated West Beach club house as well. Hyannis Port's golf club, which had suffered extensive hurricane damage, had been refurbished to include a bar and lounge, a solarium and a dining room, where golfers could lunch without leaving the vicinity of the links. It also provided facilities for dinner parties for members and guests.

Yacht races were revived in Hyannis Port's pretty harbor. Ted Kennedy added to the family's reputation for winning, taking firsts in several races with *Tenovus* that summer, while his brother Jack was content to skim the choppy waters of Nantucket Sound in non-competitive sails aboard the *Victura*, his back heavily braced against the recurrence of the pain his wartime injuries intermittently gave him.

As he sat reading Stendhal through spectacles, his long legs propped against the rail of his father's veranda, Jack Kennedy looked more like a schoolboy home for the holidays than a 29-year-old Democratic nominee for Congress, a position won after a grueling debut the previous spring in which his political career had been securely launched. In the election in November, his Republican opponent was granted not the remotest chance. Nomination in the heavily Democratic and skillfully gerrymandered Eleventh District was tantamount to election.

Following his discharge from the Navy in early 1945, Kennedy had turned his hand to writing occasional book reviews for the Boston *Globe* before joining International News Service as a special correspondent. But the author of *Why England Slept* and *As We Remember Joe*—a slim, 75-page, maroon-bound book of tributes to his brother—found small satisfaction in day-to-day journalism, particularly as his measured, lackluster writing style found little favor in a Hearst enterprise ever happy to eschew scholarship for spice and sentimentality in its reportage. Room at the bottom of a wire-service pyramid attracted Jack Kennedy not at all.

A frequent habitué of Leon and Eddie's and The Diamond Horseshoe, he was more prone to sample Manhattan's glittering postwar night life, particularly after the austerity of Chelsea Naval Hospital and a young manhood marred by illness and administered by a rigidly wholesome set of parental strictures.

But neither journalism nor *la dolce vita* of New York's café society was ever seriously considered a fit occupation for Jack Kennedy. A long-time friend of Joseph P. Kennedy, Morton Downey was at the height of his popularity, with many friendships in high political circles. Downey gently took Jack to task for his playboy proclivities that could do him injury later when he entered political life. Even in 1945, Downey was convinced that Jack Kennedy "would some day be president of the United States," [2] for his entry into politics was as inevitable as it was predictable.

"It was like being drafted," Kennedy confided years later to Bob Considine, New York *Journal-American* columnist. "My father wanted his eldest son in politics. 'Wanted' isn't the right word. He *demanded* it. You know my father."

Returning to Boston in mid-1945 to establish a political base, Jack stayed first at the Hotel Bellevue in Cambridge, where Honey Fitz held sway. Later he leased a three-room apartment at 122 Bowdoin

Street on Beacon Hill, an address that would later serve as "home" for brother Ted's political aspirations; Kennedy was laying the groundwork for a campaign, but the office he was to seek was yet to be chosen.

The interim period, however, was accounted for by a series of "warm-up" speeches, a sort of dress rehearsal for the campaign itself.

As good a place as any to begin his forensic apprenticeship was the Hyannis Rotary Club, where he appeared in September 1945. Joseph P. Kennedy had addressed the same audience only two months before. Jack Kennedy learned a valuable lesson from his father, who never hesitated to address his frequently formidable opinions to any forum, no matter how small or parochial.

Taking as his subject "England and Germany: Victor and Vanquished," Jack Kennedy more closely resembled a high-school senior chosen as Boys' State representative—more traditional fare from Rotary program chairmen—than a young man on the threshold of his political career. His loss of weight made the collar of his white shirt gape at the neck above the conservative, uncertainly knotted, blue-patterned tie. His suit of gray cheviot hung slackly from his wide, but frail-seeming, shoulders and gave him the look, a Rotarian recalled, "of a little boy dressed up in his father's clothes."

The speech was not a memorable one, giving Rotarians no more to digest than the standard mediocre group-rate luncheon they had been served. In a voice somewhat scratchy and tensely high-pitched, Jack Kennedy projected a quality of grave seriousness that masked his discomfiture. No trace of humor leavened his talk. Hardly diverging from his prepared text, he stood as if before a blackboard addressing a classroom full of pupils who could be expected at any moment to become unruly. Although he was not a natural speaker, some of his own personality irrepressibly shone through. Stumbling over a word, he flashed a quick, self-deprecating grin that, a member of his audience remembered, "could light up the room." An appealing waif-like quality showed through, and above all a winning sincerity impressed his audience more than did the frequently high-flown language of his speech.

Despite the externals that seemed to preclude much success in public forums, the general feeling in the meeting room that day was that Jack Kennedy "was going places," even though it was perhaps caused by awareness of the power that loomed behind the slim figure at the speaker's lectern: his famous multimillionaire father, an interested member of the audience.

Then James Michael Curley, the erstwhile "Purple Shamrock," yearning for the home fields of Boston and finding Washington colorless and inhospitable in comparison, gave up his seat in the House of Representatives for another fling at running for mayor and provided the tyro politician with his first opportunity.

In late April 1946, eight days before the filing deadline, John F. Kennedy announced his candidacy for the vacated seat: "The temper of the times imposes an obligation upon every citizen to work diligently in peace, as we served tirelessly in war."

The statement was hardly calculated to set off stampedes toward election booths, but it was nonetheless preferable to the flash and bombast, the magniloquent din of rhetoric that the electorate was used to hearing in the continuing "shoot 'em up" melodramas of Boston politics.

Jack Kennedy was not the only candidate who sought to fill the vacuum created by Curley's municipal longings. The election brought a scramble of nine others eager to serve the Eleventh District, among them John Cotter, Curley's long-time secretary.[3] Kennedy's most serious rival was conceded to be Mike Neville, a former state representative and Mayor of Cambridge, a promising and able politician.

Other candidates attacked Kennedy as a "carpetbagger" because he lived neither in the North End (birthplace of his mother and Honey Fitz) nor in Charlestown, Brighton or East Boston (his father's "home town") nor in any of the wards of Somerville and Cambridge that he wished to represent. But the Kennedy name was hardly alien in the polyglot district, which included large numbers of Italians and Irish, as well as Boston's Chinatown and Syrian neighborhood. Although the district had its swank sectors, it was predominantly a poor and volatile one, rife with postwar dissatisfactions.

Although Jack Kennedy appeared uneasy in these areas of three-story tenements, he nonetheless set himself the task of getting to know his constituents during fourteen-hour days, in which he drove himself—sometimes on crutches—to make the rounds in every precinct, diffidently but determinedly seeking out the voters on their home grounds.

Mounting a campaign that emphasized housing, unemployment,

prices, inflation versus deflation, military training, veterans' benefits and Russia—something, in other words, for everyone—Kennedy made a sharp and curiously affecting impression on a district used to ward-heeling politics. Confronting his constituents directly was a flattering and formidable tactic, particularly as his manner was so different from the heartier but impersonal blasts that his opponents' sound drucks delivered throughout the neighborhoods.

Kennedy's unease with people at least suggested that he was enough aware of them to be nervous and uncertain in their presence. Talking with plain people of his district he was a convincing and sympathetic figure: "He looked like a kid who'd been sick a lot," one of the electorate remembered, "but he sure didn't act like one."

> He came around one Saturday and asked me to shake hands with him. We talked about nothing for a minute and then he asked me to vote for him, only he said: "I'd appreciate your support," or something like that. So I said to him: "Why should I vote for you? What can you do for the district if you're elected?" And right away he comes back at me: "What do you want done?" he says. It was the first time anybody running for office ever asked *me* what I wanted. So I told him. My nephew got shot up pretty good on Okinawa. After the war, like a lot of the boys in the neighborhood used to hang around together, he couldn't find a job. He went out to California because there was supposed to be better chances out there but he was having it rough. So I told Kennedy, I said, the government should do something for veterans. Should help them get a start in life. Then my wife comes out on the porch and by this time a bunch of people are hanging around so I introduce him to everybody and I said: "I'm voting for this guy and you better do the same." He thanked me and then went down the block, heading for the bowling alley there. He came around again, about two days before the election. "Just to say hello," he said.

But some of Jack Kennedy's "have not" constituents could not be won over so easily; they begrudged their votes to this rich man's son. Rumors about the vast sums of money being spent on his campaign to "buy" the election were spread by his opponents. "With the money I'm spending, I could elect my chauffeur," Joseph P. Kennedy was alleged to have said.

His father's money bought the trappings of the campaign: the posters on every empty space, the placards on streetcars and buses, spot commercials on every radio station and widely circulated reprints of a *Reader's Digest* condensation of an article by John Hersey, originally published in *The New Yorker,* on Jack Kennedy's heroic action aboard PT-109. And money had bought too the support of the district's "pols," who were known to "go to bed with their hands outside the covers in case somebody was giving anything away while they were asleep."

But, according to his young, vociferously partisan volunteers, Jack Kennedy could have won the election "on a dime" if his father had wanted to risk the chance of failure.

Vacationing at Hyannis Port after the primary election, in which he won the nomination with more than 42 percent of the votes cast in the ten-man contest, Jack Kennedy struck one observer as being "characteristically unassuming," a singularly inappropriate phrase to describe any Kennedy.

Reclining in a wicker armchair and shaded from the sun by the veranda's roof, Kennedy wore a baggy gray sweat shirt. Faint water marks were perceptible halfway up the legs of his wrinkled wash pants. The sun had given him a faint flush of health, lessening the effect of deep hollows beneath his cheekbones and lightening his bush of hair. He smiled frequently—most often to fend off questions that he did not have answers for—and paced his answers by moving restlessly about a short stretch of space, alternately sitting and pacing.

Although he knew the major problems of his district and "along what lines solutions should be sought," Kennedy would not hazard a guess about those of Cape Cod.

His victory in the primary was attributable to the support of "those who are tired of politics," those who had nominated him "not for what I have done, but for what they hope I can do." Support had come, too, from veterans, he said, "who are as split as anybody." He admitted that "what complicates campaigns is that there are veterans on all sides." He gave the major credit of his campaign's success, however, to the work done by his volunteers. "It was the young and enthusiastic workers who did the job," [4] he said.

There were many echoes of his father and grandfather in the casual pronouncements that the vacationing novice, so imprudently forthright, tossed off. Pointing out that the state department of commerce his father had worked so hard to have approved would have been of great benefit to Cape Cod, Jack Kennedy expressed his disappointment at its defeat.

"We've got to come to it, or something like it eventually," he said, "or else our young men are going to have to look for jobs in the West and the South." Then, harking back to the old boom-and-booster days of the 1920s, when a new Miami or Los Angeles had been envisioned on Cape Cod's shores, he added, "We've got to sell Massachusetts as California and Florida have been sold." He reiterated, too, his grandfather's oft-repeated cry of a "bigger and busier" Boston, linking the future of the state's economic development to the enhancement of its port.

Expressing the fear that another great depression could bring socialism to the United States, a dread straight out of his father's favorite "doomsday book," Kennedy expressed sentiments better suited to Taft Republicans on Cape Cod than to Fair Deal-oriented constituents of the Eleventh Congressional District: "Socialism can be democratic, as it is in England, but I think it is inefficient and tends toward more and more control. It is, of course, difficult to say at what point socialism comes in, whether it begins with public health provisions, workmen's compensation or what . . ."

Although Kennedy seemed content to spend the rest of the summer intermittently campaigning and renewing old acquaintances at dances at Wianno and Hyannis Port's clubs, or, when his back allowed, swimming from his father's private beach or sailing the *Victura*, in August there came a striking reminder of the older brother he had, by his own admission, replaced on the hustings. (He told campaign workers during a rare moment of discouragement during his campaign for the nomination: "I'm just filling Joe's shoes. If he were alive, I'd never be in this.")

One of the first manifestations of Joseph P. Kennedy's commemorative impulses—none of which ever seemed to assuage the grief he continued to feel at the death of his firstborn son [5]—appeared in midsummer. At a solemn high mass presided over by the Most Reverend Bishop James C. Cassidy of Fall River and celebrated by the pastor, a new main altar was dedicated at St. Francis Xavier Church on South Street in Hyannis to the memory of the late Lieutenant Joseph P. Kennedy, Jr.

The altar was a uniquely personal and unusual one, itself something of a tourist attraction. Along with traditional religious symbols was a design incorporating the story of Joe's death: a U.S. Naval Air Force plane is carved in bas-relief, and representations of St. George for England and St. Joan of Arc for France, both clad in military armor, identify the place over the English Channel where the young aviator lost his life.

In his dedicatory sermon, addressed to an audience of some eight hundred worshipers, including Jack Kennedy, his mother, his father, his sisters Eunice and Jean and his grandfather Honey Fitz, Bishop Cassidy chose the occasion to speak out boldly and at length on a more temporal subject, warning that "the country is in the clutches of a small faction of labor" and likening the skilled laborers of 1946 to the "traders of the temples of Jesus' time, who demanded much but gave little in return. Unless an understanding is worked out by labor with capital," Bishop Cassidy announced from the pulpit, "both will lose and the public will suffer."

With regard to Catholicism in Hyannis, Bishop Cassidy called upon all Catholics on the Cape to make possible more and better churches in the area, citing the need for a school for parish children.

Recalling that, when the Archbishop of Boston, Richard Cushing, had asked him what he could do for his diocese, he had whimsically replied, "a half dozen chapels to accommodate the 'swallows' [6] that come to Cape Cod each year," Bishop Cassidy pointed out that a church capable of seating at one mass the enormous crowds that now attended five masses at St. Francis each summer Sunday morning would cost an estimated $250,000.

Taking part in the dedication ceremonies as subdeacon was a young priest, the Reverend Edward C. Duffy, newly ordained at St. Mary's Cathedral in Fall River after six years at a Baltimore seminary and assigned to Hyannis for his first assistant pastorate. Square-jawed and broad-shouldered, he was no ascetic with pale hands turning the pages of his breviary. He was a robust, sports-minded young man who played ball with the town league and coached two Catholic Youth Organization basketball teams to championships.

After the ceremony Jack Kennedy introduced himself to the newcomer and invited him to go sailing. He impressed Joseph P. Kennedy as well. Some three weeks after the dedication the young priest was surprised to receive a telephone call from the former ambassador asking him if he would compose the wording for a small brass testimonial plaque to be placed, without ceremony, in the church's lobby because "a young man can better express the memorial sentiments I want." The young priest, although uneasy that his church superiors had been bypassed, was too flattered not to comply with so distinguished a parishioner's request.[7]

Opportunities for the young priest to take advantage of the Kennedy family's repeatedly offered hospitality during the busy summer season were infrequent, although each Friday evening one or another member of the family called the church's rectory to give the schedule of first-run films to be shown in the basement's projection room.

There were more occasions, however, to go sailing with Jack. Often just the two young men sat aboard the *Victura* for leisurely cruises across the windy harbor. Despite five years' difference in their ages, a friendship developed between the young priest and the young politician, for they had much in common: Each had, in his own way, responded to his own sense of mission. If the young priest held any doubts about his vocation they went unexpressed. The novice politician, however, had many, and he frequently voiced them, wondering aloud "how he would make out" once elected to the House of Representatives.

Jack Kennedy was surprised and amused to learn that the quality of his companion's seminary education had gone beyond the liturgy of the church and the ritual ceremonials attending the duties of a priest's office to cover a broad spectrum of subjects from psychology to sociology. An economics degree had preceded the seminary degree. He was particularly intrigued by the subject of the young priest's thesis, "Communist Techniques in America," written under the supervision of Father John F. Cronin, a recognized authority on the subject.

The thesis had been written in 1941 when America's outlook on the subject had been different—Bishop Fulton J. Sheen had been requested by his network to delete a reference to such methods of infiltration and subversion in one of his famous televised talks. And his thesis had not been intended, the young priest confessed, as a definitive discussion of the subject. Nevertheless, when Jack Kennedy asked if he might read it, the young priest sent home to Fall River for a copy. After keeping it for several weeks, Kennedy returned the thesis with a "well done" during a weekly visit to the church. On these visits, more often than not, he dropped to his knees on the rug in the rectory's living room to deliver his confession *vis-à-vis* his young confessor rather than in the darkened cabinet in the church proper, a natural and unself-conscious expression of his faith. (It has been a surprise to many people that no member of the devout Kennedy family has sought the life of a religious. Bobby, in particular, has often distinguished himself by passing behind the railing to serve the mass in street clothes when altar boys have failed to appear.) *

Disasters both national and local, a railroad strike and chronic food shortages harassed Cape Codders, but August's weather came close to providing the *coup de grâce* to the summer. A long series of "Cape Cod fogs" dampened the spirits of tourists and natives alike. The rainiest August in many years, though nourishing the beach plum, cast cold water on the monetary hopes of businessmen. The cool and overcast weather did not, however, altogether dissuade large crowds from clamoring onto the Cape for Labor Day weekend, traditionally the end of the summer season.

By mid-September, many were bemoaning the belatedly beautiful weather, as the Cape sweltered under uniformly hot and cloudless days, prompting the Chamber of Commerce to suggest: "Every visitor who came to Cape Cod this summer should be told before next summer what kind of weather we're having this September."

In the face of such a relentless series of catastrophes, it was a singular tribute to the energy and resilience of Cape Codders that they not only survived the season but also found strength to launch that autumn an ambitious campaign to locate United Nations headquarters in an area on Cape Cod that could be made available "almost instantly."

It was an ideal site, approximately mid-Cape and bordering what is now the Mid-Cape highway, according to the Chairman of the New England United Nations Committee at a $20-a-plate committee lunch on a private estate at Bass River, as plans for an "active and vigorous campaign" to bring the permanent site of the United Nations to Cape Cod were made public:

* In 1961, a recently ordained priest from County Cork was only partly aware of the young man in a light-blue sports jacket who volunteered to serve at the altar with him during an early-morning midweek mass. Informed afterwards that his altar boy had been the Attorney General of the United States, the priest said in a rich brogue: "I feel greatly honored. I would like to get his autograph."

Cape Codders are eager to welcome the United Nations into their midst. The United Nations groups will be unanimously welcome because the Cape location can meet their demands as to size and still not encroach on those areas that are now occupied by buildings of permanent and summer residents.

It was charged that United Nations delegates in New York were constantly being subjected to pressures from communists and other pressure groups, and Cape Cod was pointed out as "a location steeped in the democratic traditions of the American town hall and free from schemers who seek to exploit the United Nations assembly for their own selfish ends." There was also at Otis Field in Camp Edwards "the largest airport in New England," which could be made available as an international landing field to give United Nations personnel quick and direct access to all parts of the world.

But as Honey Fitz and other loyal Boston Red Sox fans had the rare opportunity to line up for World Series tickets at Fenway Park, such Cape-nurtured United Nations hopes grew slim, as the possibility increased that a former stockyard site on Manhattan's East River front would be chosen as the location of the complex of United Nations buildings.

In November, as Republicans captured both houses of Congress, John F. Kennedy was elected to office for the first time, by a majority of better than two to one over his Republican opponent, Lester W. Bowen.

Six

The Blessing of the Fleet was held for the first time in Province-town in late June 1948. Modeled after Gloucester's famed annual event, the celebration was a huge success, offering the rich anomaly of a public Roman Catholic ceremony in a community that prided itself on being "the first landing place of the Pilgrims."

Provincetown's association with the rest of the Cape was a tenuous one at best. Isolated at the peninsula's tip, like an island thrust fifty miles out to sea, "P'town" still had a flourishing fishing industry. Fishermen continued to mend their nets, and "the catch" was a topic of day-to-day conversation, as housewives kept track of their husbands on their boats via two-way citizen-band radios while doing the breakfast dishes.

The crooked narrowness of Commercial Street could lay claim to considerable, if well-rehearsed, charm. A summer town crier in Pilgrim breeches, white collar and stockings (and buckles snapped over his oxfords) tolled his bell announcing the number of frequently rowdy day trippers to be expected off the afternoon Boston excursion boat, to the delight of camera-carrying vacationers. Many of them paid admission to mount the steep stairway to the top of a 250-foot Florentine bell tower that commemorated the *Mayflower*'s brief stay in Provincetown's harbor.

Provincetown, however, extended its hospitality without the need for seminars. Proud of its early O'Neill associations, it provided refuge not only for such famous artists as Franz Kline and Hans Hofmann, but also for such young artists at the beginning of their careers as Red Grooms, whose first one-man show had taken place in a storefront ·gallery on Commercial Street. Provincetown also offered sanctuary for birds of more exotic plumage, periodically tolerating invasions of homosexuals of both sexes.

Although some of the local color caused raised eyebrows, scandalizing the rest of Barnstable County, there was no denying the exquisiteness of Provincetown's geography, the magnificent breadth of its beach at Race Point or the bleak majesty of shifting high dunes that threatened to spill over and envelop Route 6 itself at Province-town's outskirts. A solid row of motels and cottage colonies was packed on Beach Point along the edge of a curving and resplendent waterfront.

Provincetown's first Blessing of the Fleet was led by a procession of altar boys in white and scarlet surplices bearing crozier, miter and cross past thousands along Commercial Street, gaily draped with bunting and American and Portuguese flags. Members of Bishop Feehan Assembly, 4th Degree Knights of Columbus, wearing red-lined capes, swords and tricorn hats, escorted Bishop James E. Cassidy from Provincetown's Church of St. Peter the Apostle to the roped-off wharf, where some four thousand people were crowded in close to witness the opening ceremonies. They began with the singing of the national anthem of Portugal and the "Star Spangled Banner," and then a maroon-robed choir sang "Full of Glory, Full of Wonder" before Bishop Cassidy, his white and gold vestments gleaming under an intermittent sun, gave his benediction to those gathered about him.

While a light ocean-borne wind lightly furled the Bishop's vest-ments, the fishermen sought their boats; crosses had been affixed to masts, and brightly colored flags fluttered from halyards. Sounding their whistles and bells, the boats of the fleet, some with freshly painted hulls gleaming above water lines and decks ceremonially scrubbed clean, pushed out from the wharf and into the harbor to form a complete circle, maneuvering slowly counterclockwise for the eastward approach to the wharf.

Led by the draggers, first in status among fishermen, with the trap boats behind and the trawling dories waiting their turn, the proces-sion began. All boats slowed passing the bunting-decked pier to re-ceive the individual blessings from Bishop Cassidy standing atop a jutting platform erected for the ceremony at the pier's southeast corner.

Bowing slightly as each vessel passed, Bishop Cassidy murmured, "good luck," as he sprinkled holy water on the boats that slowed beneath the spray close to the edge of the wharf. The families and friends of crew members blessed themselves before the boats turned

97

back to sea. A band accompanied the blessing of more than 75 boats during the three-hour ceremony, then followed with a short concert on the wharf.

The celebration was not over, but few tourists were invited to participate in the parties and street dance that followed or to sample the buffet of spicy *chourico* sausage, *masa* (chopped fruit and sweetbreads), sweet doughnut-shaped *muisadas* with large helpings of guava jelly, quantities of *vinho* and a particularly potent local liquor made from fermented raisins.

Although most Cape Cod communities, like Provincetown, strove to enhance their attractiveness to the summer visitor, there were others who fought the incursion of tourism every step of the way. And one such village in the Town of Barnstable even managed to reverse the process of development that was going on apace elsewhere on the Cape. Cotuit, some eight miles west of Hyannis, once the summer home of Abbot Lawrence Lowell, former President of Harvard University—a baseball diamond now memorializes his wife—and something of a commercial center during its years as a busy seafaring and oystering village (when it could boast "in every house at least one man who went to sea"), replaced its major business block with a small park. In 1958 "The Pines," Cotuit's largest and most famous resort hotel closed its doors after 65 summers. Its collection of fine furniture was sold at auction when the hotel was dismantled. While seminars preached the gospel of hospitality, Cotuiters voted instead to restrict three beaches in or near its village to use by year-round and summer residents only and instructed selectmen to obtain state legislation permitting such action.

It was to this obscure and frequently bypassed corner—beautiful but simply too dull for most vacationers—that John F. Kennedy came, during one of his few visits to Cape Cod in 1947, to pay honor to a dead colleague, Congressman Charles L. Gifford, long-time Republican representative and a man who, according to the simple graveside eulogy at Mosswood Cemetery, had "found his place among men."

Jack Kennedy spent little time on Cape Cod during his first year as a congressman, which was undistinguished, although the United States Junior Chamber of Commerce had singled him out as one of America's Ten Outstanding Young Men.

During one short August visit, however, Kennedy recorded something of his first impressions of Congress: "Of all the important problems facing the nation," he said, "housing is the most ignored." There were simply "too few homes at too high a price," he added, suggesting that a program should be initiated to build "from 1,250,-000 to 1,500,000 homes every year for the next decade."

Calling veterans' priorities "a joke," Kennedy criticized Congress for refusing to pass a housing bill, charging that "the investigating committee set up to look into the housing problem is nothing more than a political sop."

Kennedy favored Federal aid to education, but the bill's terms had to be made clearer with regard to aid in nonpublic schools, as well as to which states were to receive such aid.

Kennedy lamented that the minimum-wage bill had met defeat in committee but expressed confidence that it would be passed when it came around again: "To pay a man less than 60 cents an hour in these times is simply not justifiable," he said. "There must be some guarantee that workers can get a living wage at the very least."

It was "very important that the government have the power and the means to protect itself," Kennedy said of plans to investigate Federal employees with communist sympathies or affiliation, "but the whole investigation should be very carefully done."

He had wholeheartedly supported the Truman Doctrine of aid to Greece and Turkey without feeling that such a program was bypassing the United Nations, for "we are doing what the United Nations is not equipped to do."

Later that summer Kennedy announced that he would request the War Department to set aside ground near Boston for a national cemetery for war dead from overseas. In October Kennedy left for Europe with Representatives Charles Kersten (Democrat, Wisconsin) and Richard M. Nixon (Republican, California), members of the House Subcommittee on Education and Labor investigating the extent of communist infiltration of the French and Italian labor movements. "It will be very valuable to know what is going on in those countries," Kennedy said, "especially in view of our foreign aid program."

During that summer the man whose former seat Kennedy was occupying in the House of Representatives began a six-to-eighteen-month term at the Federal correctional institute at Danbury. "You are sentencing me to death," James Michael Curley said when a

Federal judge in Washington rejected his plea for clemency on the grounds of ill health.

As he entered prison toward the end of June after his conviction for using the mails to defraud in matters of war contracts, Curley appealed to his old friend, House Majority Leader John McCormack, long-time political power and dispenser of patronage. McCormack drew up a petition to President Truman seeking pardon for the Boston Mayor and secured the signatures of all Massachusetts representatives, both Democratic and Republican, but one: John F. Kennedy.*

Kennedy's frequent return to Cape Cod for traditional summer family reunions at Hyannis Port were often marred by a recurrence of malaria or the continuing distress he suffered from his injured back. One such gathering of the clan in May 1948 was a tragic occasion. Word was received that Kathleen Kennedy Cavendish, Lady Hartington, had been killed in an airplane crash in the Ardèche Mountains while her father awaited her arrival in Paris.

The first Kennedy to break the chain of family solidarity, Kathleen had taken the agonizing decision to defy her parents' strict opposition to her marriage on religious grounds. An attractive, vivacious girl who markedly resembled her mother, Kathleen had chosen, upon her husband's death, to continue living in England.

While Bobby went to join his father in France, the rest of the family gathered at Hyannis Port; Jack arrived from Washington with his sister Jean for a high memorial mass at St. Francis Xavier in Hyannis, amid rumors that Kathleen might be buried on Cape Cod. But funeral services were held at the Church of the Immaculate Conception in London and burial in the village of Edensor, a mile from Sheffield, in the Devonshire family plot beside her husband, who had been killed in France in 1944.

* Freed when Truman later commuted his sentence, Curley ran for a fifth term as mayor. He was defeated, and his flamboyant career came to an end when he dropped out of a subsequent mayoralty race in 1951 because of ill health.

In retirement, however, Curley retained power sufficient to bring Joseph P. Kennedy to his apartment early in the senatorial campaign of 1952 to ask him to make a radio speech supporting his son.

"When I refused on the grounds . . . that I would have to do likewise for other candidates . . ." Curley recalled in his autobiography, *I'd Do It Again,* Kennedy asked him if he would agree not to speak against his son's candidacy, a request that Curley granted.

That June, Jack Kennedy sailed from New York for England to settle his sister's affairs. Upon his return he ducked questions about his rumored candidacy for Governor of Massachusetts, while nomination papers containing about 150 New Bedford signatures were filed for verification with Kennedy's signature of acceptance affixed. Similar documents had been circulated in Fall River and filed a few hours before the deadline.

In Boston, however, Joseph P. Kennedy was announcing firmly, "John's running for Congress again," baffling those who were pushing his son's candidacy as the only Democratic candidate who wasn't "shopworn or tarnished."

John F. Kennedy's candidacy had run into an insoluble block: Massachusetts' constitution specifically required a governor to have seven years' continuous residency in the commonwealth as a prerequisite to seeking the office. The arrangement was not so flexible as that which had allowed him to seek a seat in Congress representing a district in which he could claim at best only a transient residence for a little more than a year. Kennedy had designated Palm Beach as his residence in filing income tax prior to his enlistment in the Navy in 1941.

Re-elected to Congress without difficulty in 1948, Jack Kennedy continued to accept many speaking engagements across the whole of the commonwealth, most of them beyond the narrow precincts of the congressional district he represented in Washington.

With an address to the 63rd annual convention of the Massachusetts Federation of Labor in 1949, Kennedy began to involve himself more directly in statewide affairs, telling the convention that communities with unemployment ratios of at least 17 percent would be eligible for Federal assistance under a program being mapped out to aid unemployment-striken areas in New England. Pointing out that such aid would be in the form of increased allocations of government contracts and Federal construction projects, Kennedy mentioned New Bedford and Worcester as qualifying but made no mention of Cape Cod, which suffered from chronic unemployment in the off-season.

That summer Joseph P. Kennedy vehemently denied, from his Hyannis Port veranda, statements taken from some four hundred tons of captured official German documents and made public by the State Department. "It is complete poppycock, as far as I'm concerned!" the former Ambassador to the Court of St. James snapped, commenting on reports by Herbert von Dirksen, German Ambassador to Britain, that the American Ambassador had told him in London in 1938 that Roosevelt was "not anti-German, but received spotty advice."

These reports represented Kennedy as strongly impressed by descriptions of Germany supplied to him by Colonel Charles A. Lindbergh and blaming worsening German-American relations on the Jewish question: "not so much because the Nazis want to be rid of the Jews, but because of the loud noise they're making going about it." Most of Roosevelt's advisers, according to von Dirksen, "were afraid of the Jews and did not dare say anything good about Germany"; others "did not know any better because they were not informed about Germany."

Receiving from Ambassador Kennedy the judgment that "when he [Kennedy] spoke favorably of Germany, people would have absolute confidence in his statements because he was a Catholic," von Dirksen reported that he believed Kennedy to be sincere in his efforts to better relations between their two countries but confessed uncertainty about the American Ambassador's motives, concluding that they might be "tactical considerations relating to the next presidential election" or "personal political motives for bringing himself into prominence."

Kennedy's rebuttal made Hyannis Port a front-page dateline in newspapers all over the country: "Ambassador von Dirksen, in the few conversations I had with him, must have been trying very hard to set himself right in Germany by telling the German Foreign Office the things he thought they'd like to hear." *

In June a gay prenuptial party was held at Hyannis Port's golf club to celebrate Bobby Kennedy's forthcoming marriage to Ethel Skakel. The Great Lakes Carbon Corporation's Douglas DC-6—owned by

---

* Toward the close of the 1952 senatorial campaign, leaflets captioned *German Documents Allege Kennedy Held Anti-Semitic Views* were widely distributed in Jewish districts outside Boston giving new exposure to the controversy.

Rebuttal leaflets were hurriedly circulated in the same areas by Kennedy supporters, who accused Lodge of using McCarthy tactics, the first and only time McCarthy's name was injected into the campaign by either candidate.

Later Jack Kennedy, addressing a noticeably unresponsive gathering of three hundred prominent Boston Jews, reminded his audience: "Remember, *I'm* running for the Senate, not my father."

the Skakel family—arrived at Hyannis' airport from Bridgeport with 21 guests, then returned for another load of celebrants.

That July Senator Joseph McCarthy came to Cape Cod on a Northeast Airlines flight, arriving discreetly on a quiet Sunday morning at Barnstable Municipal Airport, to be taken to Hyannis Port for an unpublicized holiday-weekend visit at the Kennedy house.[1] A close friend of Eunice and her husband-to-be, Robert Sargent Shriver, McCarthy was warmly received by Joseph P. Kennedy, an unabashed admirer who in later years remembered only McCarthy's affability and *bonhomie*. "He went out on my boat one time and he almost drowned swimming behind it," Joseph P. Kennedy said, "but he never complained."

McCarthy was invited to play an infield position on the Kennedy family's "Barefoot Boys" team during its traditional Fourth of July softball game on the lawn abutting the Kennedy veranda. He was retired after committing four errors. Also sidelined on the porch from a flare-up of his back injury, was Jack Kennedy.

That September Kennedy addressed a joint meeting of the Hyannis and Lower Cape Kiwanis Clubs at the Wayside Inn in Chatham.

Reinforcing his remarks on the tense world situation, Kennedy called the number of West European troops facing a growing communist threat "pitiful" and urged that the United States send more troops. "Supplying arms is not enough," he said, warning that "here in this country we must be prepared for all the controls we had during World War II."

He then gave evidence of his growing unhappiness in the House, where, although conscientiously supporting legislation of the most significant interest and benefit to his constituents in the Eleventh District, he was frequently bored, restless and absent because of illness, the social season at Palm Beach or speech making in Massachusetts.

Making no secret of his dissatisfaction, Kennedy pointed out that, although there were more younger men in Congress than there had been before the war, most of the power still resided with older members because of "archaic rulings" and suggested two changes: a revised system of seniority and a speeded-up method for taking roll calls.

After Christmas Kennedy took a five-week tour of Europe, visiting NATO headquarters to confer with General Eisenhower. He delivered a radio report upon his return in February 1951. A round-the-world tour the following October, in which he was accompanied by Patricia and Bobby, included "study stops" in the Middle East, Pakistan, India, Indochina and Korea. It gave him the benefit of eye witness briefings and investigations and reinforced a growing interest in foreign affairs that went far beyond the ken of his constituents but provided material for a growing itinerary of speaking engagements.

While Jack Kennedy stepped up his public appearances, his father melted into self-imposed obscurity, a deliberate inconspicuousness he had assumed during the 1946 campaign when the Boston advertising agency that labored on a rum account (part of Kennedy's lucrative liquor-import firm) and handled his public relations had been told: "No more speeches. Jack's gone into politics."

In November, Henry Cabot Lodge, addressing meetings in Hyannis and Falmouth, predicted a Republican victory in the next year's election and promised a well-directed effort "of utmost vigor" to rid the government of communists. He assailed the Truman administration for postwar Soviet gains, as well as for the nation's comparative unreadiness for war. He spoke of his own efforts to reduce waste in government and to secure a 150-group air force to give the United States defense program additional strength.

Strappingly handsome, Lodge looked the very model of assurance during what had been called a "nonpolitical" appearance, for surely Lodge didn't have to chase votes after three enormously successful campaigns for the Senate.

A week later Jack Kennedy addressed a speech to the Boston Chamber of Commerce. He had embarked on a much-accelerated speaking tour that would bring him before Kiwanis, Elks, Exchange Clubs, regular town Democratic gatherings and communion breakfasts all over the commonwealth, the answer to every program-committee chairman's prayers. No matter how obscure the occasion or organization issuing the invitation, Kennedy accepted; at least he tried to accept them all. "We must, I suggest," Kennedy told his Chamber of Commerce audience, "try and think in terms of three categories of things: the things we cannot and must not do; the things we are doing that should not be done, and the things we are not doing that we should be doing."

Jawaharlal Nehru of India had told him that Americans could not preach freedom and independence on one hand and attempt to shore up the remnants of European colonial empires on the other. India would continue to resist communism, Nehru had told him, but he protested the right of the United States to insist on a choice between the West and Russia. "We cannot reform the world," Kennedy said. "We should not impose upon the Eastern world our values, institutions or customs. However much we may value our concepts, our mechanical well-being, even our bathtubs, the East may think little or nothing of them."

Urging that the United States make no "broad unlimited grants [of money] to any government," Kennedy said he hoped that such aid would be in the "concrete and businesslike" areas of aid in techniques and know-how.

> As some of our recent experience demonstrates, mere grants of money are debilitating and wasteful. . . . We cannot abolish poverty that for centuries has characterized this area. There is not enough money in the world to relieve the poverty of all the millions in this world who may be threatened by communism. We cannot and should not attempt to buy their freedom from this threat; all we can do is help them achieve that freedom if they really wish to do so. Our resources are not limitless.

Two days later Kennedy told the Acushnet Men's Catholic Association Annual Banquet that "Uncle Sugar is as dangerous a role for us to play as Uncle Shylock." He expressed displeasure at some of the diplomatic representatives he'd met during his world tour—especially in the Far East—who had struck him, Kennedy said, "as a breed of their own, moving mainly in their own limited circles and unconscious of the fact that their role is not tennis and cocktails." He went on to list what should be done to defeat communism in those areas.

In January 1952 Kennedy returned to Cape Cod. His plane was grounded in Boston by fog, and he was driven the remaining distance to address a meeting of Hyannis and Orleans Rotarians, joined by members from Harwich and Falmouth.

His appearance marked a return to the speaker's platform where he had served part of his apprenticeship in 1945 at the beginning of his career. Six years had made considerable difference. He was still slender and boyish. The intervening years had only enhanced his extraordinary good looks. The diffidence, the earnestness of a "characteristically unassuming" candidate were gone, however. They had been replaced by a no less serious purposefulness and a poised self-command, the results of long hours of practice.

At the lectern he was an assured and easy speaker, without notes. His text was largely drawn from his Chamber of Commerce speech and an earlier radio report following a European tour. A more forcible voice with a somewhat tense edge commanded attention, impressing an overflow crowd of about two hundred, who noticed the developing mannerisms—the pointed finger, the downward stab of the hand for emphasis—that most particularly characterized his new and more direct style.

Reviewing his previous year's world tour with particular reference to the critical areas he had visited in Southeast Asia, Kennedy placed considerable stress on Indochina, a country, he said, that would unquestionably vote communist if elections were held that year.

Noting that Russia would be ahead of the United States in plane production for the next nine months, after which the United States would have caught up, Kennedy said, "The next nine months are crucial and dangerous ones for our country."

His speech was frequently interrupted with warm applause, by far the most enthusiastic reception yet accorded Jack Kennedy on Cape Cod. A brief handshaking session followed the speech; then, very late that night, Kennedy was driven back to fogbound Boston to meet another speech-making commitment early the following day.

Two weeks later Kennedy was in Fairhaven across the bridge from New Bedford. "If war comes, it will come this summer," Kennedy told three hundred men at a communion breakfast of the Holy Name Society of St. Joseph's Church. "Because the balance of air power will shift to our side by 1953, this summer will prove to be, in my estimate, the most dangerous period, for if there will be a war, that's when it will begin . . ."

Again taking up the crisis in Indochina, Kennedy pointed out that reports of Chinese troop concentrations above the northern border could be the forerunner of an invasion within "five or six weeks. I was the first congressman to go to French Indochina in three years," Kennedy said, "a discouraging state of affairs when one realizes the importance of this area."

Russian control there would "give them tremendous balance of power in Asia," Kennedy said, "and communist forces could start a westward roll across India and on through Europe, utilizing the huge manpower pool of the East."

Referring to the "$64 question": what the United States should do if Indochina was invaded, he said, "We would give air and sea support, but as to sending troops to that area, that's a decision that I wouldn't want to have the responsiblity of making." [2]

He participated in a radio forum, "Reducing the Federal Waste-line," which was sponsored by the Massachusetts Committee for the Hoover Report in early 1952, and continued to tour the state as election-year political fever swept the country. The first rumored candidacy of General Dwight D. Eisenhower was being skillfully furthered by Henry Cabot Lodge, already an announced candidate for re-election to the Senate.

Basil Brewer, publisher of the New Bedford *Standard-Times* and Massachusetts campaign manager for Senator Robert A. Taft, quickly sought to stop the momentum of the "draft Eisenhower" drive: "It is, of course, perfectly obvious that General Eisenhower cannot and will not be drafted," Brewer said, in a front page statement. "It is known the General has been so advised by his own supporters . . ." Commenting on Lodge's previous press-conference remark that he was "warily confident Ike would respond," Brewer quoted an earlier Eisenhower statement: "Under no circumstances will I ask for relief from this assignment in Europe in order to seek nomination to political office and I shall not participate in the preconvention activities of others who may have such an intention with respect to me."

Brewer, a fiercely partisan Taft supporter, privately conceded the strong possibility that he would realize a long-cherished desire for the ambassadorship to Portugal if Taft were elected president. He had not only serialized Taft's *A Foreign Policy for Americans* in the *Standard-Times* but had also been responsible for the Ohio Senator's first visit to southeastern Massachusetts, for a reception in his honor at the Wamsutta club earlier in 1952.

Taft's "infectious grin" and the warmth of his personality surprised and delighted even his most partisan supporters. His flat, dry voice; his spectacles and thinning hair, and the suggestion of a paunch under the vest of his open suit jacket gave him the homely quality of a country lawyer and struck a responsive chord. Ohioan or not, Taft strongly suggested the tang and snap of a New England Yankee. "It is with great pleasure that I come to the home town of my old friend Basil Brewer," Taft said at the reception. "I have had his unwavering support for many years and his exaggeration of my merits has, I hope, produced many friends in New Bedford for me."

Taft did have many friends, not only in New Bedford, but on Cape Cod as well. Advertisements extolling Taft's candidacy appeared well in advance of the Massachusetts primary, and bumper stickers and posters blossomed in profusion, thanks to a large and well-staffed "Cape Cod for Taft" headquarters.

In April 1952, however, an "Eisenhower for President" committee was formed on Cape Cod, with Sheriff Donald P. Tulloch as chairman. Tulloch admitted that Eisenhower headquarters on the Cape "hasn't much money to ballyhoo its crusade"—an obvious reference to well-financed Taft headquarters. But, he continued, "it has something which money can't buy, a deep and abiding faith that our country can elect a leader untouched by the weary and compromising racket of professional politics. The vast majority of Cape voters has hitched its hopes to the star that is sweeping America."

Eisenhower swept the free-for-all, write-in presidential primary in April, capturing 29 of 32 Massachusetts convention delegates. Those pledged to Taft's candidacy won election on Cape Cod, although voters gave the edge in the preferential balloting to Eisenhower by a small margin.

Already mentioned as the probable candidate for either governor or senator—his announced candidacy for either awaited the decision of Governor Paul Dever—Kennedy urged the re-examination of Federal fiscal policies unfavorable to New England during an appearance before the New Bedford Lions Club and Junior Chamber of Commerce, which presented him with an award for "outstanding community service."

Expressing disappointment at the failure of the 81st Congress to increase minimum wages from 75 cents to $1 an hour, on a selective basis, Kennedy proposed a "concerted effort" to wipe out North-South wage differentials before shifting from regional economic issues to foreign affairs.

Calling the explosive situation in Southeast Asia, "Russia's greatest opportunity for immediate extension of communist rule," Kennedy charged that the State Department, through lack of understanding of its importance, had virtually ignored the area. He predicted that it would be taken over by communists unless technical assistance, military aid and propaganda measures were stepped up.

In early April, the Boston *Globe* headlined its prediction that Dever would seek re-election as governor, as he was loath to risk his political career on a foredoomed challenge to the apparently invincible Henry Cabot Lodge.

After conferring with Dever, a "favorite son" candidate for the Democratic presidential nomination, who did not choose to reveal his intentions until after Easter, John F. Kennedy, a month before his 35th birthday, announced his candidacy for the Senate:

> For entirely too long the representatives of Massachusetts in the Senate have stood by helplessly while our industries and jobs disappear. Because of this, thousands of families today are denied the opportunity for successful and decent living. Other states have vigorous leaders, men who have definite goals based on constructive principles and who move toward these goals unswervingly. Massachusetts has need for such leadership.

Whether or not the electorate would decide that John F. Kennedy could provide such leadership was, of course, the big question. Joseph P. Kennedy thought so. His privately financed opinion polls had indicated to him that his son had as good a chance of beating Lodge as anybody. At precampaign strategy meetings in Hyannis Port, which he dominated, the former Ambassador urged John to challenge the incumbent and pointed out: "When you've beaten him you've beaten the best. Why try for something less?"

His father's optimism notwithstanding, Jack Kennedy, with only a lackluster record of accomplishment in the lower house of Congress, where, he himself admitted, "we were only worms," hardly seemed a serious threat to the re-election of Lodge. The latter was a man who not only enjoyed an incumbent's advantage but who also was the closest political ally of General Eisenhower, the "captive hero," in Marquis Childs' phrase, and generally conceded to be the one man who could lead the Republican Party back into the White House.*

Although Jack Kennedy's announced candidacy caused only a small flurry of interest on Cape Cod at first, local ears pricked up when a Kennedy speech criticized cuts in air-force appropriations, for more than $2.5 million to expand Otis base facilities located in Camp

---

* When Jack Kennedy announced his candidacy, Henry Cabot Lodge sent a message through Arthur Krock to "tell Joe not to waste his money on Jack because he can't win. I'm going to win by 300,000 votes." If Lodge seemed overconfident, he had good reason to be. Beginning in 1936 he had successively beaten three popular Irish politicians, James M. Curley, David I. Walsh and Joseph Casey.

Edwards had already been appropriated in the house, part of a bill slated for passage in June.

Speaking to more than one thousand women during one of the first of the famous "teas" at the Hotel Mellen in Fall River, Kennedy declared that unless the cuts were restored America would not have the air strength it desperately needed for survival.

The New Bedford *Standard-Times* publicly applauded Kennedy's stand, taken several weeks later during the early-summer session of Congress, in defense of Massachusetts' fishing industry against the threat of vastly increased imports of groundfish fillets.

Taking a short breather at the beginning of the most vigorous statewide campaign Massachusetts had ever seen, Kennedy joined the biggest crowd in Cape Cod's history and celebrated the Fourth of July weekend at his father's house. He was more fortunate than many holiday visitors, who had to spend the night in their cars because not enough accommodations were available.

A week later Kennedy watched the Republican national convention in Chicago, broadcast on television for the first time. The battle raged between the Taft and Eisenhower forces, led by the skilled maneuverings of Lodge, who, in his dedicated crusade to capture the Republican presidential nomination for Eisenhower, was absent from the political arenas in his own backyard.

Eisenhower's nomination in the first roll call on a hot, muggy Friday afternoon brought from Basil Brewer the following comment:

> I wouldn't be honest if I did not say there are scars, deep ones, in the Republican party as a result of the late primary campaign.
>
> Fortunately in Massachusetts, I and my associates have conducted a campaign which at no time was derogatory to Ike. Therefore, in supporting him we have nothing to take back.
>
> I pledge my own individual support of Eisenhower to the limit of my talents and ability, that of my newspapers * and that of all my associates in the campaign with whom I have influence.

Brewer then urged all Republicans to get wholeheartedly behind the Eisenhower-Nixon team in order to drive the "crooks and starry-eyed liberals from Washington." No mention was made of Lodge.

* The Cape Cod *Standard-Times* is distributed on Cape Cod with its parent newspaper, the New Bedford *Standard-Times*, so that Cape residents had direct access to Mr. Brewer's view.

A lingering bitterness, however, did cling. Two weeks later an ill-concealed note of waspishness crept into Brewer's review of the Democratic national convention: "The 'draft' for Governor Stevenson of Illinois for the Democratic presidential nomination was about as spontaneous as the 'groundswell' for General Eisenhower."

On August 17, 1952, the New Bedford Sunday *Standard-Times* reprinted "by special permission of *The Reader's Digest*," the condensed article "Survival" by John Hersey that had originally appeared in *The New Yorker*. It was virtually a piece of Kennedy campaign literature by the summer of 1952. Reprints had been widely circulated in the 1946 campaign, and 900,000 copies were being distributed as part of a tabloid rotogravure giveaway at Kennedy headquarters all over the state.

The significance of the article's appearance in the *Standard-Times* during an election campaign was not lost on outraged Lodge supporters. It created an immediate, if unpublicized, furor centering on editorial motives.

In Hyannis in mid-August, Jack Kennedy opened his Cape Cod campaign, one that managed to rouse even Barnstable's near-moribund Democratic committee. The Cape's traditional, rock-like Republican stance had varied little throughout its history; neither time, tide nor Roosevelt had made any noticeable difference.

The special effort Jack Kennedy made to meet with members of the Barnstable "Kennedy for Senator" committee in the basement hearing room of Barnstable's town offices, to discuss the local aspects of his campaign and to outline statewide plans was an enormously winning gesture for any candidate to make. "You wouldn't catch anybody as high falutin' as Lodge doing it," a committee member said.

Committee members found the candidate confident, deeply tanned and *au courant* with local problems relative to his candidacy—and most receptive and sympathetic to the committee's difficulties and suggestions. At ease in sports clothes, Jack Kennedy created an enormously likable impression in relaxed give-and-take with a small group. The warmth of his personality inspired the committee to mount what for Cape Cod was a major campaign effort to elect a Democratic candidate; the discouraging prospects for its success were temporarily overlooked.

As a practicing pragmatist, however, Jack Kennedy could have viewed Cape Cod only as the least likely place in the state to gain new adherents, and he didn't waste much more time campaigning there; he appeared only briefly at a fairly well-attended tea at his father's house in Hyannis Port that August. There the Kennedy bandwagon encountered its first palpable resistance. Most natives were preoccupied by their busiest season yet and prone to sniff at "summer people" anyway. But familiarity had bred, in some local cases, if not contempt, at least a strong and active dislike of the Kennedys.

Others cherished instances of Kennedy family rudeness or displays races, whereas some held "no happy memories working for the of arrogance at Hyannis Port's pier after fiercely contested yachting Kennedys." Accused of pretentiousness and snobbery on one hand, the Kennedys were put down on the other for being "too rough and raw" and "lacking in culture." And it was an indisputable fact that the Kennedys had never courted general popularity on Cape Cod until Jack's entry into politics.

The natives were too sharply aware perhaps that the invitation to tea was part of the political campaign and had been tendered, in the words of one resistant voter, "only because they wanted something," after which "they wouldn't know you the next day if they fell over you." Of course, Henry Cabot Lodge was not likely to recognize everyone who had voted for him the day after the election either.

"I suppose we were all dying to see the inside of that house," a disappointed guest at the tea confessed, finding it less luxurious than she had hoped and not commensurate with the reputed Kennedy millions.

The residents of Hyannis Port raised their eyebrows just a little when their calm village became, for one afternoon, a political camp ground—and a Democratic one, at that. Although some of those attending the tea found the candidate's famed allure insincere, many others thought that the event provided the high point of the summer season.

The Hyannis Port experience, however, hardly typified the success such receptions were having all over the rest of the state. A more representative example occurred some two weeks later, a tea given for women of the New Bedford area and attended by a small, loyal contingent of Kennedy supporters from Cape Cod.

White-satin hostess badges identified a corps of local Democratic ladies: they were assisted by relays of "pourers" working in shifts.

Others aided the chairman, who had received, well in advance of the occasion, instructions and assistance from Kennedy campaign workers, who overlooked no detail to ensure the smooth running of the reception.

Most particularly, the air of a political rally was shunned. While an orchestra played background music throughout the evening, repeating at intervals a catchy strain identified as the "Kennedy for Senator Song," more than one thousand women gathered in the main ballroom of the New Bedford Hotel.

The candidate was introduced by New Bedford's then district attorney: "When an entire family renders many services, kindnesses and charitable acts to people, nations and the world, our hearts go out to them completely and we adopt that family as our family."

Turning his attention to the guest of honor—tanned, still boyish at 35, extraordinarily handsome and superbly turned out in a lightweight dark blue suit and his customarily conservative silk tie—the District Attorney glowingly introduced him as having "served his country well in government and in war."

Wisely, after such an introduction, Kennedy limited his own remarks. It was his eighth public appearance that day.

> You women are interested not so much in the success of a party or of a candidate as in the success of your country. We realize women will be highly important factors in the coming election. Because you are interested, because there are more of you, because you live longer and have all the money, all the politicians will be talking to you.

After the appreciative and flattered laughter died down, with his audience beaming at him, Kennedy went on, graciously thanking the local chairman of the committee on arrangements for the tea.[3]

He looked at his slender, vibrantly attractive mother, chic in a brilliant red-draped crepe frock "straght from Paris," long black gloves and a small red and black hat. "I am very grateful, too, to my mother. We expect our mothers to help, but she hurried home from a visit to my brother Ted who is in the Army overseas which I think was doing a great deal . . ." Applause from the other mothers present drowned out the remainder of the sentence. "She used to campaign 55 years ago with my grandfather[4] John F. Fitzgerald when he was running for Congress," Kennedy went on, while the ladies present murmured their disbelief.

Kennedy wasted little time on issues. He grew serious:

> We are faced by an enemy whose goal is to conquer the world by subversion and infiltration if possible, or, if necessary, by open war.
>
> This year and the year after are the years of maximum risk for the United States. By the end of 1954 and 1955 the United States and our allies will be strong. But two or three years must elapse before the balance of military power shifts in favor of the West.
>
> I believe nevertheless the danger of war is not so near as we may fear. Four factors lead me to this point of view. We have atomic superiority. Even if the Soviets marched into Western Europe they would run the risk of guerilla action by the unwilling satellite nations in their rear. Even if they could seize West Europe, they still would be at war with the United States in a war we would win.
>
> Finally, a restraining factor is the feeling the communists have that time is on their side, and that they will be able to seize large areas of the Middle East and Southeast Asia without resorting to war, taking advantage of widespread illiteracy, ignorance, disease and poverty. These are two areas to which we have given far too little attention.

Turning very briefly to the statewide matters, Kennedy alluded quickly to the need for Massachusetts to preserve its industrial position, mentioning the hard-pressed local fishing industry and concluding with a sentimental and subliminal appeal for support:

> My grandfather, John F. Fitzgerald ran for the Senate against my Republican opponent's grandfather, and, I am sorry to say, he was defeated. Now, the two grandsons are running and I hope the Fitzgeralds and the Kennedys will be more successful this time than the Cabots and the Lodges.

Smiling his thanks as the applause reached a crescendo, Kennedy turned the platform over to his mother. She began, her eyes sparkling:

> I'm tremendously excited about all this. It is something that never has happened to me before. When I was a girl, my father John F. Fitzgerald was Mayor of Boston and any little talk by me was out of the question.
>
> When my husband became Ambassador to Britain, any public talk by me was even more out of the question.
>
> And now, I'll tell you something you may find interesting. I have just come home from Paris, and skirts are longer and tighter there!

The roar of appreciative and surprised laughter and applause that greeted this superb change of pace was testimony to her skill as a public speaker, inexperienced or not. When the applause began to die down, she added, "You are wonderful to come out on this very hot night as you have to see us."

The platform was then turned over to Jean Kennedy, on whose attractive shoulders, in charcoal-gray organza over matching taffeta, fell the more businesslike portion of the reception. In a gracious but firm talk, she invited every woman who would like to help the Democratic cause to sign a card volunteering for campaign work, getting out the vote and helping at Kennedy headquarters. A troop of volunteers with pencils and index cards began circulating among the women, and the reception ended.[5]

Two days later the rivals met on the same platform when "the issues facing the Republican and Democratic Parties" were debated for the first time in the campaign, an event sponsored by the League of Women Voters of Waltham. An interested group of Jack Kennedy's neighbors—curious to see "what Jack would look like next to Lodge"—arrived to find the auditorium of South Junior High School already rapidly filling up. It was primary day, but, as both candidates were running unopposed, the results of the voting were not crucial except perhaps to Kennedy strategists as indicators of how well the race was going.

It was soon apparent that the candidates bore more striking similarities than differences. Both seemed charming, urbane and effortlessly articulate men who had decided not to take too seriously the League's invitation to do public battle. The fact that Kennedy had "won" the debate, however, was pretty well established, when the question of tariffs was injected into the evening's discussion. Lodge could only reiterate his liberal and well-known views on the lowering of such tariffs, views that did not sit well with an audience of residents of Waltham, Massachusetts' erstwhile "Watch City," whose industry had suffered irreparable harm from foreign competition.*

Throughout the debate, Joseph P. Kennedy was stationed high at the top of the auditorium balcony, leaning against a radiator, where he scribbled short, informative notes and arguments for delivery to his son on the platform by two runners alternately at his disposal.

---

* Had Lodge done his homework as well as Kennedy had done his, he could have easily turned the tables by pointing to Kennedy's opposition to an RFC loan to the bankrupt Waltham Watch Company in 1947, when he argued, "It's a question of how far Government can go in propping up a private business that can't keep going on its own."

In the primaries, Kennedy was the most popular Democratic candidate for office in Barnstable County, receiving a total of 431 votes—78 more than were received by Governor Dever, also a Cape Cod summer resident, with a sumptuous house in Centerville. But the disparity in numbers between Republicans and Democrats was visible in Lodge's Capewide primary total of 4,781. In the Town of Barnstable Lodge scored 1,110 to Kennedy's 105.

In New Bedford, a short 35-mile journey away, where 772 more regular Republicans than Democrats were registered, Kennedy had polled 9,362 votes, almost 2,000 more votes than Lodge, who received 7,434 votes (with 2,403 blanks against his name). Statewide the primary vote had been very close; Kennedy polled 394,138 in the Democratic primary and Lodge 394,896 in the Republican primary.

Charter flights of the Cape and Islands service taxied Kennedy to Hyannis Port for short "breathers" from the rigors of stumping the state, but friends and supporters crowded the veranda to argue politics (they were cautioned to make less noise when Joseph P. Kennedy was napping). Jack, like all local candidates, did enjoy the brief respite provided by the furor at the disclosure of a "Nixon Fund." The vice-presidential candidate's television appearance, during which he divulged his personal finances in the celebrated "Checkers" speech, resulted in a flood of sympathetic telegrams from Cape Codders.

Although the Nixon controversy was to create a nationwide uproar, no less a one was created on a statewide level: The bombshell burst over the senatorial campaign on Friday, September 26, when Basil Brewer, publisher of the New Bedford *Standard-Times* not only announced his support for John F. Kennedy but also particularly and emphatically repudiated Henry Cabot Lodge, who, he charged, had "bolted the Republican party."

More than 24 of the state's leading newspapers sent representatives to the Brewer press conference. Reporters from Chicago and New York papers, as well as wire-service representatives, were also on hand, drawn by widespread rumors that Brewer's announcement could have explosive repercussions on the now hotly contested senatorial campaign. The crowded, coolly impersonal suite of the Sheraton Plaza in Boston was charged with anticipation. Members of the press came early, and the hotel's staff graciously supplied additional chairs for the unexpected crowd.

Finally Brewer made his appearance. He was a small, dapper man with milk-white skin, thinning white hair and a benign, almost sweet, smile, who nonetheless bore a marked physical resemblance to Joseph P. Kennedy. He wore a jaunty, brightly patterned tie and a rosette in the lapel of his impeccable dark-gray suit. His rather old-fashioned black-rimmed spectacles were misleadingly like those of elderly gentlemen who feed pigeons in the park.

Armed with a thick folder of notes and memoranda, of which he would make lethal use, Brewer took his place in one of the striped arm chairs, placing the folder on a small table beside him. He was calm and completely at ease, betraying no visible hint of the nature of his announcement.

Opening the conference, Brewer said, "Many Republicans as well as others have inquired as to our position" in the senatorial race between Kennedy and Lodge. "I have been subjected to great pressure from supporters of Senator Lodge, some claiming to represent the Senator himself, to induce myself and the *Standard-Times*, if we were not to support Lodge, at least to be neutral."

While reporters stirred restlessly, sensing that Brewer's opening remarks were only the preamble to an unprecedented announcement, he went on:

> The interest is wide, and not confined to the Commonwealth of Massachusetts. Also, the issues are of critical importance. Therefore, this press conference to give all newspapers and press associations equal opportunity to publish the story if they care to do so.
>
> In stating my position with reference to the Lodge-Kennedy contest and as former manager of the Taft campaign in the Commonwealth, I am, of course, not speaking for Senator Taft or for any Taft supporters in the state. I am expressing the views of myself, of the *Standard-Times* and of my associates in the New Bedford newspapers.
>
> On Friday afternoon, July 11, after the nomination of General Eisenhower and Senator Nixon I announced my support and that of our newspapers for the Eisenhower-Nixon team, for Congressman Herter,* candidate for governor and for others of the Republican state ticket. This was reiterated that same evening at a Republican get-together in Chicago and published the following day in the *Standard-Times*.
>
> On September 12, following the historic meeting between General

---

* Questioned on how his support of Kennedy affected his support of Herter, closely aligned with Lodge, Brewer said, "I am supporting Herter, but I am not supporting Herter's support of Lodge," a semantic stroke that brought appreciative smiles from reporters present.

Eisenhower and Senator Taft, I said the two "had again demonstrated the greatness of their stature," and that Taft and Eisenhower supporters may now "join forces with enthusiasm and with assurance of victory." That still is our position and we already are devoting all our energies and the influence of our newspapers to Eisenhower, Nixon, Herter and others of the Republican state ticket.

At a previous press conference on August 7, discussing an exchange with . . . the chairman of the Massachusetts State Committee, I was asked our position with reference to the Lodge-Kennedy contest. At that time, I declined to state our position because it would have confused a greater issue then under discussion, the getting together of the Eisenhower and Taft forces for victory in the presidential election.

After a short pause, during which Brewer scanned his audience of expectant reporters, he said:

Today the union of the Taft and Eisenhower forces is an accomplished fact in Massachusetts and elsewhere. Therefore, there need be no further delay in announcing our wholehearted support of Congressman John Kennedy and opposition to Henry Cabot Lodge in the current senatorial contest . . .

While the suite buzzed with comment and several newsmen hurried out to file bulletins for the last editions of their newspapers, Brewer sat placidly waiting for his chance to go on:

In so doing, we are not "bolting the Republican Party," for Senator Lodge long ago bolted his party by votes for the Truman Socialistic "New Deal" as we shall show. Also, he deserted his constituents by a record of absentations from roll calls which in 1952 was the largest of any senator except one, as we shall show.

Brewer promptly produced a tabulated chart from his folder, which he said "shows Lodge was absent on 98 of 129 roll calls in 1952 . . . exceeded only by Senator Carlson of Kansas who missed 100 roll calls." He pointed out that Lodge had been absent on 74 of 202 roll calls taken in 1951. Brewer not only attacked Lodge's absenteeism, but he also performed the service of defending Kennedy's:

Senator Lodge's absentations in the 1951–1952 session far exceed those of his opponent Kennedy, though Kennedy's absentations, including war service-connected illnesses, were the key emphasis in $60,000 or more of advertising by which Senator Lodge on September 8 opened his attack on Congressman Kennedy.

After his Primary victory, the candidate for the Democratic nomination for Congress visits his father at Hyannis Port. June 1946. (New Bedford *Standard-Times*)

John F. Kennedy instructs 14-year-old Ted in the arts of sailing the Wianno Junior *Onemore*. July 1946. (New Bedford *Standard-Times*)

The famous "tea" at the New Bedford Hotel in August of 1952. John F. Kennedy addresses the audience under the watchful eyes of his mother. (New Bedford *Standard-Times*)

A month after declaring his candidacy for the Senate, John F. Kennedy makes a rare public appearance on crutches. May 1952. (New Bedford *Standard-Times*)

Kennedy shares a convertible with Adlai Stevenson during a motorcade in New
Bedford in October 1952. (New Bedford *Standard-Times*)

Jacqueline Bouvier and John F. Kennedy ride a "Sailfish" following the announcement of their engagement. June 1953. (New Bedford *Standard-Times*)

On the beach at Hyannis Port. August 1957.

Following his address at the United Fund's "Kickoff Dinner" at New Bedford, Kennedy was presented with a cartoon booming his presidential candidacy in 1960. October 13, 1957. (New Bedford *Standard-Times*)

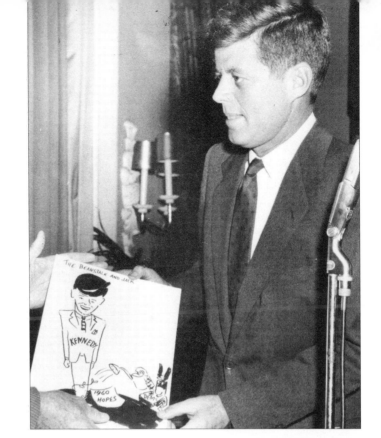

Jacqueline and John F. Kennedy at the National Guard Armory in Hyannis after the only campaign speech of his career made on Cape Cod. October 1958. (Barnstable *Patriot*)

The famed "Kennedy Compound": John F. Kennedy's house left foreground (1),
Bobby Kennedy's house (2) and Joseph P. Kennedy's house (3). (Chick Craig)

Caroline meeting the press. July 1960. (New Bedford *Standard-Times*)

Jacqueline waves from the porch of her father-in-law's house the day after her husband won the presidential nomination in Los Angeles. July 1960. (New Bedford *Standard-Times*)

The Brothers Kennedy. July 1960. (New Bedford *Standard-Times*)

John F. Kennedy greets well-wishers at the fence at his house on Irving Avenue in Hyannis Port during the campaign summer of 1960. (New Bedford *Standard-Times*)

Homecoming parade down Main Street. July 1960.

The President-Elect at National Guard Armory in Hyannis. November 1960. (New Bedford *Standard-Times*)

John F. Kennedy leads the way to the News Store in Hyannis Port, accompanied by secret servicemen and niece and nephews. July 1961. (New Bedford *Standard-Times*)

John F. Kennedy and the First Lady leave St. Francis Xavier Church in Hyannis. (Harold Cobb)

John F. Kennedy accompanies John, Jr. on a visit to Jacqueline at Otis Base Hospital following the birth and death of Patrick Bouvier Kennedy. August 1963. (New Bedford *Standard-Times*)

John F. Kennedy salutes those watching at the fence at Otis Air Force Base for the last time before returning to Washington. October 21, 1963. (New Bedford *Standard-Times*)

The Lodge advertisements [6] had been so skillfully written that, according to Brewer, "even the Boston *Herald*, which is so strongly supporting Lodge was deceived—in my opinion, intentionally—and published an editorial commending Lodge's attendance record."

Dipping into his well-stocked file folder again, Brewer produced a copy of the *Herald*'s editorial and quoted from it: "One of the factors Bay State voters should consider carefully next November is whether they want a part-time or a full-time spokesman in the Senate for the next six years."

"Based on that statement," Brewer said, "the voters could not possibly want Senator Lodge and his absenteeism record."

The most vigorous and lively questioning from reporters centered on whether or not Brewer's resentment at the treatment of Taft during the Chicago convention had played any part in his opposition to Lodge. Re-emphasizing that his opposition to Lodge was not based on the Senator's prominent role in depriving Taft of the nomination, Brewer answered:

> Neither I nor our newspapers are supporting Kennedy because Lodge assisted in the defeat of Taft. But I would not be entirely fair if I did not say that some of the techniques of the Duff, Lodge, Dewey faction revealed character weaknesses which should be taken into consideration in judging whether a man is qualified to hold a seat in the Senate of the United States.

Asked what he thought would be the effects of a Republican's announcing support for a Democratic candidate, Brewer unhesitatingly said:

> I hope it will elect Kennedy! As for the presidential campaign, in my opinion it will help Eisenhower and Nixon. I don't expect any strong preconvention Eisenhower supporters to agree, but I believe a Republican announcing support for Kennedy is going to help.

Pressed for a further explanation of this view, Brewer outlined two reasons for his belief. First, Democrats who might be wavering could be influenced to support a Republican presidential team because, "they, too, want a change"; second, "some of the Taft people will be influenced to follow me in supporting Kennedy, I believe, and they will feel freer to support Eisenhower and Nixon . . . as up to now many have not been inclined to do."

If Lodge, then, was going to be used as a kind of sacrificial lamb in order to propitiate Taft supporters, another reporter wanted to know if Brewer's endorsement had been "above party considerations."

"What do you mean by 'above party'?" Brewer asked sharply.

"Is it a choice between party or between two men?" the reporter said.

"The difference between the two men outweighs party considerations," Brewer said, taking another well-aimed thrust at Lodge. "I think Kennedy will make a better senator."

After Brewer had discussed at length the seating of disputed southern delegations at the Republican convention, still stubbornly insisting that Taft's convention experience had no connection with the Kennedy endorsement except "insofar as it reflected on the character and good faith" of Lodge and on "whether he was equipped for the Senate," a reporter asked about the *Standard-Times'* support for Democratic Senator David I. Walsh when Lodge successfully defended his Senate seat in 1946.

"We supported Lodge wholeheartedly in 1936 against Curley," Brewer explained. "When he ran against Walsh, we supported Walsh." He pointed out that his newspaper had supported Walsh in his political campaigns for more than 25 years.

Asked if Kennedy had been told that he was to receive the endorsement of the New Bedford *Standard-Times*, Brewer said, "Yes," adding matter-of-factly, "He was very pleased."

To the question, "What steps do you plan to take in supporting Mr. Kennedy?" Brewer replied: "Just whatever two newspapers, The New Bedford *Standard-Times* and the Cape Cod *Standard-Times*, can do to legitimately support Congressman Kennedy as well as all other nominees whom we are and will be supporting." [7]

Reviewing Kennedy's record, Brewer cited his service as a PT-boat commander and noted as well that Kennedy had been a "vigorous supporter of aid to combat communism in Greece, Turkey and Italy, having voted for the Marshall Plan aid to China and Korea as well as other mutual defense legislation." But he had, at the same time, been alert to point out that "the countries of Europe were not doing their just share in the vital task in the defense of the West."

Four years previously Kennedy had attacked the China policy of the United States, declaring the "responsibility for the failure of our foreign policy in the Far East rests squarely with the White House and the Department of State," Brewer quoted, adding, "Does that sound like a Republican talking?" Kennedy's support of the Republican view that Congress should have a voice in the matter of sending United States troops to Europe and his denunciation in May 1951 of the "trade in blood" between allies and communist China, Brewer said, struck him as "virtually identical to the views of Robert A. Taft."

The conference closed after Brewer commented on the question of whether or not the election of a Democrat in Massachusetts to replace a Republican in the Senate might prevent the Republicans from gaining a majority and thus the power to organize the Senate, including committee membership. Brewer's reply was resourceful: "If Republicans depend on the election of one senator for their chance of being able to organize, they won't get that opportunity," he said tartly. Then, thanking the members of the press present, Brewer gathered up his papers and left the suite.

It had been a magnificent, superbly calculated piece of vindictiveness, despite Brewer's tepid remonstrances to the contrary, and a massive vengeance on the man who had led the anti-Taft forces at the convention. Brewer had brought it off for maximum damage to Lodge's candidacy. The devastation was manifest in the extensive coverage his press conference won in the statewide press—it was easily the single most newsworthy event in the campaign.

Brewer's announcement was a shattering blow to Lodge's already wobbling campaign. Lodge was tired from his preconvention exertions on Ike's behalf, but, even under normal circumstances, he was hardly Kennedy's match when it came to campaign "hustle." Brewer's press conference raised a howl of protest from Lodge's Cape Cod supporters. During a day-long tour hailed as "the most successful on Cape Cod in 50 years," Lodge the following week got his first chance to answer Brewer's stunning denunciation of his candidacy.

He was traveling with Christian Herter, whose candidacy had received Brewer's blessing and who, somewhat confusingly, as he was running for governor, vowed to rid the government of "minks, pinks and stinks." He preceded Lodge to the speaker's platform. But Lodge's attempt to refute Brewer's stinging attack could hardly duplicate the impact of Brewer's press conference, despite an enthusiastic and partisan audience of some 450 people crammed into Hyannis' VFW hall. Lodge said:

If you are going to be represented by a man of conviction you are not always going to agree with him. I am not content to sit back. If there is something I can do I will go out and do it, and for that I know I have been criticized. In fact, there is an individual in New Bedford who said I ought not to take any part in the campaign to nominate a Republican candidate.

Lodge told the gathering sponsored by the Barnstable Town Republican Committee that he was "a friend of Taft's" but that he had been for Ike long before Taft became a candidate. Defending himself against Brewer's charges of absenteeism as best he could, Lodge admitted that he had been "absent at various times in 1952 . . . because I was trying to put over General Eisenhower as the Republican candidate. My opponent, Representative John F. Kennedy was absent too," Lodge said, "but for a different reason. He was campaigning for himself in Massachusetts. He was campaigning for himself and having teas—legal and non-fattening, I am sure," Lodge added, bringing down the house.

Lodge's sarcasm was faintly tinged with desperation, bearing out the fact that Lodge had at last become aware enough of the outstanding success the teas were having to attack them. In the campaign in which he had originally been regarded as front runner, Lodge was rapidly losing ground.

Pointing to Kennedy's voting record as the "worst Bay State voting record ever recorded during the last six years"—Kennedy had failed to record his position 179 times—Lodge added: "Kennedy's slogan of 'Do more for Massachusetts,' means only more than he has done, and candidly, ladies and gentlemen, that isn't very much."

Lodge concluded:

I want to work with Ike to build a durable peace. With him in the White House we will really build military strength as well as economic strength. We can have prosperity without war. We can have greater prosperity in peace than in war as production will move into productive things.

He also vowed that he would work to continue Camp Edwards as a permanent military post.

About one hundred people from Orleans, Eastham, Wellfleet and Brewster were on hand when Lodge spoke at Orleans Town Hall at a meeting sponsored by the town Republican committee. Again defending himself against Brewster's charges of absenteeism, Lodge said:

> My opponent has never denied he missed more roll calls. I was absent some of the time campaigning for Eisenhower while my opponent was campaigning for himself. On several occasions when it was claimed I was absent I called my secretary and through my office was recorded as voting for or against matters. This was not done by my opponent.

To his audience, of solidly Taft persuasion, Lodge took pains to explain that "I was *for* Ike—not *against* Taft. I felt strongly for Eisenhower, but would have supported Taft with vigor if he had been nominated."

Two hundred people loudly greeted Herter and Lodge in Falmouth. With Camp Edwards close by, Lodge wisely injected the "local issue" in his preliminary remarks and spoke reassuringly of his efforts to preserve the installation on a permanent basis. "This camp means much to Cape Cod," Lodge said.*

Lashing out at Basil Brewer, Lodge made his strongest public statement against the New Bedford publisher's charges:

> I think the people in the circulation area of the New Bedford *Standard-Times* are being denied their rights under the Constitution to have a free press. Brewer says I'm not a Republican. He must be the Supreme Court judge as to who is a Republican. There are 767,000 voters in Massachusetts who think I am a Republican. That's 767,000 to 1.

Later in his speech Lodge referred to Brewer once again: "Maybe he's done the right thing. He's against the civil rights bill and progressive legislation. He ought to be with the Kennedy family—they're where he is."

The following evening Jack Kennedy addressed Cape Cod via radio station WOCB in West Yarmouth—also owned by *Standard-Times*

---

* Although Lodge promised what he "would" do if elected, Kennedy appeared already to have taken action, a sample of the sort of deft one-upmanship against which Lodge was fighting a losing battle.

In reply to a direct appeal from Kennedy, President Truman had promised an inquiry into the proposed abandonment of Camp Edwards. Kennedy's campaign headquarters made public a telegram received from Major General Harry H. Vaughan, Truman's military aide, which said, "The President directs me to advise you that Camp Edwards will be utilized to the fullest extent consistent with service needs."

interests—in a talk that had been prerecorded in Boston the night before. The talk was not calculated as an answer to Lodge's successful tour. That would come two weeks later in a whirlwind barnstorming tour, undertaken by two of the Kennedy sisters, at which Cape Codders could only marvel. Some natives shook their heads in disbelief when one day's itinerary was announced:

Falmouth Recreation Building, 9:30 A.M.
Bourne Memorial Community Building, 11:00 A.M.
Sandwich, Clark's Block, Jarves Street, 11:45 A.M.
Hyannis, Hearing Room, Basement Town Hall, Main Street, 2:00 P.M.
South Yarmouth, The Owl Club, 3:15 P.M.
Harwich, Exchange Hall, 4:15 P.M.
Orleans, Orleans Inn, 6:45 P.M.
Wellfleet, Town Office Building, 7:45 P.M.
Provincetown, Town Hall, Caucus Hall, 8:30 P.M.

Taking into consideration the automobile trip from Hyannis Port to keep the morning's first appointment in Falmouth and the return that evening from Provincetown, the day of campaigning ran better than fourteen hours.

The appearance of the Kennedy sisters to "discuss with voters the issues of the campaign" had been arranged in conjunction with various "secretaries" in Cape towns. "Voters and friends regardless of party" were invited to greet the Kennedy girls, who were accompanied by Edward Moore of Osterville, former secretary to Joseph P. Kennedy; officials of the Barnstable Kennedy for United States Senate Club, and Judge Robert A. Welsh of Provincetown.

"John F. Kennedy has dedicated his life for the benefit of the people," Eunice Kennedy told fifty Falmouth women gathered for an informal reception at the town's former U.S.O. building on Main Street. While coffee, doughnuts and cookies were served, she added, "Jack Kennedy is responsible for firing the opening shot against communism in this country," and appealed to her audience to offer their automobiles for transportation to the polls on Election Day. And she urged Democratic committee members to telephone friends and neighbors "to get out the vote for Kennedy."

Both attractive sisters wore earrings inscribed "Vote for Kennedy" and flared, bright-colored skirts embroidered with their brother's name and a superimposed photograph of the United States capital.

A small but enthusiastic group greeted them in Bourne. Patricia outlined her brother's public and military career. "It would be wonderful if Cape Cod would send one of its own sons to the United States Senate," she said. "We have lived on the Cape in Hyannis Port for so many years that it is home to the whole family."

Accompanied by Ethel Kennedy, who had given birth to the candidate's first nephew a mere three weeks before, the group proceeded to Sandwich.

In Hyannis, they were joined by the candidate's mother, who was introduced by Judge Welsh: "The Kennedys are our neighbors," he said. "We know them and their qualities of leadership, integrity and honesty. But this is a fight and in a political fight it is up to us to let the electorate know that Congressman Kennedy does possess such traits."

To the audience of fifty women, Rose Kennedy said: "Our family would rather be in Hyannis Port in the summer than any place else in the world. After a 'get-acquainted' period of 26 years, Cape Cod is very close to the Kennedy family's heart." A consummate public speaker, Mrs. Kennedy again deprecated her own efforts:

> As you probably know, my father was John F. Fitzgerald, congressman and former Mayor of Boston. I married Joseph P. Kennedy, former Ambassador to the Court of St. James, and now my son John is in Congress. So you see there hasn't been much opportunity for me to practice in a family where the men did most of the public speaking.

Where the Herter-Lodge invasion had encountered dismal raw cold and rainy drizzle, the sun shone for the Kennedy sisters, as they moved down-Cape past serene offseason landscapes splashed with remnants of autumn foliage and lit by a clear, crisp blue sky and occasional glimpses of a sparkling, empty sea.

At Harwich, Patricia spoke to a small audience of women gathered at huge and quaintly ornate Exchange Hall, pointing out that Jack Kennedy's familiarity with local problems made him an excellent candidate for Cape Cod voters.

About 25 people greeted the sisters at the Orleans Inn, overlooking a chill and glittering waterside. Orleans was solid Republican territory, a lovely quiet town, its silent streets splashed with tall tree shadows. It had voted overwhelmingly against Roosevelt during the biggest Democratic landslide in the nation's history. Undaunted,

Patricia tirelessly reiterated the merits of her brother's candidacy, particularly stressing his fight against communism and for aid to veterans.

But it was at the day's final appearance, after a brief stop at Wellfleet to speak with 35 residents there, that the Kennedy girls met with a truly warm and sizable welcome, for Provincetown was that rarity on Cape Cod: a Democratic stronghold. With its large Portuguese population, Provincetown was more likely to reflect Old World mores than typical Cape Cod political stances. And with a large percentage of its population unemployed in winter and lined up every Tuesday morning at Town Hall to "sign up" for unemployment-insurance benefits, it was more likely to welcome proponents of social legislation.

In a rousing climax to a breathless day's campaigning, the meeting was held at Provincetown's large white clapboard Town Hall on Commercial Street. It was led by Judge Welsh. Patricia spoke, summarizing her brother's life on the Cape, his education and wartime experiences, his entrance into politics and his record in Congress. Even Ethel got into the act in Provincetown. She gave what was unquestionably the shortest speech of the tour: "I'm crazy about Jack," she said, "and I'm only an in-law."

With characteristic superb timing and a thoroughness that left nothing to chance and no possible advantage unexplored, the next coup in Kennedy's campaign was delivered in the New Bedford *Standard-Times* of Sunday, October 19, 1952. It appeared to be an endorsement of Kennedy's candidacy by a former wartime adversary:

> A pleasant echo from the desperate South Pacific sea battle that almost took the life of Congressman John F. Kennedy, then a PT-boat commander has just reached him. In an earnest if not perfect English translation, the commander of the Japanese destroyer that cut Kennedy's boat in two, nine years ago wrote him:
> "I am firmly convinced that a person who practice tolerance * to your former enemy like you, if elected to the high office in your country, would no doubt contribute not only to the promotion of genuine friendship between Japan and the United States, but also the establishment of a universal peace."

The letter was from Kohei Hanami, former commander of the destroyer *Amagiri*.

Realizing how quickly he was losing ground to Kennedy in the campaign, Lodge persuaded Eisenhower to come to Massachusetts. Ike's appearance in New Bedford was a huge success, with more than 40,000 people cheering his route to Buttonwood Park, where another 10,000 listened to his speech despite fair but very cold weather.

A week later Adlai Stevenson appeared in New Bedford.

"You know I don't campaign on Sunday and I'm just a tourist passing through New England this afternoon with two of the finest citizens I know—my old friend Paul Dever and Jack Kennedy. And, I'm delighted to see that these two fine citizens of Massachusetts seem to known an awful lot of friends along the road."

Stevenson announced he would "resume my campaigning tomorrow in case you want to hear what I'm saying."

About 3,500 people heard Stevenson's short outdoor address before he appeared at the New Bedford Hotel where 1,200 Democratic women were being feted at a tea given by Marie Dever, sister of Governor Paul Dever who was seeking re-election and Mrs. Joseph P. Kennedy.

(Accepting a gift of locally manufactured shirts from representatives of the United Textile Workers of America, Stevenson quipped, "If anyone had any idea how dirty my shirts are by this time, they couldn't have done better by me. This will save me from going to the laundry.")

Touring Massachusetts with Kennedy that October, Stevenson made it clear at every stop of his campaign train that he regarded Jack Kennedy as "my type of guy," referring to him as "perhaps one of the most promising men in American public life."

As he drove himself relentlessly toward the campaign's end, Kennedy's health broke. Hating to appear on crutches, he was in such frequent pain that he dragged one foot as he doggedly crisscrossed the state during the last, long, exhausting days, sipping soup from paper cups and downing daily frappes—Massachusetts idiom for ice-cream milk shakes—between campaign appearances.

Although Cape Cod remained steadfastly Republican, declaring itself overwhelmingly for Eisenhower (he received 20,943 votes to only 4,984 for Stevenson), Kennedy's total was by far the largest any Democrat had ever received there: 8,035 votes to 17,370 for Lodge. In Kennedy's "home town" of Barnstable, he polled 1,942 to 3,977 for Lodge, a remarkably good showing compared to Cape Cod's usually lopsided results and representing a loss from Lodge's 1946 victory edge over David I. Walsh from 78 per cent of votes cast to 67.5 percent.

Statewide the vote was Kennedy 1,211,974 and Lodge 1,141,247, a margin of 70,727 votes. Eisenhower had overwhelmingly defeated Stevenson by more than 200,000 votes—the first time a Republican presidential candidate had won in Massachusetts since Coolidge in 1924—sweeping into office all other major Republican candidates but Lodge, including Christian Herter, who narrowly defeated Paul Denver by 14,456 votes. New Bedford's results were astonishing. Kennedy had carried it by 37,350 votes to 15,812 for Lodge.

Lodge's concession of defeat to Kennedy was a message ripe with innuendo and anything but "kind" or "extremely generous," as Kennedy described it in his edgy answer. "I extend congratulations and express the hope that you will derive from your term in the Senate all the satisfaction which comes from courageous, sincere and effective public service," Lodge wired.

Kennedy replied:

> We have just heard after a long night of waiting that Senator Lodge has been kind enough to send a telegram conceding the election. I appreciate very much Lodge's extremely generous telegram.
> I am impressed by the tremendous responsibility of representing a great State like Massachusetts and am grateful to the people of Massachusetts for their confidence in me.

Only two other Democrats from Massachusetts—Marcus Coolidge and David I. Walsh—had ever been elected to serve in the Senate.

The New Bedford *Standard-Times* purred its gratification at seeing the entire slate of candidates it had endorsed elected to office and, with some justification, claimed it had won the election for Kennedy by withdrawing its support from Lodge.

Kennedy later added, "I'm glad it's over."

Still trying to puzzle out what had happened to him, Lodge said, "It was those damned tea parties."

Immediately after his election Jack Kennedy returned to Hyannis Port. Expressing surprise and regret over the defeat of Stevenson and Dever in Massachusetts, Kennedy said: "I feel keen disappointment in Governor Stevenson's loss, as I took part in the draft Stevenson campaign. He waged an excellent campaign, no one could have done better. But he ran into a whirlwind."

With his son safely elected to the Senate, Joseph P. Kennedy allowed himself to appear once again on a public platform, coming out of self-imposed obscurity to keep his first speaking engagement in many months at the Osterville Rotary Club. In obvious high spirits, he could not keep his feelings from being reflected in a speech that was conciliatory and good-natured in the extreme, a remarkable change of pace from his usual dire warnings of "tough times ahead" and the deep pessimism that usually marked his public utterances.

Expressing concern over the enormity of the problems that confronted the newly elected government—problems so "complex, ramified and changing that it is amazing we expect humans to come up with answers"—Kennedy expressed the hope that "a different kind of thinking at the top will do a great deal to help us all know where we stand." But he cautioned his listeners to have "patience, hope and prayer" for the new administration. Recommending patience with public officials, Kennedy pointed out that a man in Washington must "not only be a good administrator, he must be able to get along with reporters, columnists and Congress."

The merest shadow of criticism crept into his address as he urged his listeners not to accept the opinions of newspapers or columnists on "what is really good or bad. Actually," he said, reaching the pinnacle of forbearance, "only a low proportion of government officials were involved in the corruption that has received such attention in the press."

Warmly applauded and later surrounded by well-wishers, Kennedy was approached by an acquaintance and former tennis opponent. "I'd never seen Joe look so happy as he looked that night. I congratulated him on Jack's winning. I suppose everybody was doing it that night."

Grinning with delight and flashing the charm that had so captivated the British during his first popular year as ambassador, Kennedy said: "Jack's on his way now. This'll do it. You wait and see. In twelve years he'll be president."

As his listener gaped at him in astonishment, Joseph P. Kennedy went on: "When it happens, just remember who told you," he said and walked off.

Seven

No matter how facetiously Cape Codders might refer to secession —the idea of an independent Cape Cod, to be called "Cod Island Republic," wasn't a new one, having first been broached in the 1930s—the idea reflected a genuine reaction against the Cape's headlong, postwar plunge into vastly expanded summer tourism. "Just think what it would mean," the Orleans weekly *Cape Codder* editorialized, resurrecting the idea in 1953. "The bridges would be torn down and the Cape returned to the Cape Codders, native and adopted—with the adopted being sort of on probation subject to being tossed into the canal."

Taking inventory of the benefits that would accrue from such lovingly worked-out details of the plan as "restrictive immigration quotas" and the lapse of "summer complaints everybody seems to be so unfond of anyway," the paper only thinly masked genuine dissatisfaction.

Pointing out that in truth "we'd probably all starve to death," the editorial summed up: "Maybe we ought to stick around a little longer and give the country to the west another chance."

For Cape Cod it was, of course, too late for another chance. Those who hungered for the primitive simplicities of a Cape Cod past could only despair at the changes "progress" had wrought. Neither their protests nor the marked upsurge in activity of militant garden clubs guarding every elm could hope to halt the bulldozer. In vain did architectural preservationists claim as relics various edifices that were doomed to destruction; their piazzas, widow's walks and 12 over 12 windows yielded to plate glass, plywood and ceramic tile.

Most important, control of the summer economy was passing from native hands to a disturbing degree. The impact of the off-Cape capital poured into business ventures and development schemes could not be better illustrated than in the curious turn of events that signaled the new controversy over Cape Cod's traditional "blue" laws.

Through the office of the Chatham Board of Trade, businessmen of that beautiful community, noted for its wealth and style, announced plans to stay open "on Sunday as usual"; the selectmen immediately replied that they would have "no choice but to enforce the statutes governing operation of businesses on the Lord's Day."

Chatham businessmen, however, were also supporting enforcement, suggesting that the whole "blue law" question provided opportunities for religious organizations to "do a great and worthwhile deed in all towns on Cape Cod and Massachusetts." According to one spokesman:

> We are willing to close our stores as required by law if all business enterprises on Cape Cod do the same. The law for us in Chatham is no different than that of any town in Massachusetts. It is not our intent to break down the laws, but trying to get enforcement without discrimination.

However well-intentioned the good businessmen of Chatham were in their crusade to revivify the blue laws, they had not reckoned with the new breed of summer businessmen, who had few off-season connections with Cape Cod and who looked for only one thing there: the quickest possible return on their investment dollars.

Despite the Hyannis Board of Trade's compliance with such blue laws a year later, the issue was stirred up again the following summer. At a mass protest meeting at the Ezra Taft Baker School in South Dennis, about seven hundred members of the audience called for a resolution that would allow Cape merchants to "carry on their businesses on Sundays until corrected measures to the law are adopted by the state legislature." They pointed out that business in Nantasket, Revere and Salisbury was open on Sunday, arguing that "Cape Cod is losing customers by the thousands to these resorts."

Where "the protection of the sabbath" had once been a formidable bulwark few had dared to oppose, the local clergy feebly attempted to stem the tide, devising a committee "to make a study and report its findings." It was too late. By the following June, the incredible was actual: The blue laws were changed.[1]

Other cherished traditions were breaking down as well. In 1953 the first Democrat ever to hold the office of selectman in the Town of

Barnstable, E. Thomas Murphy, was easily re-elected for a second term, proving that his election in 1950—after five successive defeats —was neither an accident nor, as one year-rounder put it at the time, "an act of God."

The depot that had stood as a landmark at Main and Center Streets of Hyannis' East End for nearly one hundred years was torn down in June 1953, signifying the railroad's dwindling importance and the victory of the automobile. A new railroad station was built, appropriately, on the outskirts.

Plagued since postwar years with frequent and rumored stoppages, the railroad had become more a problem than a benefit to the summer economy. Its difficulties reached a climax one summer day in 1958 when, for the first time in 86 years, Cape Cod was without seasonal passenger-train service. Service was later resumed on a temporary basis; however there have been no trains since 1964.

Although the abandonment of the Boston-to-Hyannis Old Colony line had been forecast, cancellation of the New York-Hyannis run caught Chamber of Commerce officials by surprise, as "for the last ten years the railroad has been assuring us that they would never abandon passenger service between New York and Cape Cod."

But fears that loss of rail service might curtail the tourist industry proved groundless. The next problem the Cape found itself confronted with was directly attributable to the faster access from the "mainland" made possible by the new mid-Cape highway, which brought larger numbers to Cape Cod's waterside than had ever come before.

The problem of rowdyism in Hyannis' West End and elsewhere, which had been gathering momentum since postwar years but had become a serious threat in the early 1950s, was finally brought to public attention when the Barnstable *Patriot* boldly spoke out in the vernacular in July 1954:

> Once it was the Queen's Buyway, a street of fine shops and dignified eating places. Here, twenty-five years ago, well-dressed couples and family groups came to shop and see a movie.
>
> There was no jostling crowd, no hole in the wall cut-price shops, or jazz blaring from garish nightclubs and no gangs of girls on the make and youths on the prowl.

Although there "are still some excellent shops and eating places in the West End," the *Patriot* went on, "the area has a honky tonk flavor that would have been out of place 25 years ago."

The wartime year-round boom was blamed by many for the ruination of the area, for then a dwindling wealthy clientele had been replaced by the earthier and freer-spending soldiers from Camp Edwards, who flocked on passes to West End night clubs to stand four deep at the bar while the proprietors coined money too fast to worry much about *lèse majesté*.

By the following year, maintaining order in the West End had become so difficult that the problem received more than local publicity, erupting into ugly headlines, as the general tension finally spilled over into violence during the largest influx on a Fourth of July weekend in the Cape's history. Natives were horrified to pick up their Boston newspapers that morning and read: "48 Seized in Hyannis Spree."

"Our sedate West End resembled Scollay Square on a New Years' Eve," said one observer at the scene. Windows were smashed, signs were pulled down and beer cans littered the streets, as police battled some two thousand teenagers and adults, allegedly from the Boston and Worcester areas.

Reaffirming his determination to rid the town of such undesirables, Hyannis' chief of police, with great good sense, offered no hope for the implementation of a suggested inspection system at the two entrances to Cape Cod: "It would be impossible to sort out the good and bad at the canal bridges," he said, "and let only the desirables through."

The physical changes taking place on Cape Cod were not limited to the deterioration of Hyannis' once-swank West End or the removal of an old railroad depot. Hallett's Field, a major green area on Main Street, which had acted as a sort of arbitrary boundary separating the summer and year-round business districts of Hyannis and had been the site of many civic and athletic activities, was bulldozed, and a shopping plaza on a rectangle of hard blacktop took its place. The summer Music Circus, renamed "Melody Tent," was moved to its present location at the West Main Street rotary in 1954.

More serious was the motel-building boom that was blighting the entire face of Cape Cod. There were those who boasted that "there was a time, and it wasn't too long ago, when some of Cape Cod's so-called overnight cabins were not much better than hen coops. Those days are passed . . . the motel is now part and parcel of Cape Cod and some of the newest are far and away classier and more stylish than some of the Cape's better hotels."

"Classier and more stylish" some were, no one could argue, but

133

many were blatantly unbeautiful, particularly those that tumbled one over the other, in stall-like rows of flashing neon "Vacancy" signs from Mill Hill in West Yarmouth straight to Bass River and beyond. They turned Route 28 into a gaudy wasteland of highway snack shacks, gifte shoppes, pizza towers, "amusement centers" and drive-ins.

Despite protests of spoliation at town meetings and appeals-board hearings, the voices of reason were frequently drowned out by the ring of the cash register and the renascent pitch of the booster.[2] Tawdry, jerry-built "modern" architecture—eschewing the famed simplicities that had once characterized the Cape—provided deliberately "different," attention-getting structures. One pink motel, with a "dude-ranch" facade, pretended it was in Arizona, whereas Polynesia appeared, complete with Easter Island figures, at the busy hardtop curbing on West Yarmouth's fluorescent roadside.

Most disturbing to the protesters was the fact that such vulgar precincts appeared to be thriving, apparently successfully serving the vacationers who preferred seashore holidays in deck chairs at flagstone-paved swimming pools with views of the relentless traffic passing close by.

Of a survey it undertook prior to the summer season of 1956, the Cape Cod *Standard-Times* ebulliently reported:

> While the vacationer will find the same Cape Cod in 1956 he knew in 1955 there are changes. All over Cape Cod construction, improvement and physical refinement is under way. New schools, home construction, harbor development, beach improvement, new roads and accommodations and business . . .

Yet, the article charged, the Cape had lost none of its former charm. Rebuttal was swift. The following week the letters-to-the-editor columns published this reply:

> To the Editor
> Cape Cod *Standard-Times*
> Dear Sir:
> Of all the ridiculous statements I have read is that contained in the opening paragraphs of an article in the July 4 issue of your paper.
> The paragraph in question opens a lengthy portrayal of how "Cape Cod expands facilities for visitors and residents alike . . ." It reads: "What a difference a year makes on Cape Cod. None of the quaintness has disappeared . . ."

Perfectly ridiculous! Today there is scarcely to be found anywhere a trace of Cape Cod's quaintness; that is unless the writer of the article considers flashing neon signs are quaint and preferable to inspiring starlight; that the ring of the cash register is quaint and preferable to the call of the bob white; that hideous road signs are quaint and preferable to pine woods. Is the writer one of those who would commercialize the very soul of Cape Cod? The quaintness of Cape Cod of thirty years ago has disappeared.

Although the newspaper had looked only on the bright side and overstated its case, the outraged letter writer had cited only the offending portion of Cape Cod that reinforced his opinions, shutting his eyes to areas where there was still a great deal of the Cape's former charm.

One had only to follow the curving and leisurely ribbon of pavement marking Route 6A—the old Cranberry Highway on the North Shore, largely bypassed after construction of the Mid-Cape and the gaudier attractions on Route 28 to the south. One could stand beside a cool pond in Sandwich to watch a waterwheel slowly agitate the reflection of a "Christopher Wren" church tower or pause at the range of high dunes descending to a magnificent space of perfect beach at Sandy Neck. There was the untouched perfection of the great marshes, where colonials had harvested their salt hay, still lazily growing wild, turned a sere yellow in the hot August sun.

Much more than a trace of charm was left in the Village of Barnstable—the "real" Barnstable, as villagers hastened to point out—which was drenched green in summer, its huge arched trees splattering the route ahead with bits of sunlight. Farther on were the fastidious landscapes of Yarmouth Port, a lesson in Cape Cod history by its very architecture; the quiet fields of Harwich; Eastham's peaceful meadows, and Brewster's immutable scenery, so strongly rooted in the soil that it seemed untouched by this century—even though an occasional motel bravely displayed its sign and roadside stands dispensed beach-plum jelly and asparagus in season.

There were many such places if one chose to look: Centerville's quasi suburbia, rural Forestdale and the lushly forested Mystic Lake in Marstons Mills. And, of course, there was always Hyannis Port, in 1953 as constant and invariable as ever.

No bulldozer rearranged those complacent landscapes. Rather, great attention was lavished on overlarge, often homely structures that, located elsewhere but at such a superb harborside, would have long since fallen under the auctioneer's gavel for whatever prices white elephants could bring.

Not only did the houses remain and flourish, but so also, with remarkable fidelity, did many of their occupants. The old summer families, some of them in their second and third generations, returned to Hyannis Port year after year, more determined than ever to preserve its "way of life." Less than a hundred years old and a johnny-come-lately as natives reckoned it, Hyannis Port began to look upon itself as the repository of "unspoiled" Cape Cod traditionalism that it had never owned.

In June 1953 Hyannis Port's golf club house was the scene of an engagement party for the United States Senator described as "the most eligible bachelor of capital society" and his fiancée, "a girl from Newport," Jacqueline Lee Bouvier.

The wedding, announced for September 12, was to be the second in the Kennedy family that year. Eunice had been married to Robert Sargent Shriver, Jr., in a May ceremony performed by Francis Cardinal Spellman at St. Patrick's Cathedral in New York; the wedding was followed by a luncheon for 1,700 guests at the Waldorf-Astoria Hotel and was described as "the highlight of the New York social season."

A press conference was hurriedly arranged "to keep confusion within bounds" when word leaked out that Jack Kennedy and his fiancée were together at Hyannis Port for the first time since the formal announcement on June 24 of their engagement, and urgent telephoned requests for interviews began pouring into the Kennedy summer house.

The following Saturday, Hyannis Port's usual afternoon calm was ruffled for slightly more than three hours as Jack Kennedy and Jacqueline Bouvier obliged the press, posing for formal photographs in street clothes, then changing to take their places together near a "sailfish" moored on shore close to the breakwater.

With her dark clipped curls framing a face of exquisite prettiness, Jacqueline seemed not to mind being so unexpectedly thrust into the limelight. (During the summer of 1952 she had, on two occasions, attended campaign teas in Fall River and Quincy, making her first acquaintance with her husband-to-be's constituents.)

Jack Kennedy, in rumpled white shirt and bermudas, his brush of hair blown over his tanned forehead in the harbor's brisk wind, seemed hardly to be Jacqueline's senior by thirteen years. He cheerfully traded quips with newsmen while Jacqueline chatted vivaciously with photographers, describing her former employment as an "inquiring photographer"; she had wielded a graflex on behalf of the Washington *Times Herald*. The couple, showing no resentment at so massive an invasion of their privacy, entirely captivated the more than twenty typically hard-bitten newspapermen.

That weekend Kennedy inspected tornado damage at Worcester. The following week, accompanied by Jacqueline, he returned to present a check for $150,000 from the Joseph P. Kennedy, Jr., Foundation to Assumption College, which had been severely damaged by the storm. A chartered plane waited to take them back to Hyannis Port.

In midsummer, Robert Kennedy resigned as special counsel to the McCarthy investigating committee—"to enter private law practice" —and received bipartisan commendation for his work with the committee. He went immediately from Washington to Hyannis Port to join his wife and children. Joseph P. Kennedy announced from his veranda that the death of Robert A. Taft was "the greatest tragedy to befall the American people in the loss of a statesman since the assassination of Abraham Lincoln."

The prenuptial summer was a happy activity-filled one. Jacqueline was a frequent guest at Hyannis Port, where she and her fiancé reviewed their wedding-invitation lists together, sailed the *Victura* and took long walks along the beach. Jacqueline even participated gamely in the rough-and-tumble family touch-football games on the lawn behind her future father-in-law's house. An ankle injury and her own predispositions soon retired her to the sidelines as a permanent spectator.

In Hyannis, the young priest whom Jack Kennedy had befriended in the year of his political debut was engaged in preparing sacramental records and composing the standard letter of freedom to marry—routine documentation required for every communicant prior to his marriage—to be sent to St. Mary's Church in Newport, where Archbishop Richard J. Cushing would officiate at the nuptial mass.

The forthcoming marriage aroused enormous interest on Cape Cod, not centered on the "home grown" Senator, however. Enthralled at the prospect of a "picture-book wedding," local ladies doted on details of Jacqueline's trousseau from the portrait neckline of her ivory silk-taffeta wedding gown to the heirloom veil of rose-point lace, originally worn by her grandmother, which was to be held in place by a tiara of lace and orange blossoms.

Jean and Ethel Kennedy were among the eight attendants, "wearing long pink taffeta dresses with cap sleeves, cummerbund sashes and matching Tudor caps," in a wedding party that included a matron of honor, a maid of honor, a flower girl and a page who wore "short black velvet trousers, and a white silk shirt with jabot and cuffs."

Robert Kennedy was his brother's best man—in a reversal of the roles at his own wedding in 1950. Fourteen ushers headed by brother "Ted" included Charles Bartlett, Senator George Smathers, and old friends LeMoyne Billings and Torbert McDonald.

More than one thousand spectators outside the Newport church surged forward when the ceremony began, attempting to glimpse the couple through the open doors of the church. Encircling the crowd with ropes, police pulled them back toward the opposite side of the street, while inside the church seven hundred guests took their places in space that normally accommodated six hundred; an unidentified woman fainted.

Under a bower of oak leaves and smilax, the couple was married to the accompaniment of "Ave Maria" and "Panis Angelicus." It was, indeed, "a picture-book wedding," although Jack experienced a moment's difficulty kneeling during the nuptial mass, celebrated at an altar decorated with white gladioli and chrysanthemums, before marching confidently down a pure-white carpet in the church's center aisle.

Horses roamed the spacious fields adjoining Hammersmith Farm during a champagne buffet and dance following the wedding, while the couple distributed pieces of the five-tiered, four-foot-tall, flower-topped wedding cake, which was so huge that it had been delivered in two sections by the Fall River baker, who described it as "the biggest, the finest, the most important cake of my career."

White-jacketed waiters served what appeared to be endless trays of champagne to guests, who kept the bride and groom standing in the receiving line for more than four hours. The society orchestra of Meyer Davis played before a specially erected dance floor on a terrace that overlooked Narragansett Bay.

Included in the list of 1,400 guests were Don Fernando Berk-

Meyer, Peruvian Ambassador to the United States; Mrs. Bernard Gimbel; Westbrook Pegler; Marion Davies, and Basil Brewer.

Henry Cabot Lodge sent his regrets and a Steuben glass ashtray.

The couple returned to Hyannis Port the second week in October after a Caribbean honeymoon and before moving to Washington; Kennedy was prevented from coming back to Cape Cod until late the following summer by the marathon and frequently tumultuous session of the 83rd Congress.

A full-scale investigation was under way in Washington; one that was occupying the attention of many Americans. Their television sets were tuned in to the Army hearings being conducted by Senator Joseph McCarthy, decried as "cruel and reckless" by attorney Joseph N. Welsh.[3]

Although Kennedy stood aside from the controversy while his colleagues in the Senate sought a middle-of-the-road committee to investigate McCarthy's conduct, he applied himself to matters of strict concern to his constituents. He took Eisenhower to task for not aiding New England's economy in the face of growing unemployment, claiming that the area had not received its fair share of Federal contracts and seeking to have the fourth Forrestal-class aircraft carrier built at Quincy—although laws required that the vessel be built in a naval shipyard.

One member of the Kennedy family, however, clashed directly and publicly with Senator McCarthy's committee. During Senator Henry Jackson's cross-examination of McCarthy, a psychological-warfare campaign suggested by G. David Schine, in which anti-Communist propaganda would be distributed abroad via cartoons and pinups, was derided. The incident provoked a shouting match, in full view of astonished observers, between Roy Cohn, McCarthy's chief counsel, and Robert Kennedy, a former assistant counsel on McCarthy's committee and, since February 1953, counsel for the Democratic members of the Senate Investigations Subcommittee.

Beginning as a whispered conversation, the dialogue had quickly increased in volume. According to Robert Kennedy:

Cohn was mad. It seemed that something was about to explode within him. His voice was low. He was speaking between his teeth. He said, and I don't remember the exact words, "You tell Jackson we're going to get him Monday. We're going to bring out things about him, things that he has written favorably inclined toward communists."

Then Robert Kennedy exploded.* "Don't warn me," he said loudly. "Don't try it again, Cohn, you won't get away with it. You tried it with the Army. You tried it with Democratic senators. Now you're trying it with me . . ."

"Do you think you're qualified to take part in this case?" Cohn said, scrambling to his feet. "Do you think you're qualified when you've got a personal hatred for one of the principals?"

"If I do," Kennedy answered, "it's justified . . ."

"Do you think you're qualified to sit here . . ." Cohn began again, but Kennedy, his face flushing darkly, walked away.

To reporters who asked him what the argument was all about, Cohn replied: "Ah, we've got a cute kid here. Before the hearings he told someone in McCarthy's office he hated me and was going to get me in these hearings."

By the last day's session of Congress, Jack Kennedy was in extreme pain and forced onto crutches again. When the Senate voted adjournment, he was on a chartered plane en route to Hyannis Port, hoping that a long rest there would improve his back. Instead, the pain grew more intense.

On the veranda of his father's house overlooking the familiar rippling flatness of Nantucket Sound, Kennedy heard Dr. Sara Jordan of Boston's Leahy Clinic candidly express her alarm, then document the slim chances her patient had of surviving the spinal-fusion operation required to correct his back condition. It was an operation that could involve grave risks because an adrenal insufficiency provided him with little defense against infection and shock.

When she left, Kennedy pushed his crutches aside and, turning to

---

* The Cape Cod *Standard-Times* recorded the incident as follows:

Bashful Robert F. Kennedy swept from the sidelines to the limelight today in a burst of temper which amazed his friends and seemed to surprise himself.

The 28-year-old counsel for Democrats on the Senate Investigations Subcommittee was embarrassed after his brush with Cohn, the unit's chief counsel over what he said was a threat by Cohn against a committee member.

Kennedy's hesitancy to talk about it was in keeping with the easy-going manner he has displayed since first going to work for McCarthy's subcommittee as an assistant counsel in February, 1953.

a friend beside him in a wicker armchair, said, "I'd rather die than spend the rest of my life on these damned things!"

Two weeks later Hurricane Carol's roaring wind struck a blow at Cape Cod. All but five boats moored off the Hyannis Port Civic Association's pier were sunk or smashed on the shore, and damage to the pier itself was estimated at $5,000. The Kennedy family's bathhouse lay on its side, its roof half covered with churned-up sand and its green-painted shutters neatly in place.

Compared with Falmouth and Buzzards Bay, where property losses exceeded $1 million from winds of more than one hundred miles an hour and three people lay dead in the wreckage, Hyannis suffered minor damage: Winds had shattered shop windows on Main Street and buckled the Melody Tent's big orange and blue-striped canvas, prematurely ending the season. Serious harm had been done to the last big holiday weekend of the summer, according to the Chamber of Commerce, for the usual Labor Day crowds failed to materialize.

James ("See Me First") Woodward, thanking the Cape and Vineyard Electric Company and repairmen of the New England Telephone Company for the work they had done to restore service, paid tribute as well to "the oil-burner man" and the electrician who had given him hot water and heat. Then with irrepressible optimism he announced: "Now that we have the beach grass and mudflats out of our basement, we will see if we can sell some real estate to live through the winter." He advertised a special bargain in West Dennis, where "a man bleeds to death, bitten by a quahog, because there's no doctor."

The Cape had cleared away the invasion of mudflats and beach grass sponsored by Hurricane Carol when Hurricane Edna loomed on the horizon. Regional civil-defense units again prepared to go into action in the event an alert was sounded, and shop windows were barricaded as the hurricane watch began.

Jack Kennedy remained at his father's house alone except for two warring servants—one of them drunk—awaiting the second storm. An eerie copper-gray light intensified the green of the trees, casting an invisible but oppressive pall that clung with a penetrating heaviness in the air until Edna blew out to sea.

Another storm was brewing as the special session of Congress that would decide the question of a McCarthy censure drew closer.

While many public figures were publicly deferring judgment on McCarthy—including Senator Margaret Chase Smith, a long-time opponent who had "no immediate comment"—one public figure did not hesitate to speak out boldly in McCarthy's favor: Returning from a three-month trip abroad, during which he had accepted a post-humous *croix de guerre* for his dead son at ceremonies in the French Foreign Ministry, Joseph P. Kennedy conceded a growing trend toward anti-Americanism in Europe but said that it was "certainly not due to Senator McCarthy, but to lack of confidence in American diplomatic leadership under both the GOP and Democratic administrations." "The people resent the United States telling them what to do on every question," Kennedy said. "They fear our anxiety."

Not having read the report of the Senate committee investigating McCarthy, Kennedy refused to comment on that aspect of the controversy. He had gained a "definite impression," however, that anti-McCarthy propaganda in Europe came from communists:

As for McCarthy, I found that it is the communists in Europe who seem to be most interested in condemning him. I have run across people who were critical of him because he called General Marshall a traitor. I found, however, that those who resented his remarks were willing to agree that Marshall was responsible to a very considerable degree for the loss of China, and certainly was not one of our best Secretaries of State.

"I certainly want to hear all the arguments before I reach a final decision," Senator Leverett Saltonstall said, adroitly avoiding the subject of McCarthy censure in the face of Governor Foster Furcolo's heavy-handed campaign to unseat him in the off-year election.

Jack Kennedy, in seclusion at Hyannis Port and "not available for comment," had never made any secret of his admiration for his senior colleague and had issued joint communiques with Saltonstall listing the achievements of "The New England Bloc," emphasizing their nonpartisan cooperation. Kennedy's lack of enthusiasm for Foster Furcolo, who had come up through the ranks of regular Massachusetts Democratic party machinery—the labyrinthine way that Kennedy himself had disdained—was no secret either.

Persuaded, nevertheless, to endorse the whole Democratic ticket, including Furcolo, during a joint televised appearance, Kennedy flew to Boston from Hyannis despite a fever and growing distress from his back. Increasingly irritable and short-tempered, his patience frayed by unremitting severe pain, Kennedy arrived to wait more than an hour for Furcolo to appear. After quickly scanning the prepared script, the senatorial candidate began protesting that Kennedy's endorsement of him wasn't "strong enough."

"You've got a hell of a nerve coming in here and asking for last-minute changes," Kennedy said.

"But Jack, it's not an outright endorsement!" Furcolo said. The argument came to an abrupt end when Kennedy reached for his crutches to hobble out of the studio, thrown into an uproar as broadcast time drew closer.

Returning in time for the program, Kennedy stonily read endorsements for the "Democratic ticket," mentioned only gubernatorial candidate Robert Murphy by name and omitted any reference whatever to Furcolo, who went on to lose an election he never had much hope of winning.

Several days later, Jack Kennedy arrived in Hyannis on a warm and radiant Indian Summer Sunday. Very pale and taut, his lips pressed together, Kennedy was slowly helped up the stairway for the one-hour trip to New York. He was to undergo the perilous operation at Manhattan's Hospital for Special Surgery because "I can't stand any more pain."

A telegraphed blessing from Pope Pius XII, the first message of its kind ever sent by the Holy Father, was received at the hospital just prior to the operation. The message offered "as pledge of heavenly assistance for your complete recovery his paternal apostolic benediction". The telegram was signed by Cardinal Dellacqua, acting Secretary of State for the Vatican.

Dr. Philip Wilson headed the medical team that performed a double fusion on Kennedy's spine, an operation that was postponed three times until it was decided that Kennedy was strong enough to undergo it. "The Senator passed a comfortable night and is in good condition this morning," Dr. Wilson said, in an official bulletin following the operation.

Another 48 hours passed, however, before a final judgment on the results of the operation could be made, although reports indicated that Kennedy would take two months to recover; it was announced that he could resume his duties in Washington in February.

Then there was silence. No further bulletins were issued, and rumors flew that Kennedy was near death. His family was summoned. Last rites of the church were administered at his bedside while doctors struggled to save him. After surviving two crises, he lay immobile for a month, closely attended by his wife, family and friends.

"My son, U.S. Senator John F. Kennedy is making good progress after his recent operation and is in no danger," Joseph P. Kennedy told the New Bedford *Standard-Times* on November 11th from his home at Hyannis Port.

"I am issuing this report on the senator's condition in behalf of the Kennedy family because of unfounded and disturbing rumors that are being circulated, especially in Washington. These reports imply Senator Kennedy's condition is such that he will be unable to resume his seat in the Senate. Such reports are not in accordance with the facts."

In December Kennedy was taken from the hospital on a stretcher and flown to Palm Beach for Christmas with his family. But his condition appeared unchanged. In mid-February 1955 Kennedy returned to the hospital again. Another operation was performed. Once again last rites were administered, and once again he survived.

By the end of February he was sufficiently recovered to leave the hospital for a long and difficult period of convalescence at his father's Florida house. Exhausted by his double ordeal, still in great pain and deeply depressed by the possibility that he might never walk again, he suffered the darkest period of his life.

"Then one day the letter came," Kennedy remembered in an article, "What My Illness Taught Me," published in *American Weekly* for April 29, 1956. "It was from a 90 year old lady who had always lived in a small Cape Cod village. She, too, was bed-ridden, she wrote, perhaps for the rest of her life, but she was full of hope and good humor."

"I've never voted for a Democrat in my life, Mr. Kennedy," she started right out, "but I want to vote for at least one before I die—might stand me in good stead up above. So I want you to be up to running in 1958. Don't waste away feeling sorry for yourself, young man. Keep busy. Do all the things you've never had time to do . . ."

Ninety years old, I thought, and telling me to keep busy, just as she must be keeping busy. It was a tonic for my spirits. I think if I hadn't received that letter I'd never have got around to writing my book, *Profiles in Courage.*

After reading the letter, I realized there were a lot of things I wanted to do for which time had never been available. The Library of Congress kept a steady stream of books flowing to me during all the months of my convalescence . . .

Kennedy returned to the Senate that May, but his periodic reliance on crutches and frequent weekends at the Hospital for Special Surgery gave rise to new anxieties among friends and constituents about his ability to carry on his duties as senator as he plunged back into the business of doing more for Massachusetts. In his first major appearance in the Senate, he delivered a statement before the Joint Congressional Atomic Energy Committee, urging a New England site for "pilot plant activity" in the development of commercial electric power from atomic energy. (In later years plans for an "atomic park" on Cape Cod were approved but never carried out.)

At a Massachusetts Jefferson-Jackson Day "harmony dinner" the following week, Democratic National Committee Chairman Paul M. Butler was "happy to see this inspiring gathering," adding, "it is especially good to see John Kennedy back in harness again."

It was a fence-mending occasion. Kennedy shared the dais with Paul Dever, James Michael Curley and former Governor Foster Furcolo, who provided the evening's major surprise when he introduced Kennedy as a "natural hero" and recalled "our shoulder-to-shoulder service in the House of Representatives."

Acknowledging Furcolo's remarks, "as nice an introduction as I've ever gotten—and I am grateful," Kennedy provided a surprise of his own:

> We were and are good friends. I am confident Foster is going to be one of the leaders of the party and of the State. When I came here tonight, I knew we were going to bury hatchets, but I wasn't sure just where. I think the only place to bury hatchets is in the ground.

Later, referring to Furcolo again, Kennedy said, "You know, relationships take turns, and our relationship did last fall," indirectly referring to Furcolo's unsuccessful candidacy for the Senate. "I hope we'll hear no more about Kennedy and Furcolo."

The following day Jack Kennedy returned to Hyannis Port for the first time since his operation to host a huge party for 280 members of the Massachusetts legislature, the state-house press corps and the congressional delegation in Washington, who arrived at Hyannis' depot aboard a special-charter train to be taken by bus—escorted by privately detailed police—to the home of Joseph P. Kennedy, who had left that morning for Europe.[4]

Hired for the occasion was a personable young photographer from East Dennis who filled Kennedy's requirement for a "photographer who looked like a guest." He was to work with a 35-millimeter camera and was given explicit instructions: "Some of these men today are going to want me to pose for pictures with them they can use in the upcoming elections," Kennedy said. He arranged a signal with the photographer to indicate when he did not wish a picture to be taken. The prearrangement was to be complicated by the fact that some of his politician guests had taken the precaution of bringing their own photographers with them.

A rapidly moving target that sunny, warm early summer day, Jack Kennedy greeted his guests in chinos, sweat shirt and sneakers, circulating among them on the spacious harbor-front grounds and taking part in the day's golf, swimming, volleyball and softball activities before and after the lobster dinner served at the golf club's dining room.

According to a Kennedy spokesman, the gathering was intended "to bring Federal and state legislators together as a means of promoting better co-operation and understanding between both groups for the further benefit of the State." But more specifically, if indirectly, the party was meant also to lay to rest the persistent rumors about Kennedy's health. No one witnessing his day's activities could doubt his recovery. His tanned leanness offered a contrast to the jowls and broad, soft midriffs of many of his guests.

That July Kennedy was reported in good condition at New England Baptist Hospital. Two weeks later, after another checkup at the Hospital for Special Surgery in New York, Kennedy said: "I feel just fine," and pointed to the hated crutches in a corner of his Senate office. He disclosed that for the last two months he had been returning to the New York hospital on weekends for muscular therapy in order to strengthen his back.

At the same time he announced plans for a trip to Asia and the Middle East in the fall as a member of a special Senate subcommittee investigating at first hand the effectiveness of the United States technical-assistance program. He acknowledged with thanks the gifts and letters that had poured into his office during his convalescence, reflecting wide interest in his illness, but he smilingly added that the concern expressed for his condition was now "needless."

In an exclusive interview granted the New Bedford *Standard-Times* before he boarded *United States* for England Kennedy said:

> Indochina is the area of most critical importance to American foreign policy today. There, more than in any other area, the communists and non-communist world are struggling for power. There, more than in any other area, a power vacuum exists and the outcome of the struggle is undecided.

Outlining the crisis that had risen out of the Geneva agreements of 1954, under which national elections were required by the following July in North Vietnam (controlled by Ho Chi Minh and the Viet Minh communists) and the area south of the 17th parallel under the anti-government forces of Premier Ngo Dinh Diem, Kennedy explained:

> Despite the free world's faith in free elections, it is doubtful whether such elections in the North can be truly free and whether, in view of the larger population in the North and the terroristic tactics of its communist rulers, the outcome could be anything other than a victory for the communists.
>
> If Premier Diem refuses to agree to elections—and he has already indicated such refusal—we should not push Diem into an election he does not want and cannot win simply because the French desire it.

Pointing out that the Viet Minh had been building up their military forces in violation of the Geneva agreements, while France and the United States were reducing theirs, Kennedy warned: "If war broke out as a result of South Vietnam's refusal to agree to elections, the military situation would be very critical indeed."

Calling Vietnam the "key to Southeast Asia, not only in terms of military defense, but also as a potential bulwark in the economic and democratic development of that continent," Kennedy spoke of the area as being "a danger spot, where war is most likely to erupt within the next twelve months."

That fall Joseph P. Kennedy called a meeting at his Hyannis Port home, which was attended by representatives of such diverse organizations as the Cape Cod Synagogue, St. Francis Xavier and the Federated Church of Hyannis and the Rotary and Kiwanis Clubs— people with "broad, first-hand knowledge of the recreational needs of young people." The purpose of the meeting: the first proposal and discussion of a memorial gift of $150,000 that Joseph P. Kennedy was prepared to make to the Town of Barnstable, "which had meant so much to Joe, and the family."

Those present were touched and impressed by the sincerity of Joseph P. Kennedy's philanthropy. To the unofficial committee formed to determine what shape the memorial would take, Kennedy made only one condition: A suitable site would have to be provided by the town and, once the memorial facility was built, funds from other sources made available to maintain it.

From the beginning all agreed that no information on the project should be made public until plans were complete and the check actually in the selectmen's hands. All interested newspapers would be given the same opportunity to break the story at the proper time.[5]

In December, Ted Kennedy, first-string left end on Harvard's varsity football team, and Bob Margarita, Harvard's head freshman coach and a former star of the Chicago Bears were guests of honor at the annual banquet given by the Barnstable Boosters Club to honor members of Barnstable High School's "Red Raiders" football team.

A ruggedly handsome two hundred-pounder, Ted, a senior majoring in government, made a strong impression on his audience. Already a poised public speaker, he made of his address a wholesome locker-room pep talk, sprinkled with a dash of anti-intellectualism.

Declaring that, in high school, some people mistakenly think that "the toughest characters are those who drink the most, smoke the most or have the biggest vocabulary" but that, in college, they discover that "the toughest are those who block and tackle the hardest. In football," Ted said, "you learn the value of that little extra effort."

An unusual full-page review greeted the publication of *Profiles in Courage* by John F. Kennedy in the New Bedford *Standard-Times* of January 1, 1956.

> . . . the book itself is a testimony to Mr. Kennedy's own perseverance. He wrote it while making the long, slow painful climb back to health from an operation designed to correct the results of a war-time

injury. It was written by a man enduring intense pain for whom even routine research was an agonizing ordeal.

There is no trace of that personal travail in the book. He has written a literate, lively book marked by thoughtfulness, maturity of judgment and completeness.

Particularly pleased at the inclusion of Senator Robert A. Taft in the list of distinguished men honored by testimonials in the book, the reviewer quoted the author's comment that, although "insufficient time had lapsed to be able to measure Taft's life with historical perspective," sufficient time "has passed to enable something of a detached view" of Senator Taft's act of courage.*

In the rotogravure section of the following week's Sunday issue, a modest ad for the book, destined to be awarded the Pulitzer Prize for biography, appeared with a testimonial by Bernard Baruch.

At Barnstable's town meeting that March, the site of the proposed Joseph Kennedy, Jr., memorial on Cape Cod was selected: the William A. Baldwin Memorial Park on Bearse's Way in Hyannis. To what purpose the location would be put was yet to be decided.

Because of the secrecy that had to be maintained, Article 98 of the warrant presented at the meeting was necessarily vague:

> To see if the town will vote permission for a charitable corporation, or an individual to erect on land of the Town at or near the junction of Bearse's Way and Bassett's Lane, a building for public recreational purposes and accept such building when completed as a gift to the town.

Only slight opposition was expressed by one voter, a resident of Bearse's Way, who had heard that a gymnasium was to be built there. In his opinion the town had enough of them in its schools and elsewhere. A committee member asked the meeting "to have confidence in the wisdom of the committee," giving first public utterance to the idea of a skating rink. (In October "the best recreational plant obtainable for the amount available" was decided by the committee

---

* Taft's "profile in courage" described his widely criticized opposition to the Nuremberg trials and the death sentences meted out to eleven Nazis. "We cannot teach them government in Germany by suppressing liberty and justice," Taft had said. "As I see it, the English-speaking peoples have a great responsibility. That is to restore to the minds of men a devotion to equal justice under the law." Taft accused the allies of accepting "the Russian idea of the purpose of the trials: government policy and not justice."

to be an outdoor skating rink, with a building for dressing rooms, snack bar and other facilities. Work was begun on the Joseph P. Kennedy Memorial Skating Center that December.)

Amid growing speculation that he would be named Adlai Stevenson's running mate during the coming Democratic convention, Jack Kennedy involved himself for the first time directly in Massachusetts state politics, an area he had formerly scorned and one usually confused and splintered by bitterly warring factions. The year 1956 was no exception.

The chairmanship of the Democratic State Committee had, following a court order, been turned over to William H. Burke, Jr., replacing John C. Carr, who, the court ruled, had not been legally elected in 1952.

Two weeks before the state convention Kennedy announced that "it would be a serious mistake" to retain Burke as chairman. When John McCormack, House Majority Leader and a long-time power in regular Democratic state politics, challenged him and came out in support of Burke, the rival forces of Kennedy and McCormack drew their battle lines. A tumult was anticipated at the committee's next meeting.

Jack Kennedy, who usually preferred to dissociate himself from the frequently operatic antics of Massachusetts intramural politics, thrust himself into the thick of the fight, flying from New York after the wedding of his sister Jean and Stephen Smith in St. Patrick's Cathedral for a last-minute luncheon strategy meeting.

John ("Pat") Lynch, former Mayor of Somerville, beat Burke for the committee chairmanship in a loudly contested election, by a vote of 47 to 31 on a secret ballot. Kennedy then took control of the Democratic Party in Massachusetts, carrying all other offices on the committee as well. Burke, in a fury, shouted a bitter denunciation from the floor claiming that the election had been "bought by Kennedy henchmen." Swearing vengeance, Burke announced that he would seek Kennedy's Senate seat in 1958: [6]

> The Senator will be asked by me to place his record before the rank and record . . . and I think the rank and file of the Democratic voters of this state will agree with me that the finger of suspicion and the finger of scorn can be pointed out at him.

Hailing the election as the start of a new era in the Massachusetts Democratic Party, Jack Kennedy said, "This fight was undertaken because many Democrats thought the party needed new and responsible leadership."

Kennedy's unannounced candidacy for the vice-presidential nomination received a tremendous, if somewhat excessive boost during an unprecedented "birthday testimonial" staged in his honor on Memorial Day by Fall River and New Bedford, "the first time the two cities, with a total population of more than 200,000, have joined to honor one man."

Although the event was advertised as "nonpartisan," in the words of a former Barnstable town committeeman who attended the New Bedford portion of the festivities, "nothing is ever 'nonpartisan' during an election year." He pointed out that the testimonial had been regarded, ". . . as a great way to launch Jack's vice-presidential campaign."

The day began with a public reception at Fall River's city hall, where Kennedy arrived to review the parade and the beginning roar of a 2½-hour air show staged by army, navy, marine and air-force planes. He greeted Joseph Martin of Attleboro, long-time House Leader, in the cool, drizzling rain: "Joe, you look like you're lashed down for a hurricane," Kennedy said, as he took his place at the head of the column, wearing only a light jacket. He saluted more than thirty thousand cheering spectators lining the route of the march, two-thirds of a mile to Fall River's South Park, where Martin, who made the trip by car, was the main speaker.

In New Bedford, about twenty thousand people cheered Kennedy's appearance on the reviewing stand before that city's parade, after which he was joined by Jacqueline, who had arrived by chartered plane to be greeted by "his best smile of the day" and—in a rare public demonstration of affection—a kiss before the reception at New Bedford's Municipal Building, where she was presented with a bouquet of red roses and Kennedy received a set of whalemen bookends.

Immediately after the reception and following the arrival of Senators Albert Gore, Henry Jackson and George Smathers—kept on the Senate floor until that morning and flown to New Bedford despite bad flying conditions—the Kennedy party left for Lincoln Park and another reception, during which telegraphed tributes were read, including one from former President Herbert Hoover expressing his appreciation "for the way you have been carrying the ball for the reports of the Commission on the Organization of the Executive Branch of Government."

There were messages too from some of his Senate colleagues like Lyndon B. Johnson:

> It's good to know John Kennedy is to be honored by his friends in Massachusetts. Here is a man eminently qualified to talk and write about dignity and courage and integrity. The qualities that have endeared him to his people have brought him the respect and affection of his colleagues in the Senate. He is a real profile in courage.

Senate Minority Leader William Knowland of California sent his congratulations:

> Dear Jack: I am advised a number of your friends are meeting in your honor today. I would not want to let such an occasion pass without extending my personal best wishes on this event. It has been a pleasure to serve with you in the Senate.

Other messages were received and read from Senators George Payne and Hubert Humphrey.

More than 1,400 people filled Lincoln Park's clambake pavilion to overflowing and listened as Martin, opening the speeches, took note that it was "a happy omen for New England that both parties were so well represented."

> We've come here to honor a young man who has brought great fame to himself and his State. He is a man of character and substance for whom we have universal respect. Unlike so many others who don't have faith in New England, he believes in New England. I am happy to pay tribute to this young man, and my best wishes go to this faithful public servant.

Senator John O. Pastore, Democrat of Rhode Island, was honored to be invited to attend "this neighborly demonstration of affection and respect for our esteemed colleague."

Throughout the encomiums that followed, Jack Kennedy maintained a somewhat noncommittal half-smile, his head cocked attentively, listening. If he was discomfited by the growing lushness of phrase, the elaborate flights of rhetoric, he did not show it. Jacqueline, seated alongside, frequently glanced at her husband, as if for reassurance.

Basil Brewer, representing New Bedford, cited Kennedy's courage and faith, his dedication and determination, which had carried him through wartime exploits and illness.

But it was Senator Albert Gore of Tennessee, describing the clambake as "a gathering of the friends of your distinguished son from the four corners and the interior of the nation" in a soft, gently persuasive Tennessee drawl, who drew the strongest response from the audience and made the most significant speech of the day: "We like what he says, and we like the way he says it. He speaks the voice of America, the voice of a courageous Christian of vision, imagination and intelligence." When the outburst of applause quieted, Gore added, "I'd love to see Jack Kennedy on the first or second place in the Democratic ticket in 1956, 1960 or 1964. . . ." The audience burst into cheers, whistling and vigorous applause as Jack Kennedy ducked his head and grinned.

Senator Henry Jackson also made reference to future candidacy for higher office. Senator Smathers, speaking of "the difficulty in telling of your affection and high esteem for another man," said, "You have a real champion representing you in the United States Senate."

Climaxing the program was the presentation of a silver bowl, tray and cups by a feature writer of the New Bedford *Standard-Times*. He recalled a long-ago interview with the then Congressman Kennedy, who had answered a question about his romantic interests. "It's getting so I prefer a vote to a date—that's politics for you." The gifts were presented with the sentiment that the citizens of New Bedford and Fall River were happy that the Senator had been mistaken and that "politics had replaced its hold on you long enough to permit a few dates and thereby the attainment of your greatest achievement, Mrs. Kennedy."

Jack Kennedy did not attempt to match the fervor of the afternoon's oratory. His speech was stiff, perfunctory and curiously out of key with the previous panegyrics.

"It's been a long day and a cold one," Kennedy began, referring to the weather, for surely the temperature of the occasion had been warm enough. "I want to thank all of you," he went on, expressing gratitude to the respective chairmen of the New Bedford and Fall River committees. "We have a great state here," Kennedy said. "We agree about more things than we disagree about." The honors tendered to him that afternoon "would make it even more of a pleasure than it's been in the past to represent you in the United States Senate."

If the speech seemed an anticlimax, it mattered little to the hundreds who eagerly crowded around the pavilion to listen and accorded a standing ovation as the guest of honor and his wife left the premises.

A week later an unusually orderly Democratic state convention listened as Kennedy, urging party unity, warned that intraparty strife could make Democrats "their own worst enemies in November."

"I will support all nominees of the party in November," he said unequivocally. "If Furcolo is the nominee for Governor, I will support him."

He was not actively seeking the Democratic nomination for vice-president, Kennedy said, nor did he "expect it to be offered." He declined, however, to say whether or not he would accept the nomination if it were tendered and advanced Senator Gore's name as the likeliest for vice-presidential nominee.

As Kennedy's unofficial campaign gathered steam, preconvention endorsements were being more pointedly advanced. At the Friday session of the state convention Governor Abe Ribicoff said that the Democratic Party could "do no better" than to nominate Kennedy as running mate.[7]

The season was in full swing on Cape Cod when Adlai Stevenson told a New Hampshire news conference that he considered John F. Kennedy an excellent candidate for the Democratic vice-presidential nomination; rumors that Stevenson was expected on Cape Cod to "confer" with Kennedy at Hyannis Port proved to be unfounded, however, much to the Chamber of Commerce's disappointment.

On June 14 Harvard University conferred an honorary degree upon Senator John F. Kennedy. The citation read: "Brave officer, able Senator, son of Harvard, loyal to party, he remains steadfast to principle."

The conferring of the honorary doctorate of laws, rumored for weeks, had been kept secret until commencement day and was his third such honor in a week. Both Boston College and Northeastern University had conferred honorary degrees on him as well.

Kennedy's address to the annual meeting of Harvard's alumni association in Harvard Yard marked a significant change from the vocabulary and sensibility of his usual public pronouncements. If some doubts were left regarding Kennedy's credentials as a liberal, the speech he delivered that day was well contrived to lay them all to rest, pleading as it did for understanding between the intellectual and the politician.

"The American politician of today and the American intellectual of today are descended from a common ancestry," Kennedy said. The authors of the American Constitution had been founders of American scholarship as well, Kennedy went on, citing the works of Jefferson, Madison and Hamilton among others as having "influenced the literature of the world as well as its geography."

Concluding the enormously well-received speech—a speech, it was to be pointed out, that his father never could have made—Kennedy quoted a British matron's letter to the provost of Harrow: "Don't teach my boy poetry," she wrote. "He's going to stand for Parliament." Then he commented, "If more politicians knew poetry and more poets knew politics, I am convinced the world would be a little better place to live in on this commencement day of 1956."

With the July adjournment of Congress national politics began in earnest. Flown from Hyannis to the state Federation of Labor's seventieth annual convention in Springfield, where delegates gave him a wildly enthusiastic ovation, Kennedy announced again that he was not an active candidate for the vice-presidential nomination. He told his audience that he believed the second man on the Democratic ticket should be "someone from another part of the country," as the delegates chanted "No! No!" in a clamorous demonstration. "Next October I will be back in Massachusetts," Kennedy said, "and I will be working as hard as I can for the election of a Democratic governor."

At the Democratic national convention in Chicago, John F. Kennedy was the object of a first small, "favorite son" demonstration following the showing of the film, *The Pursuit of Happiness*, which he had narrated. The Chicago *Sun-Times* openly endorsed a Stevenson-Kennedy ticket.

"Jack should stick with it," Governor Abraham Ribicoff of Connecticut said. "Anything can happen. And if it goes to the floor, Jack can win."

Kennedy's close defeat in his bid for the nomination—after becoming an "open and avowed candidate"—and his loss to Kefauver by a scant twenty votes stirred the only Cape Cod interest in the Democratic convention.

"It was close," Kennedy told the *Standard-Times*. "We didn't get started until Thursday night. At noon today we really didn't know how many votes we had. Then, Pennsylvania didn't come through as we had hoped. In any case, it's over."

A gracious televised speech during which Kennedy thanked his supporters, pledged his own support of the ticket and moved to make Kefauver's nomination unanimous was warmly applauded by delegates favorably impressed with a political figure conceded to be by far the most attractive to turn his smile toward the watching television cameras.

He flew to Europe for a postconvention vacation at his father's Riviera villa but was almost immediately recalled home when Jacqueline, seriously ill from an emergency operation, suffered a miscarriage of a baby expected that fall.

On October 9, 1956, Jack Kennedy became a Cape Cod real-estate taxpayer, purchasing for the sum of $45,948 the Irving Avenue property in Hyannis Port destined to become "the Summer White House." [8]

The arrival of *Mayflower II* at Provincetown [9] in June 1957 was delayed when it was becalmed sixty miles south of Nantucket Lightship. Towed the final miles into port, it was nevertheless given a tumultuous greeting by thousands who lined the fogbound shore. The ceremony marked the beginning of Cape Cod's most spectacularly prosperous season in its history, helped by a record heat wave during June. The mellow voice of Patti Page crooned the charms of "Old Cape Cod," a veritable singing commercial that could have been written by the Chamber of Commerce.

In August Elizabeth Taylor and Mike Todd ate popcorn in the back row of a Hyannis movie theater; and the Senate put aside such explosive issues as Eisenhower's civil-rights program to pay tribute to the late Senator Joseph McCarthy who had died on May 2. His body was placed in state in the Senate chamber, and funeral services were conducted from the rostrum where the roll call was taken to censure him on December 2, 1954.

Although Senators Wiley, Knowland, Goldwater and Dirksen spoke eulogies, Jack Kennedy made no tribute. He concerned himself with an emergency immigration bill and with filing a protest with the Secretary of the Treasury and the Commander of the Coast Guard about the proposed closing of Nauset Lifeboat Station in Eastham.

In September a new $500,000 Joseph P. Kennedy, Jr., Youth Community Center, a combined gymnasium-auditorium with facilities to accommodate 1,200 people was formally dedicated in New Bedford.

The Most Reverend James Connolly, Bishop of the Fall River Diocese, who accepted a check for $250,000 from the Joseph P. Kennedy, Jr., Foundation that had launched the project, officiated. Joseph P. Kennedy and his niece, Ann Gargan, were driven from Hyannis Port to take part in the ceremonies, during which the former Ambassador was introduced as "the greatest Catholic philanthropist in the world."

In his brief remarks, Kennedy spoke affectionately of New Bedford, but when he tried to say something about his son—after taking note of his death twelve years before—his voice quavered, then stopped.

In November Joseph P. Kennedy presented the new skating center in Hyannis to the Town of Barnstable during a ceremony that began with the national anthem and a blessing by Reverend Leonard J. Daley, Pastor of St. Francis Xavier. Reverend Carl Fearing Schultz of the Federated Church delivered the benediction, and Joseph P. Kennedy made a "presentation" speech in which he mirrored views he had earlier expressed in a letter:

Dear Neighbors of Hyannis and Barnstable:
For many years my family has maintained its summer residence at Hyannisport. Here, in this lovely and friendly area, our son, Joe, and his brothers and sisters lived and laughed and grew through many sunny, happy days.
It was, therefore, an especial pleasure to make available through the Joseph P. Kennedy, Jr., Foundation the funds for constructing the Skating Center which is being dedicated tonight, November 1, 1957.
With sincere good wishes to all our neighbors, and thanks to all who have contributed to the planning and execution of this building and skating rink and with the hope that the Center will be a source of community pleasure for years to come.
Very sincerely,
(signed) Joseph P. Kennedy

In his acceptance speech, Victor F. Adams, Chairman of the Selectmen of the Town of Barnstable reiterated sentiments conveyed in a letter sent to Joseph P. Kennedy that morning.

Expressing gratitude on behalf of the town for the "fitting and appropriate memorial" that was to be dedicated, he commended the donor's stipulation that "this rink be opened to all the young people of Barnstable without regard to race, religion, national origin or any other arbitrary designation."

"This fine and worthwhile gift will help to promote good fun, good health and good citizenship," Adams said. "As long as this facility is used, Lieutenant Joseph P. Kennedy will not be forgotten."

Jack Kennedy, the new father of a seven-pound, two-ounce daughter, could not witness the rink's dedication, as a speaking engagement precluded his attendance. Following a protest by Hyannis clergymen two weeks later, the Barnstable Recreation Commission ruled that the skating center would not be open for any activity on Sundays until 1:00.

Another ceremony took place in March 1958, an open house to honor the dedication of the new National Guard Armory on South Street in Hyannis, "a building which seems destined," a somewhat prophetic speaker announced, "to play an important part in the civic, social and recreational future of the town of Barnstable."

At another ceremony, Barnstable County Municipal Airport's sleek new modern administration building was dedicated by Senator Leverett Saltonstall, assisted by representative Donald W. Nicholson of Wareham. A week later, Cape and Island charter-flight service flew Jack Kennedy on a trip to Boston on the first leg of a return journey to Washington, where a labor bill aimed at corruption in labor unions was being attacked by Secretary of Labor Mitchell as "too weak."

Cosponsored by Kennedy with Senator Irving Ives of New York, the bill passed the Senate, despite the defeat of many floor amendments from Republicans, who insisted that the bill would not curb the labor racketeering that Kennedy's brother Robert had unearthed as chief counsel to the Senate Rackets Investigating Committee. That committee was headed by Senator John McClellan, an occasional weekend guest at Hyannis Port during the investigations.

Kennedy called the bill an "effective weapon in the hands of responsible leaders, honest members and the Federal Government in driving racketeers and mobsters out of the labor movement."

In July, as cancellation of railroad service between New York and Hyannis forced new arrangements for children of the *Herald-Tribune* Fresh Air Fund programs, Jack Kennedy spent frequent weekends at Hyannis Port replenishing his energies.

Twenty-six-year-old Ted, manager [10] of the senatorial campaign in which Kennedy sought re-election, visited Hyannis and Falmouth as part of a five-week statewide tour. He was accompanied by Lawrence F. O'Brien, director of organizations for the "Kennedy for Senator" committee and Kenneth O'Donnell of Jack Kennedy's staff. The explained purpose of the tour: "To put our finger on the pulse of the people in every section of Massachusetts." Ted declared:

> We wish to determine the position of the Senator in the minds of the voters. This is the start of a vigorous and detailed campaign designed to assure Senator Kennedy's re-election. We want to know what the voters are thinking and their feeling on the vital issues of the day. We are going directly to the people to find out and by the middle of August, I plan to speak with voters in every part of Massachusetts.

Kennedy's opponent in the election was Vincent J. Celeste. Appearing at the annual clambake of the Bristol County Republican club in Rehoboth, Massachusetts, Celeste castigated his opponent for voting for the St. Lawrence Seaway and opposing the civil-rights bill; he accused Kennedy of seeking re-election by the use of a "financial steamroller" and "abstract publicity that paints him as a saint," as well as "of a political marriage with Walter Reuther."

"I am going to defeat John F. Kennedy," Celeste said, to an audience that remained unconvinced despite the decibels. "I tell you this not as a boast, but as a practical lawyer and a man who knows what it is to be defeated." Celeste did, indeed, know defeat. In the 1950 congressional election Congressman Kennedy had scored a record victory, with 87,000 votes to Celeste's 15,000.

More than 125 people attended the Cape Cod Republican club's rally at the Hyannis yacht club to hear Celeste reiterate: "I can defeat the junior Senator and I will. Kennedy was elected in 1952 on the promise that he would avoid national and international affairs and concentrate on Massachusetts, and this promise surely must be embarrassing to the junior Senator."

A fiery yet ineffectual speaker, Celeste called Kennedy's opposition to the civil-rights bill, "soliciting the support of Southern Democrats" and labeled the Kennedy-Ives labor measure "a phony bill, which doesn't remedy one per cent of the wrongs."

In August, when the House killed the bill by a vote of 198 to 190, Kennedy said, "Old Jimmy Hoffa can rejoice at his continued good luck," and denounced the bill's defeat.

In August Eunice and Jean were hostesses at a social hour following a documentary entitled, *A Day in the Life of John F. Kennedy*, shown for the first time in the new National Guard Armory to an audience of 250 people, who were addressed by Ted Kennedy and Lawrence O'Brien.

In the midst of the campaign, Cape Cod heaved a huge sigh of relief when Hurricane Daisy battered her way out to sea, completely bypassing a fully prepared * but apprehensive Cape Cod.

On September 18, 1958, the Barnstable *Patriot* published an editorial entitled, "Muscle for the Labor Bill," [11] in which it attacked the newly defeated Kennedy-Ives bill for weakness and ineffectuality. Shortly thereafter, the *Patriot's* readers were astonished to read in the letters-to-the-editor column John F. Kennedy's rebuttal, published in full, in which he defended the bill and castigated the editorialist for being "uninformed." [12]

In October Celeste again attacked "the financial steamroller" tactics of Kennedy's campaign and again predicted his own election "even against the fabulous Kennedy millions . . . although I'm the only one who seems to think so."

Describing Kennedy's pre-election report of expenditures as "an insult to a moron's intelligence," Celeste said that a report of no contributions and no expenditures by the Democratic incumbent was "fantastic": "Every time you pick up a newspaper, read your mail, walk past billboards or turn on television or the radio you have conclusive proof of the breathtaking sums the Kennedys are dumping into this campaign."

A week later Jack Kennedy made his first and only political appearance on Cape Cod during an election campaign—in Hyannis on a late October evening in 1958. A drenching rainstorm did not, however, discourage an audience of nearly five hundred people who arrived half an hour before the meeting, sponsored by the Cape Cod "Kennedy for U.S. Senator" committee, began.

While his constituents gathered at the National Guard Armory, Kennedy and his wife were putting in a courtesy appearance at an

---

* Four New York radio stations swung immediately into action with messages costing $1,500 each, pointing out that the hurricane danger had passed, all roads were clear and all resort facilities available, part of a program conceived by the Cape Cod Chamber of Commerce to inform the public of weather conditions, a promotion to "recoup an estimated 1 million dollar loss caused by hurricane warnings that had discouraged vacationers away from Cape Cod."

"open-house preview" of newly modernized facilities at the Cape Cod *Standard-Times*. Jack Kennedy was greeted by Basil Brewer, who introduced him during a special broadcast from the newsroom over radio station WOCB.

When Kennedy and Jacqueline entered the Armory by a side door, the audience rose to its feet and burst into applause. The couple made its way to a temporary speaker's platform raised for the occasion and crowded with candidates for state and county offices, all of whom were to be introduced during the program.

Robert O'Neil of Hyannis Port, chairman of the committee, preceded Kennedy to the microphone, thanking those assembled for braving bad weather to attend; with little preamble, he introduced the main speaker.

Kennedy stood up and from his place behind the slanted wooden lectern beside the microphone acknowledged the ovation that followed with a wide smile, a smile that did not seem the reflex action of a candidate on the stump.

Dressed in a dark-blue pin-striped two-button suit, with a white handkerchief showing at the breast pocket and a blue silver-patterned tie, he partly obscured with his shoulder a political poster that had temporarily been affixed to the Armory's plaster- and ceramic-tiled wall with brown wrapping tape; it advertised his candidacy for re-election with the slogan, "He has served *all* Massachusetts with distinction."

In his speech, during which he thanked his audience for coming on such a stormy night, Kennedy spoke of the many pleasant memories he had of summers spent at Hyannis Port, telling his listeners that hardly a week went by that he did not have to consider one matter or another that in some way affected the Cape Cod "I proudly call home."

Although he touched on such national issues as the defeat of the labor bill he had cosponsored and national defense (pointing out that it was "an established fact we are behind the Soviet Union in phases of military preparedness"), he stuck pretty close to home.

Moves out of the state by certain industries were regarded as "natural" and no cause for alarm: ". . . Massachusetts, which long enjoyed a near-monopoly of certain types of industry is losing some of its factories to other areas . . . but the future of our State is in a sound, diversified group of industries . . ."

Kennedy's appearance had been advertised as "nonpartisan," echoing Lodge's 1951 appearance in Falmouth. But his speech did indeed seem to be no more than a "fireside chat," casual and deceptively low-key, rather than a political campaign speech. He was by now an extraordinarily effective public speaker, assured but not smug or self-consciously oratorical. Speaking without notes, he frequently glanced at the audience, singling out the rapt faces of his attentive and demonstrative listeners in the well-lit armory.

At the conclusion of his half-hour's talk, Jack Kennedy and Jacqueline stood below the speaker's platform to shake hands with hundreds who formed a long line to greet them. One person who had a first opportunity to observe Jack Kennedy "up close" remembered that

. . . he was not so tall as I'd thought him to be from photographs, or from watching the Democratic Convention in 1956 on television. . . . He seemed very much younger than 41, although as you drew closer to him you could see lines in his forehead and around his eyes. It was his expression, I think. A sort of leaping eagerness that made him look younger than he was.

When I reached him he put out his hand and said, "Hello, nice to see you," and smiled. I told him how much I had enjoyed his speech, and he thanked me. He was about to let go of my hand when I wished him good luck for the Democratic nomination in 1960. I don't know why I said such a thing. It just popped out. He smiled and asked me my name. When I told him, he half-turned to Jackie, as if he were going to introduce me to her, but she was occupied by a woman in a plaid raincoat and spangles in her hat who was talking her ear off, so he turned back to me.

"Where do you live?" he said. When I told him, he said, "It's nice over there" and asked me if I knew a neighbor of mine. When I said I did, Kennedy said, "Tell him I said hello." I was going to say I thought I'd seen the man in the audience, but I'd already taken up more of his time than I should have so I moved on. Jacqueline was standing by herself. She took my hand. She was a very pretty girl; she didn't seem ill-at-ease exactly, but she was "out of things," standing alongside her husband, yet not really a part of what was going on. I said, "I hope you didn't get too wet getting here tonight." I couldn't hear her answer because right then, Jack laughed very loudly while talking with two men, and I went on to this sort of buffet table they had set up with cake and cookies and took a glass of punch being served in paper cups because my mouth was so dry from the excitement. But the punch was warm, so I just took a sip.

When I left about fifteen minutes later, Kennedy was bent over listening attentively to an old man with an umbrella.

Following an Americans for Democratic Action endorsement of Kennedy's candidacy, which pointedly passed over Foster Furcolo and the rest of the Democratic state ticket, came a quasi endorsement that, for Cape Cod at least, had infinitely more significance.

The Barnstable *Patriot,* a weekly that reflected more indigenous intelligence than did the Cape Cod *Standard-Times,* startled year-rounders with its October 30, 1958, editorial entitled, "Kennedy Has Set a Good Record in Senate":

> Although this has always been a Republican paper in a Republican stronghold, we are going to venture an opinion that may not set so well with some of the "dyed in the wool" Republicans in the Cape area.
>
> We are going to say that there may be some good in some Democrats after all. We refer especially to John F. Kennedy who is aspiring to succeed himself as Senator in Congress.
>
> We have found Mr. Kennedy a very able representative of the people of the State without particular regard to party affiliation, who together with Senator Saltonstall have combined to give the State of Massachusetts able and progressive representation in Washington. . . .
>
> We are satisfied that Mr. Kennedy has always and will always represent the State of Massachusetts in Washington regardless of party lines.

In the November election Jack Kennedy overturned Cape Cod's long political traditions and became the first major Democratic candidate ever to carry the area: He received 12,392 votes to 10,118 for Celeste.[13]

Statewide, Kennedy's margin was an incredible 874,608, the largest ever accorded any candidate for any office in either party in the state—and the largest margin received by any senatorial candidate in 1958—breaking the previous Massachusetts record set by Leverett Saltonstall when he received a plurality of 561,668 in 1944.

Immediately after the election, speculation about Kennedy's possible candidacy for the presidential nomination was rife. The Associated Press poll of state Democratic chairman placed his name at the top of possible contenders, along with Senator Stuart Symington who had also been re-elected overwhelmingly.

Though national politics was interesting to some, however, more parochial matters were occupying Cape Codders. At the beginning of 1959 the proposal for the establishment of a national seashore on Cape Cod created the bitterest controversy in years, provoking the selectmen of Truro to circulate 1,200 questionnaires to voters and property owners, the results of which were announced and discussed at a special town meeting on action the town would take on the park proposal. One Truro resident, however, took matters more directly in hand and wrote to Kennedy about the proposed Cape Cod National Seashore Park, which Kennedy was cosponsoring with Saltonstall and Representative Hastings Keith. Kennedy replied:

> Thank you very much for writing me your views regarding the proposal to establish the Great Outer Beach National Park on Cape Cod. . . .
> I have not as yet taken a final position on this national park proposal because there is still room for compromise and for revising the borders of the seashore area which were set in the first report of the Park Service.
> In my judgment there can be some legitimate revisions and alterations in the proposal without destroying its merits. . . .
> I shall follow this park proposal with care and with confidence that a reasonable solution can be found which does not seriously impair the rights of individual property owners.

While the controversy over the park proposal raged through the summer, Connecticut Governor Abraham Ribicoff, a guest at the Kennedy house in Hyannis Port, participated in a day-long conference, during which forthcoming presidential preconvention strategy was discussed.

Returning to Hartford, Ribicoff announced at his press conference that Kennedy intended to postpone until December any formal announcement about his rumored presidential aspirations. Ribicoff commented on speculation that Kennedy's Catholicism would hurt his chances:

> There are so many people interested in the Kennedy candidacy that it definitely is our hope that he will run. I've been convinced right along that the people of the United States will accept a man for his ability, integrity record and his personality. That is the way you should judge a man. Not based on religion.

Jack Kennedy celebrated his sixth wedding anniversary with Jacqueline in Hyannis Port that September; he returned a month later for an altogether different occasion. If it is true that, as a political novice Jack Kennedy had been told by his cousin Joe Kane in 1946: "in politics you have no friends, only coconspirators," then there was no better place for discreet convocation than Hyannis Port in the off-season.

A handful of disinterested year-round residents in the Port witnessed the procession of men and automobiles to Robert Kennedy's house, as a chill October wind swept off the Sound, ruffling the tatters of autumnal foliage on the nearly bare tree branches and scattering leaves along the deserted avenues. The only other sign of life was the indefatigable golfers on the nearly empty links at Hyannis Port's well-manicured course.

Had the absent owners of empty summer establishments been privy to the councils in their previously inviolate village, they would have been utterly astounded. For in front of a crackling fire, kindled to warm the damp living room, Jack Kennedy, dressed in a tweed jacket, slacks and cordovan loafers, took dead aim at the Democratic presidential nomination.

For three hours Kennedy delivered an astonishing recitation, an informed oral survey of the entire country, state by state, without the aid of notes or statistics—interrupting himself only on those few occasions when he had to request information from his audience of top advisers and allies.

On January 2, 1960, after the year-end controversy over the Pure Food and Drug Administration's warning about "contaminated" cranberries had thrust the disposal of $30 million worth of raw and processed cranberries into dispute, Jack Kennedy formally announced his intention to seek the Democratic presidential nomination. At the news conference held in the Senate caucus room, he was confident that he could "win both the nomination and the election." Of the presidency he said: "Through its leadership can come a more vital life for our people. In it are centered the hopes of the globe around us for freedom and a more secure life."

Kennedy had once grown impatient with the life of a "worm" in the House of Representatives and had aspired to the Senate because it could provide him with more opportunities for individual action. But seven years in the upper house of Congress had convinced him that it was "in the executive branch that the most crucial decisions of this century must be made in the next four years . . ." The announcement came not quite fourteen years after the day when, as a "characteristically unassuming" novice, Jack Kennedy had hesitantly and with many self-doubts made his debut in political life.

Part Three

THE SUMMER OF A CANDIDATE
1960

Eight

I've never made a political speech in Hyannis in thirty years and I don't intend to make one now.—John F. Kennedy, Barnstable Municipal Airport in Hyannis, July 17, 1960

"Of all the Democrats whose names have been mentioned in connection with the presidency, Senator Kennedy is by far the best qualified to receive his party's nomination . . ." the New Bedford *Standard-Times* declared, conferring its editorial benediction on Jack Kennedy's public avowal of candidacy. The announcement caused a ripple of excitement even on Cape Cod, wrapped in the cocoon of its off-season insularity.

The Cape Cod Chamber of Commerce was justifiably beside itself, already anticipating the welcome glare of national publicity that was certain to focus on Jack Kennedy and—more important, in its view —the place where he had spent his summers since boyhood. Not even the most ardent publicity seeker, however, could possibly have foretold the far-reaching impact of such national exposure on Cape Cod.

Although the coming summer—hopefully one that would compensate in large measure for the disastrous season of 1959—absorbed the interests of one portion of the winter population, others were more and more taken up with the bitterest controversy that had ever split the Cape: pending legislation in Congress to create a national seashore on Cape Cod.

While Jack Kennedy's presidential stock soared after the New Hampshire primary * and he moved toward similar victories in Wis-

---

* Launching his campaign in New Hampshire, where Jacqueline accompanied him, Jack Kennedy pointed out that the last New England Democratic President had been Franklin Pierce, "a reluctant candidate."

"I am not that," Kennedy commented with a disarming grin.

consin and West Virginia, the continuing debate on the park issue was firing emotions and causing harsh enmity among year-rounders, most particularly those between Chatham and Provincetown whose areas fell within the projected boundaries of the park.

In a letter, drafted jointly with Senator Saltonstall, to the Chairman of the Senate Committee on Internal Affairs, Kennedy urged immediate action on the park, suggesting that hearings be held in Washington and expressing the hope that passage of the bill would not be deferred. ". . . It will be damaging to the affected communities if the proposal should hang in suspense . . . and if Congress should fail to act on it."

The senators seemed somewhat out of touch with their constituents, however, for Cape Cod was anything but "ripe" or "ready" for a seashore park. "Reasonable agreement" had perhaps been achieved in Washington, but at a special meeting at Wellfleet's elementary school residents had taken special pains to make it known that "a general air of co-operation among the towns of the Lower Cape" was in no way intended as an endorsement of the park proposal.[1]

The Cape Cod Chamber of Commerce requested Senators Kennedy and Saltonstall to take whatever action was necessary to delay the establishment of the proposed park, pending a locally sponsored economic study that would "give the Cape further information regarding the impact the park could have on Barnstable County's economy."

If it were true, as the Park Service maintained, that four years after the establishment of the park, some 2.5 million visitors a year could be anticipated, then in the Chamber's view: "Who can assure us that the retired and commuter families who now are making a substantial contribution to the economy will not be driven away?"[2]

At stake was title to some 27,000 acres of relatively undeveloped land, much of it adjacent to or near the waterside and hence of tremendous potential value, particularly to those developers whose bulldozers were beginning to make inroads into some of the more obscure corners of Cape Cod.

The most serious causes for concern were the right of personal property and the fate of many year-round, as well as summer, homes located on land in the areas to be appropriated by the Park Service, property whose ownership had, in some instances, resided with families for generations. Once such property became part of a national park it would cease to be taxable, and the loss of such income, according to some year-rounders, could be expected to increase others' taxes by 33 percent in areas affected; taxes would rise proportionately even in other towns on the Cape not directly affected by the park, in order to help Barnstable County pay its bills. Both Senators Kennedy and Saltonstall continued to press for mandatory payments "in lieu of taxes" to towns where tax-paying property was to be purchased by the Federal government, a provision that had been included in their original bill but deleted by the Department of the Interior.

At June's end, the first big weekend of the season, came the good news: Action on the proposed park was being delayed until the following session of Congress.

Having, for the first time in Cape Cod history, a direct association with the making of a president, many residents were finding diversion and delight in following Jack Kennedy's progress from primary victory to primary victory. At the launching of his campaign that spring in Boston, Kennedy was wildly cheered before a huge "Welcome Home, Jack" backdrop at the annual Jefferson-Jackson Day Dinner at the Statler Hilton Hotel; 2,260 people had paid $174,000 to hear both Representative John McCormack and Governor Foster Furcolo [3] extol the candidate. They were followed by an interminable and tiresome roster of local "pols" clamoring aboard Kennedy's bandwagon. "I am not prepared to turn the destiny of this country over to Dick Nixon for the next eight years," Kennedy said during a confident but brief five-minute speech. "And that is what it will be if he is elected in November."

After the dinner Kennedy confided to friends from the Cape that his campaign was "going well." He was in better health than he had enjoyed in years and had even managed to put on weight, something he had wanted to accomplish "for the work I am trying to do."

At the state Democratic convention in mid-May Kennedy confidently predicted that "Americans are not going to show the face of Richard Nixon as the face of this country," bringing a roar of approval from the severely split convention crowd, which agreed at least on his candidacy for the Democratic nomination.

Denouncing the administration's mistakes as "sins of omission of a government frozen in the ice of its own indifference," Kennedy for the first time articulated the importance of "getting the country moving again": "We should not promise that it will be easy, but the business of this country and the business of freedom will be set before the American people and this country will begin to move forward again."

He returned frequently to Cape Cod during his primary exertions and spent the Fourth of July with his wife and child at Hyannis Port. This vacation prelude to the Democratic national convention in Los Angeles offered a first portent of the effects that his electric presence would have on the quiet summer colony as state and local police were quickly rushed in to control an unprecedented flow of traffic through the Port's usually tranquil avenues.

An enthusiastic crowd of four hundred cheered as Kennedy's car drew up in front of Barnstable County Municipal Airport's administration building a little after 9:00 P.M. for the first leg of his flight to the Democratic national convention in Los Angeles. Four plainclothesmen immediately surrounded the candidate as he helped Jacqueline from the car in which they had ridden in the front seat with the Kennedy family's long-time chauffeur.

Tanned and animated as he stood amid the crowd, flashing his wide grin and shaking as many hands as possible, Kennedy said, "It's good of you to come down here tonight," while Jacqueline, dressed in white, stood by patiently smiling at the crowd. Asked how he felt, Kennedy replied: "Great. Just great."

Police cleared a path to allow the couple to enter the airport's main building, Jacqueline stepping ahead of her husband as he slowed to shake hands, leaning far out over the tight line of spectators to grasp the fingers of small children perched on their father's shoulders. Then, striding briskly onto the field, Kennedy helped Jacqueline into the chartered yellow and green twin-engine seven-seater plane in which they were the only passengers and paused at the top of the short stairway, turning once again to salute the cheering crowd. Ducking through the plane's low doorway, Jack Kennedy was off to Los Angeles.[4]

There was a marked change in Hyannis Port's overcast afternoon several days later. Jack Kennedy's association with the place, even *in absentia*, was lure enough for the gathering crowd of press and sightseers who began to congregate around his Irving Avenue house. By nightfall the crowd had dwindled to a steadfast sixty, who remained, despite a steady, tepid drizzle. Heavy automobile traffic, restricted to passage a block away from Kennedy's house, slowly wended its way through the village under strict police supervision.

At the start of the convention's first roll call at 10:00, floodlights supporting a mobile television unit—its cables snaked along the wet edge of Irving Avenue—were turned on, and a quiver of anticipation seized the waiting crowd of well-wishers and press and television staff, reinforced by a contingent of excited college students, their olive-drab, rain-slicked ponchos slung over madras bermudas; six Hyannis policemen and a state trooper patrolled the premises.

Inside the house, watching the convention's progress on a rented seventeen-inch television set was Jacqueline Kennedy, her mother, Mrs. Hugh D. Auchincloss, her stepbrother James and stepsister Janet and two representatives of *Life* magazine, witnesses to her reception of two telephone calls from the candidate before and after his nomination on the convention's first ballot. (At her press conference the following morning, Jacqueline reported that her husband had been terribly excited about winning the nomination, first exclaiming, "Isn't it wonderful?" then asking her, "Do you think so?")

Those who had waited in the rain were finally rewarded at 2:45 A.M., a short time after John F. Kennedy's nomination, when Jacqueline appeared at the front door of her house, then stepped out.

Smiling faintly, she seemed somewhat dazed when a cheer rose from those who had made the long night's vigil.

"I thought I was all alone in the country," Jacqueline said in a softly remonstrative voice nearly drowned out by the barrage of questions flung hurriedly at her by waiting reporters.

Would she fly to Los Angeles to be with her husband when he accepted the nomination tomorrow? Her answered "no" was hardly audible above other, more strident voices calling out to her. One young female member of the crowd, who had produced a damp, wrinkled slip of paper and a stub of pencil was wriggling furiously into position for an autograph attempt while an older couple, neighbors in the Port, stepped forward hesitantly to offer tentative congratulations.

Recognizing them, Jacqueline said "thank you," above the din of the noisy, jostling crowd. With the bursting of flashbulbs against the darkness came insistent appeals from the men staffing the floodlit equipment of a Providence television station, begging her to "please step a little closer" into the range of their poised cameras, which were to supply an affiliated network with important film coverage.

Obliging finally, Jacqueline moved forward into the vivid circle of light that cast eerie shadows in the surrounding darkness, vaguely framing the house's outline and lining as well the fine tracery of rain. At once the spectators quieted as the glare struck Jacqueline's face. She flinched, blinking a little from the contrasting brightness and, with chin lifting slightly, set her profile against the light.

"I'm . . . so . . . excited," Jacqueline said breathlessly, turning to the cameras.

Then a voice called to her from behind the partly opened front door of the house: "He's coming on."

The crowd's voice, only partly subdued as Jacqueline made her way into the floodlights, now rose in volume, as people shouted last-minute messages, but already Jacqueline had turned aside, relinquishing the floodlights and moving from the noise of the crowd, pressed tightly together now and straining for one last avid glimpse of her.

"I have to see him," Jacqueline said over her shoulder, just before she closed the door.

The following morning Jacqueline stepped into a waiting car under an overcast, lightly sprinkling sky to be driven around the block to her father-in-law's big, white house to meet the press for the first time in her role as the wife of the Democratic presidential nominee.

The narrow avenues adjacent to Jack Kennedy's house were under the restrictive management of a corps of yellow-slickered policemen attempting to keep at bay the swarm of eager curiosity seekers—some armed with their lunches as well as their cameras—come to lay siege if necessary to accomplish a glimpse of the potential First Lady.

Jacqueline shook hands with each newsman in turn. Inviting the press to sit down, she took her own place in a large wing chair upholstered in tapestry in a corner of Joseph P. Kennedy's spacious living room.

Seeming poised and self-possessed, Jacqueline confessed to being "absolutely rigid and mute with excitement. I'm nervous," she said with a small, quick smile at the onset of her press conference. "How could I help it?" she added, facing more than forty reporters and press photographers.

Called "Mrs. Kennedy" by questioning newsmen—earlier she had pointedly indicated her preference for "Jacqueline," admitting, "I don't like to be called Jackie"—she offered her reaction to the events in Los Angeles. "I saw it at the same time everyone else did."

"I'm very happy for Jack," Jacqueline said. "He worked so hard for the nomination. He started planning for this convention in 1956." Admitting that she had hoped for a first-ballot victory, she added, "It was over before I realized it."

She had taken only a short nap the previous night; her husband had telephoned her again at 5:30 that morning, Jacqueline said, to tell her that he would leave Los Angeles Sunday morning and fly nonstop aboard a chartered plane to Boston.

Would she meet him at the airport in Hyannis when he landed?

"I'd like to," Jacqueline said. Then she looked about her at the crowd of men pressing in close and beyond the broad veranda leading from the living room, where a magnificent view of Nantucket Sound was wholly obscured by a confusion of television camera crews, lights, cables and clustered technicians waiting to photograph a portion of her press conference. "It depends on how many of *you* will be there," she went on with a wry grimace. Then, recovering her aplomb and her smile, she explained that neither her doctor or her husband had allowed her to go to the convention because of her pregnancy. "There would be too much pandemonium in Los Angeles for me."

A family celebration was planned, but Jacqueline would not elaborate or give details. She and Jack would try to squeeze in a two-week vacation before he returned to Washington for the August session of congress. "We plan to stay here if it can be peaceful," she said. "We'll cut off the telephone if we have to."

When asked what would she do in the event her expected baby was born on Inauguration Day, Jacqueline provoked a brief burst of laughter from those assembled by asking, "When's Inauguration Day?"

Somewhat startled at the general response to her reply, Jacqueline recovered from a moment's discomfiture and joined in the laughter. Then up went her chin for the next question. If her husband achieved the presidency would they continue to live in their own house on Cape Cod?

"We'd make our own home the summer White House," Jacqueline said. "After all, this is our home."

Jacqueline's accomplished response when asked who would she like

175

to see as her husband's running mate brought a gentler burst of laughter from her audience, tribute to so deft a demonstration of discretion. "I like everyone," Jacqueline said. "I know each of them, and they are all fine men."

Should the role of a First Lady be an active one? "It depends on the First Lady," Jacqueline answered. "Everyone has to be herself," she added, conceding that she had not made plans for that part of the future. "It's a long road ahead until then," she said. She was more interested in her husband's welfare than in anything else, Jacqueline added. "In the meantime I'm going to catch up on my reading and painting. With running the household and bringing up a young daughter, I'll have enough work to occupy my time."

Did Caroline know of the convention's outcome? "She's too young to realize what's going on," Jacqueline said. "She senses the excitement, but doesn't know what it's all about." As a father, the nominee was "a disciplinarian—not too strict—but he's very affectionate."

At the end of the press conference Jacqueline willingly posed for pictures, then rose from her chair to thank the reporters present. "You've all been very gracious," she said.

While newsmen made their way out of the room, Jacqueline rested briefly, composing herself before venturing onto the crowded veranda to face the waiting battery of television cameras.

Meanwhile, Hyannis was bracing itself for Kennedy's return from Los Angeles.

"Every possible measure provided by law will be exercised to assure reasonable privacy and protection for Senator Kennedy and members of his family at the summer homes in Hyannis Port," Barnstable selectmen announced, warning that Hyannis Port would be policed against "unreasonable invasion" by tourists.

Police, compelled to keep an around-the-clock surveillance at the candidate's house, were particularly on the alert to prevent recurrences of such incidents as a three-car invasion of the grounds surrounding Joseph P. Kennedy's house. Passengers had swarmed over the sweeping lawnscape, snapping cameras and stripping flowering shrubs of their blooms as mementos before police compelled them to leave the premises. Other groups of souvenir seekers had busily plucked every rambler rose from behind Jack Kennedy's low front fence before a tall stockade was built.

"We are mindful, too, of the rest of the residents of Hyannis Port," selectmen went on. "And we shall, through our police departments, strive to keep unnecessary traffic from causing any congestion or nuisance in the area."

Despite such avowals, the Port shuddered in the spotlight. "Hyannis Port is in for it now," a resident predicted. "Everybody and his uncle will try to get in here to take a look."

Prior to the convention, a Hyannis Port summer resident of many years had declared: "If the summer White House should ever be here, old Hyannis Port will never be the same again. We're one of the oldest and, so far, one of the least changed of any summer colony on the Cape—I'm shuddering a little."

And, indeed, it seemed that the invasion was to be accomplished from all directions at once. A low-flying aircraft, chartered by press photographers, buzzed the Kennedy houses for aerial pictures until police called airport officials to send word to the pilot that he was violating altitude limits; others used hired boats cruising near to shore to get a closer look at the presidential candidate's backyard until police patrol crafts were detailed to direct water traffic in the harbor. Hyannis Port's streets filled to overflowing with curious pedestrians. Residents found strange automobiles parked in their driveways, as visitors, restricted by a new "no parking" edict, sought temporary stopping places.

Hyannis Port's aloofness, its previous invincibility to the incursion of tourists throughout its history, was at an end.

Though Hyannis Port was filled with dismay at the loss of its vaunted privacy and exclusiveness, the mood in Hyannis was one of exultant celebration. The Democratic town committee, in communication with Kennedy's Los Angeles headquarters, was already planning to welcome the candidate when he returned to Cape Cod. "We'd like to greet the Senator at the airport and have a motorcade down Main Street of Hyannis to his home in the Port," the chairman announced. As "Kennedy's schedule is still uncertain," no exact arrangements had been made. "Be assured," the chairman said, "we will plan a welcome for him when plans are more definite."

But there was no official town welcome. "He looks tired," a selectman said. "We don't want to make it any more confusing for him." While Hyannis was the focus of a welcome-home celebration, nomination excitement was rapidly spreading across the Cape, as representatives from fourteen other peninsula towns made plans to send

177

official delegations to Hyannis. The selectmen at Bourne had already dispatched a telegram of congratulation to Kennedy in Los Angeles: "What a wonderful thing it would be to have the summer White House again at Cape Cod," the message read, referring to "Gray Gables," Grover Cleveland's summer home at Bourne from 1891 to 1904.

The proprietor of the Hyannis Inn Motel on Hyannis' Main Street was "thrilled" to accommodate a temporary press center and to become for two weeks official headquarters for Kennedy's campaign activities. Twenty rooms in the motel's main building had been leased to Kennedy's campaign committee, along with an entire banquet hall to serve for press briefings. Permanent headquarters on Cape Cod, however, were later established at the Yachtsman Hotel, a huge facility located on Ocean Street's waterfront, because of the availability there of a bar. It was suggested that "you can't have a good press headquarters without booze."

Thirty additional telephone-company workmen were pressed into service around the clock to install forty additional telephone lines at the new headquarters; a telebus, parked outside the motel's press room and manned by an operator stationed inside, provided five additional telephone booths for the convenience of reporters representing major news services and the foreign press.[5]

The official announcement came in mid-week: The Hyannis Board of Trade, in concert with the Democratic town committee, would welcome Kennedy home on Sunday evening with a short greeting at the airport, followed by a motorcade through Main Street in Hyannis to Hyannis Port.

All available local policemen would be on duty, reinforced by a detachment of state troopers from South Yarmouth barracks and by others from Middleboro and Norwell. The selectmen had approved a huge banner to be stretched across Main Street in Hyannis—"Welcome Home, Jack. We're Proud of You"—and smaller banners bearing the same message were to be displayed by merchants, urged by the Board of Trade to fly flags in honor of Kennedy's return.

On Saturday, July 16, the Cape Cod *Standard-Times* published an editorial headlined, "Welcome Home!":

Last week a young man left Cape Cod. He was departing in quest of the greatest honor that a political party can bestow upon one of its members. Perhaps there was trepidation in his heart, but if there was it was not in evidence in his demeanor. Experts said he would receive the honor he sought . . . but the ways of politics can be strange at times. So, perhaps there was a qualm.

Tomorrow, the young man comes back to Cape Cod. He comes back as the Democratic Party's candidate for the presidency of the United States, the greatest office the free world has to bestow. He has won his honor.

It was said of him as the Democratic national convention came to a close last night that he won because he had more stamina, he had more character, he had more wisdom than those who were arrayed against him in offering their candidacies to the party delegates assembled in Los Angeles.

Tomorrow, Senator John F. Kennedy returns to his home in Hyannis Port.

Senator Kennedy has been a part of the Cape since he was a boy. The Senator has played on the Cape's beaches, sailed off its shores, participated in its activities as he found the time. The Cape has watched his career, watched him emerge from World War II as one of its heroes, watched him grow in stature, as first, a representative in Congress, and then as a senator.

He'll be home tomorrow, a longer stride toward greatness, the Democratic nominee for President.

The Cape bids him an affectionate welcome.

On Sunday afternoon two hairdressers arrived at the house on Irving Avenue to dress Jacqueline's hair in the "high bouffant style she likes," preparatory to the arrival of her husband's plane at Barnstable Municipal Airport in Hyannis that evening.

Outwardly calm and betraying her excitement only when the hairstyling was interrupted in order to allow her to watch her husband's televised welcome in Boston, Jacqueline exclaimed, "How do you think I feel," when her hairdresser confessed to being "very nervous."

Families in surrounding houses in Hyannis Port gathered on their front yards when Jacqueline left the house. Joined by her fifteen-year-old half-sister, Janet Auchincloss, Jacqueline entered the white Cadillac sedan driven by the chauffeur who had been with the Kennedy family for nearly thirty years.

An escort led by Hyannis Police Chief Albert L. Hinckley drove to Scudder Avenue and, proceeding "the back way" to Hyannis, passed the Melody Tent's orange and blue canvas and the Huke-Lau Restaurant—a rare bit of Polynesia at Hyannis' West End Rotary. The three cars moved along North Street to the airport, the second automobile trailed by a police cruiser containing old friend and former "campaign manager" Judge Francis X. Morrissey of Boston and other family friends.

Arriving twenty minutes before her husband's plane was scheduled to land, Jacqueline's car was directed to one side of the airport's apron while two small private aircraft and a large press plane circled the field to land, bringing premature gasps and cheers from a crowd of about eight thousand pressed tightly against a high chain-link fence for their first glimpse of the nominee.

First to arrive was Robert Kennedy, his face drawn and pale as he spoke wearily with reporters at a fenced-off enclosure; he planned only a week's rest in Hyannis Port before returning to Washington. His wife Ethel reported that the trip and reception in Boston had been "much fun and very exciting" and saluted the waiting crowd with a broad grin as she escorted three of her children across the field to join her husband. All but five-year-old David Kennedy in a seersucker suit with knee pants looked happy and excited. Asked if he were enjoying the occasion, David said, "not much."

Jean Smith, the nominee's sister, landed in a private plane a few moments later. Then the announcement came over the airport's intercom: Kennedy's plane was coming in for a landing.

Stirring excitedly, the crowd watched as a small plane appeared in the early evening's still-blue sky, following its lowering course until it taxied to a place no more than one hundred feet from the airport's main portal. Jacqueline's car, along with those escorting her, moved at once onto the airfield's pavement. She stepped out of the car and into the plane for a private greeting, reappearing a moment later with her husband framed behind her in the plane's open doorway as a roar went up from the crowd straining against the fence and police barriers.

Jack Kennedy was triumphant. Poised on the short stairway, the figure that had so recently walked off the nation's television screens seemed in the flesh still somewhat larger than life. By now the lineaments of his person had been so well advertised that they had achieved the familiarity of mythology: the boyish handsomeness, the thick brush of hair (mitigated by a new shorter haircut), the vital springiness of his step as he descended the stairway to stand beside

Jacqueline and most of all the dynamic candlepower of his wide, illuminating smile that kindled such empathy in the overexcited crowd. Jack Kennedy needed only to raise his hand in a high spread-fingered greeting to bring an instant deafening response.

Barnstable Selectman E. Thomas Murphy stepped forward and presented Jacqueline with a dozen red roses. For an instant she looked uncomprehendingly at the proffered bouquet, bewildered by the ear-splitting noise of the long-sustained ovation.

Still grinning broadly, Kennedy left Jacqueline as he went down the waiting line of town officials and the committee of official greeters that included selectmen from other Cape towns beside Barnstable before he was brought to temporary microphones. "I would like to express my thanks . . . to all of you . . . for your kindness in coming out." Kennedy said in his familiar flat and compelling voice. "I love California . . . but it's nice being back on Cape Cod," he said, waiting for the crowd's noise to abate. "I think this is the beginning of a long and arduous road . . ." He paused again, looking at the crowd with a slight, tight smile.

"I'm delighted to be here," he began again. "Delighted to have been nominated . . . I consider it a great privilege and a great responsibility . . ." but the rest was drowned out by another prolonged wave of applause, cheers and whistles. One insistent male voice, piercing the solid wall of voices, kept up a metronomic tattoo: "Hey, Jack! Hey, Jack!"

With a resigned smile, Kennedy concluded: "I've never made a political speech in Hyannis in 30 years," he said. "And I don't intend to make one now." Taking one step away from the microphones he added, "Thank you all again."

Eight police led Kennedy through a maze of press photographers frenziedly bent on angling their cameras into focus, squinting hunched over their lenses, calling out, grimacing as the candidate reached Gate 4 and the double glass doors leading to the airport's lobby.

Turning to his escorts, Kennedy said, "I'm going to take a walk this way." Swiveling to his left, as policemen regrouped about him, Kennedy strode down the long corridor under the jutting terminal roof —while shrieks of delight rose from the crowd crammed along the high mesh barrier as it comprehended his intentions—and into the open air, passing before a waving field of hands, fingers wriggling frantically to make contact, as he walked along two hundred feet of fence, seizing all the outstretched hands he could.

Jacqueline, waiting before the doors, was herself the target of a curious crowd, which closed in as police drew a protective circle about her.

Then Kennedy rejoined his wife. After a moment's difficulty getting the double doors open without crushing the tightly packed spectators gaping at close range, the two made their way behind a phalanx of police through the airport's lobby where Kennedy again "took a walk," shaking hands with the massed group of indoor well-wishers before his escort led him to an open convertible for the motorcade. A police car went first.

A truck with a moving platform for press and movie photographers was to follow next in line, before the Kennedy convertible, but the enthusiastic throngs following the candidate spilled over the area so quickly that the truck could not safely proceed to its place ahead of the convertible, already inching its way through the spectators. Most of the photographers jumped from the truck to run alongside Kennedy's car before hitching rides in automobiles, decorated with "Kennedy for President" placards, that had found places in the cavalcade.

Slowly the convertible made its way through undisciplined crowds pressed in close and overflowing into the roadway that led from the airport to a traffic rotary. The police cruiser's siren unnecessarily heralded the approach of the nominee to thousands who had waited— some as long as three hours—crammed into the rotary's center, trampling grass and shrubbery or clinging to precarious curbside purchase in front of the Red Coach Grill's parking lot.

Slowly the convertible negotiated the rotary's curve as the crowd surged after it, chasing the motorcade as it turned onto Barnstable Road, where, on the straightaway at last, it picked up some speed heading south for Main Street.

Cutting over to Center Street, where a life-sized male mannequin dressed in black rubber skin-diving gear supported a "Welcome Home Jack" sign, the motorcade approached the East End rotary, where another crowd had spilled across the pavement.

When the convertible turned onto Main Street, a huge roar went up from the solidly packed sidewalks stretching in two dense straight lines ahead.

On the rear deck of the open convertible sat Jack Kennedy, his face flushed and grinning as he waved at well-wishers and leaned to grasp the hands of those who dashed alongside the moving car as it threaded its careful way through the huge crowd. To the good wishes shouted as he passed, Kennedy gave a smile of acknowledgment and an inaudible "thank you," while the crowd jostled forward despite two police cars, which, with their doors open, shoveled back spectators and cleared a path for the convertible. But in its wake the crowd closed ranks again.

With a broad, alert smile, Kennedy watched the familiar landscape of Main Street pass: from Martin's Bakery on the corner at the rotary and DuMont's Pharmacy to the Hyannis News and the old-fashioned facade of the Rexall drugstore (old Megathlin's, where he had begged ice-cream cones from skipper Jimmie MacClean). About him the crowd's tumultuous welcome rivaled the reception given the aviators Russell Boardman and John Polando in 1931. A fourteen-year-old Jack Kennedy had watched as his brother Joe drove the flyers down this same street in the Kennedy family's Rolls-Royce.

Moving on toward the straight white New England spire of the Federated Church, where Jack Kennedy had once addressed a Rotary Club meeting, the convertible reached the corner of Barnstable Road and Main Street. The nominee's eyes flickered with amusement at the yellow and green sign "Welcome Home Jack, We're Proud of You." Such signs were displayed from virtually every store window, building front and telephone pole along the route. This one was located above one of equal prominence advertising marked-down fountain pens stickered to the window of a stationer's next to the Center Theater, where the old Idlehour of his youth had stood, providing a private flood of memories along with a torrent of confetti from curbside dispensers, a crowd estimated at some 15,000.

Many cars parked along the route bore postered testimony not only to their presidential preferences but also to the speed and efficiency of sign makers who had produced Kennedy-Johnson placards at such short notice. But the most spectacular insignia of welcome was the huge banner spanning Main Street from Woolworth's to an anchoring post in front of Hyannis' post office.

Acknowledging the tribute with a broad smile of pleasure as his convertible traveled beneath it, Jack Kennedy focused attention only for a brief moment on Barnstable's town hall, where he had mapped

183

strategy with town Democrats in the basement hearing room during his first senatorial campaign only eight years before. At the base of the flagpole, which flew the stars and stripes in his honor, the name of his brother Joe was inscribed on an honor roll of Barnstable men killed in World War II.

Once past Kennedy's temporary headquarters at the Hyannis Inn Motel and crossing the imaginary boundary into the West End, the motorcade's progress was a little easier. There two college boys waved cardboard posters crudely lettered "Nixon" but cheered as Kennedy went by. Greetings from somewhat thinner but no less enthusiastic crowds followed the convertible as it drew up by the Hyannis Theater's French Tudor half-timbers, where ticket buyers turned from a sidewalk box office to salute the passing candidate and Kennedy, an avowed movie fan, looked toward the marquee to see what was playing; *Psycho* was the feature attraction.

As the cavalcade swept by the dilapidated relic that once had housed the elegant old Panama Club in the Queen's Buyway, the escort picked up speed, gliding past bermuda-clad spectators, who gaily waved their delight; others gathered on porches that flew flags in his honor and greeted the candidate as he sped by. En route to Hyannis Port, Kennedy slid down from the convertible's perch into a seat beside Jacqueline.

Outside Hyannis Port, the motorcade halted briefly beside a candle factory, where a large sign had been pulled across the road: "Welcome Home, President Jack: We are Not Here to Curse the Darkness, We Are Here to Light a Candle." This sign was a reference to Kennedy's acceptance speech; it lured the candidate from his convertible to touch a match to a three-foot red, white and blue candle, while a three-piece band provided musical accompaniment.

In the quiet of an expectant Hyannis Port—privately girding for "the worst summer in its history"—Jack Kennedy's neighbors, unable to resist the occasion, were waiting to extend a more sedate welcome to their fellow summer colonist. As his convertible turned into the village, a burst of applause and cheers rose from the crowd of about 250 people gathered at the corner of Scudder and Irving Avenues. The motorcade slowed, allowing the candidate to wave and smile, but it did not stop until it reached the sanctuary of Joseph P. Kennedy's driveway, tucked safely inside the Kennedy Compound.

Opening the convertible's door, Kennedy helped Jacqueline and

Janet Auchincloss from the car. As they proceeded directly across the lawn to the Irving Avenue house, Kennedy paused for a quiet moment on the steps of his father's house, speaking with Larry Newman, a special reporter for the New Bedford *Standard-Times*, who had married a childhood playmate of Kathleen Kennedy's and now made his home catercorner from Kennedy's in Hyannis Port.

"I never knew that many people could get on Cape Cod," Kennedy said. "It was a great welcome and I loved every minute of it."

His eyes paused for a moment on the waves washing up on his father's private beach in the waning daylight; he said, "I'd like to take a swim, but I want to get in the house before Caroline gets to sleep." But a small, persistent crowd of Hyannis Porters had walked through police lines and were stationed at the edge of the lawn and atop an adjacent stone wall.

To them, Kennedy said in a voice mixed with weariness and emotion: "I believe you know how you have made me feel by coming to see me tonight. You are my neighbors. I know you understand what is in my heart. I would like to talk to you all for a while, but I have to get inside before my daughter goes to sleep. Good night. May God bless you and thanks again," Kennedy said before making his way alone across his father's lawn to his own house.

Five minutes later Kennedy reappeared on his front porch holding Caroline in his arms, with Jacqueline joining him to greet those still lingering outside.

It was almost dark. Streetlights paled in the illumination from the headlights of the determined, slow pilgrimage prevented from coming closer to Kennedy's house by hard-pressed policemen at sentry posts a block away. Throughout that night and the early hours of the morning, automobiles traversed the village. At dawn a small, indomitable group was already forming at police barricades to greet a superb summer morning and the Democratic presidential nominee. Not until midafternoon was their persistence rewarded when Kennedy appeared at his fence to shake hands with well-wishers there.

Jack Kennedy rose at 8:00, breakfasted with his wife and Caroline and admired again the gift Jacqueline had painted for him: a "welcome home" picture in which her husband was shown aboard *Victura* sailing shoreward, with members of his family and others awaiting his arrival on the pier. Done in a charming, primitive style, the picture suggested, to at least one witness, "Washington Crossing the Delaware" and had allegedly been drawn as a playfully ironic comment on the occasion.

"I like it," Kennedy said, "but I wonder where she ever got the idea I had a commander-in-chief complex."

Boarding the Kennedy family cruiser *Marlin*—originally built in 1930 for Edsel Ford—for a three-hour cruise of Nantucket Sound, Kennedy successfully eluded curious onlookers, as well as newsmen and photographers, by driving the short distance to the pier. With only Bobby, Ethel, the boat's skipper and the skipper's thirteen-year-old son along, Kennedy and his wife picnicked on board.

In the early afternoon *Marlin* was met beside the breakwater by a new sixteen-foot outboard speedboat, and the Bobby Kennedys took turns water-skiing, while Jacqueline and Jack watched before boarding the outboard themselves to be taken to the family's private beach. Holding hands, they walked home together. Kennedy later appeared at his fence, to the delight of a crowd of amateur photographers, and was reported taking a nap while in Hyannis Pierre Salinger conducted his first press briefing in the new headquarters.

Reporting that Kennedy had been "excited and pleased" with the receptions tendered him in Boston and Hyannis, Salinger explained that the candidate's plans called for two days of complete rest; but held out the possibility of a press conference, however, before Kennedy plunged into the business of campaign strategy.

Commenting on Eisenhower's proposal for confidential briefings, Salinger said that Kennedy would cooperate in every way during this period but still planned to have Adlai Stevenson and Chester Bowles act as liaisons with the White House; the understanding was that only he and Lyndon Johnson would have personal access to intelligence information. At the same time, Salinger announced Kennedy's willingness to participate in suggested televised debates tentatively scheduled for the fall—if the free time offered by all networks were accepted by the candidate to be selected at the forthcoming Republican national convention.

After a two-hour boat ride on Nantucket Sound the following day, Kennedy took a nap, then walked up Sunset Hill to Hyannis Port's golf course. Beginning on the seventh hole, he played through the fifteenth, accompanied by his brother Bobby; then he stopped to chat with three of his neighbors, one of whom had known him since they both had sailed star class boats as children. One of the group passed judgment on his greens performances: "Jack is still a spray golfer."

On Wednesday Salinger, wearing baggy bermudas and a plaid sport shirt, told reporters that Kennedy would launch his campaign in Hawaii and Alaska, followed by a "vigorous stumping tour" of every section of the country.

At the end of the vacation portion of his two weeks in Hyannis Port, Jack Kennedy commenced the business of planning his campaign at a meeting attended by Lawrence O'Brien, Stephen Smith, Kenneth O'Donnell, Bobby and Connecticut Democratic Chairman John M. Bailey, who arrived from Hartford.

"Senator Johnson added great stature to the ticket," Bailey said and added praise for Bobby Kennedy's "amazing ability to organize, his astuteness politically and his tremendous energy. . . . Robert is a wonderful man," Bailey said, "a careful organizer, and a man who follows through on details. He knows hundreds of Democratic leaders and independent leaders in all the fifty states."

By now the house on Irving Avenue had altogether lost its vacation air, as the pace of Kennedy's precampaign schedule rapidly accelerated and a daily task force of visitors, including Norman Mailer in a black tropical suit and "sweating like a goat," awaited the candidate's attention. Appearing in Hyannis Port at Kennedy's invitation for an interview granted in connection with a soon-to-be-celebrated *Esquire* article, "Superman Comes to the Supermart," Mailer was admittedly "jangled" when he was introduced to Jacqueline Kennedy. (In a later article, "An Evening with Jackie Kennedy"—also published in *Esquire*—Mailer wrote a not altogether gentlemanly critique of the First Lady's performance on her televised tour of the refurbished White House, comparing her with "a starlet who is utterly without talent.")

As part of a group gathered in Jacqueline's yellow and white living room and including Arthur Schlesinger, Jr., and his wife; Prince Stanislas Radziwill (whose morning shave had been witnessed by a fascinated group of tourists stationed across Irving Avenue); *Saturday Evening Post* writer Peter Maas; campaign photographer Jacques Lowe, and Pierre Salinger, Mailer sensed Jacqueline's controlled exasperation at so total an invasion of her home. The lawn swarmed with police, newsmen and "pols" immortalizing their visit to Hyannis Port by taking flashbulb pictures on the terrace outside the living room, a practice that struck Mailer as "low and greedy."

Offering him a cool but unalcoholic drink, Jacqueline added, "We do have something harder, of course." Mailer took careful note of her "saucy regard" and her calves; they seemed "surprisingly thin and not unfeverish" to him.

Although her husband would have cause to be gratified at Mailer's significant contribution to his campaign, Jacqueline seemed uneasy in the presence of Mailer's keen perceptions, which probed deeper than the dazzled gush of workaday female journalists customarily assigned to cover the candidate's wife.

Their most successful and satisfying conversation involved Province-town, Mailer's summer home. The author's animated description of a portion of that town's attractions [6] brought from Jacqueline the comment, "Oh, I'd love to see it!" Then she added regretfully, "I suppose now I'll never get to see it." [7]

On Thursday Kennedy rose at 8:00 A.M. After breakfast he took a quick swim from his father's beach before holding conferences and strategy meetings with his brother and John Bailey; he managed a few holes of golf before submitting to an interview with Mailer, who had been invited back a second day. Mailer brought his wife along this time. Before boarding the *Victura* with her husband and brother-in-law Ted, Jacqueline confided to Adele Mailer, "I wish that I didn't have to go on this corny sail, because I would like very much to talk to you."

After lunch, Kennedy came down the back steps of his house to greet waiting cameramen. "We'll try in a few seconds and see how this works out," he said, uncertain what Caroline's reaction would be to the solid row of still and newsreel cameramen gathered on the back lawn. "She's only 2½ and we don't know exactly how well she'll co-operate, but we'll give it a try anyway."

Moments later Caroline appeared with her mother and proved to be a perfect model. Clutching a picture book, Caroline pointed to photographers as their flashbulbs competed with the sunlit afternoon, then pointed to her father's face and smiled.

"You never know, do you?" Jacqueline said. "She usually dislikes having her picture taken and sometimes fusses at the sight of the camera."

Kennedy found time during that afternoon to shake hands with a crowd of 150 congregated in front of his house; next door reporters, press photographers and their wives were guests at a cocktail party given by Bobby and Ethel on the lawn of their home, where the nominee put in a brief token appearance and a reporter had the opportunity to verify fashion details with Jacqueline.

"What was the color of that turtleneck sweater you wore on the boat yesterday? I called it tangerine."

"That's close enough," Jacqueline said, laughing. "It was orange."

Averell Harriman arrived in Hyannis the following morning for a two-hour conference with the candidate, bearing with him a letter from Harry Truman in which the former president "forgave" him for supporting Kennedy at the convention; he pledged his wholehearted support of the Democratic ticket.

At a press conference Harriman scored what he called the "weakness" of the Eisenhower administration in foreign policy, forecasting at the same time a reunification of all factions of the seriously split Democratic party in New York to work for a victorious Kennedy-Johnson ticket in November.[8]

The following morning Allen Dulles, Director of the CIA, flew to Hyannis accompanied by two aides. Met at the airport by Robert and Ethel Kennedy, Dulles confessed to being "overcome" by the reception accorded him by waiting photographers. Carrying a heavy briefcase apparently stuffed with top-secret documents, Dulles was prepared to "discuss any points the Senator wants me to cover" and to "emphasize what the Senator wants emphasized."

Not noticeably enthusiastic about his part in the courtesy briefing ordered by President Eisenhower, Dulles nonetheless submitted to a formal photographic session at Kennedy's house after a conference with the candidate, which was called "most informative" by Pierre Salinger at a later press briefing.

While her husband conferred with Dulles, Jacqueline was shopping for fresh fruit and vegetables from a produce truck parked in her driveway. After pointing out a number of items that she wanted—the East Falmouth truck gardener left four bushel-baskets full—Jacqueline hastily retreated indoors when she spotted photographers hovering close to take pictures.

After Dulles had left to spend the rest of the weekend at a CIA associate's summer house in Cotuit, Jack Kennedy took another turn at the low fence, prickly with rose thorns; he shook hands with hundreds who had waited since early morning for his now-anticipated daily appearance. He cheerfully posed for amateur photographers and, reaching over the fence's top railing, asked each his name and the state he was from. Two women in saris wished Kennedy good luck "from the people of Pakistan."

Kennedy was finishing up another conference with Harriman later that afternoon when a gleaming 1935 Rolls-Royce appeared in the driveway of the Irving Avenue house. The man who stepped out to shake Jack Kennedy's hand was Maurice Kowal, at one time a member of Kennedy's PT-boat crew. Employed as a landscape gardener in Grafton, Kowal had borrowed his employer's automobile specifically for the trip to Hyannis Port.

On Sunday morning hundreds walked and rode through Hyannis Port, many enjoying the opportunity to watch Kennedy drive out of his driveway en route to St. Francis Xavier Church in Hyannis, where word had quickly spread that Kennedy and Jacqueline planned to attend 9:00 mass.

A crowd of more than one thousand was waiting (some had arrived as early as 8:00 A.M. to select places next to the white Ionic columns of the church's distinctive facade) when Kennedy drove up to the curb in the 1956 Country Squire station wagon belonging to his wife; press photographers, newsmen and well-wishers closed in on the vehicle. After struggling to clear a passage that would allow Jacqueline to alight from the car's righthand side, Barnstable police had even more difficulty subduing the crowd so that Kennedy could walk around from the driver's side to join Jacqueline before they walked up the church steps, taking places in a pew close to the rear of the church.

Making no acknowledgment of the candidate's presence, the pastor of St. Francis Xavier celebrated mass at the altar that had been dedicated to the memory of Joseph P. Kennedy, Jr. Toward the end of services, however, the priest warned parishioners not to crowd the back lobby, as many attending had left their seats early in order to position themselves to see the candidate's passage out of the church.

Greeted by cheers as he exited, Kennedy climbed behind the steering wheel of the station wagon for an hour's visit with his grandmother Mrs. Josephine Fitzgerald, the widow of Honey Fitz, before spending the rest of the day boating. That afternoon Kennedy spoke by telephone with Lyndon Johnson for the first time since the convention. Salinger announced at the day's press briefing that Johnson was expected to visit Hyannis Port some time toward the end of the following week.

After a Monday morning conference with New York's Mayor Robert Wagner, Kennedy lunched, then took a cruise on the *Marlin*, diving off the boat at Grand Island for a swim before returning to Hyannis Port's harbor, where he grasped the wheel of a speedboat and took LeMoyne Billings in tow for a short session of water-skiing.

At that day's briefing, Salinger announced that Tom Mboya of Kenya, arriving in the United States to attend the early September session of the General Assembly of the United Nations, would visit the nominee at Hyannis Port.

The 29-year-old secretary of Kenya's Federation of Labor was met at Hyannis' airport by Eunice Shriver. Mboya informed the candidate that the greatest need of his young country was for trained technicians and people sufficiently educated to steer the future course of the nation.

Reiterating America's commitment to assist Kenya, Kennedy advanced the view that existing programs should be broadened, particularly for those countries that had recently become independent. He took the opportunity to challenge the GOP, which was convening in Chicago to select his opponent, to match the Democratic Party's civil-rights plank.

Around noon, after pictures had been taken on the terrace of his house Kennedy turned to an aide and said, "Take this guy to the Red Coach Grill, then put him on a plane," and spent the afternoon relaxing on the *Marlin*.

The following day Kennedy met with J. Leonard Reinsch of Atlanta, his radio and television coordinator for the November campaign. Perfect sailing weather brought Kennedy aboard his Wianno Senior *Victura* for a run in Hyannis Port's harbor, necessitating the last-minute cancellation of a session with press photographers slated for 12:30 at his home.

After the sail, Kennedy again cruised Nantucket Sound aboard the *Marlin*; he watched the Republican national convention on television that evening. He left his television set to walk across the lawn in a light rain and a strong harbor-driven wind to his father's house, to apologize personally to reporters he had kept waiting through the evening for a planned post-Nixon nomination conference. He made his appearance just as Salinger was telling reporters the session had been cancelled, that Kennedy was tired and was going to bed. The following morning at 11:00 A.M. a press conference was held on the porch of Joseph P. Kennedy's house, vividly spotlighted despite the brilliant sunlight, for the benefit of television and movie cameras. Kennedy presented a tanned and enormously attractive face to the more than fifty newsmen gathered beside the green hedges of rambler roses.

"I was not surprised by what I saw and heard last night," Kennedy said, offering at the same time his congratulations to Nixon on winning the nomination. "Eisenhower's influence should be very helpful to Mr. Nixon," he said.

Kennedy had a good word for his former rival, Henry Cabot Lodge, calling Nixon's running mate "an able public servant."

"I believe relative age will have little to do with the outcome of the election," Kennedy said, referring to Republican barbs at his "youth" and adding that both he and Nixon had served in Congress for fourteen years.

The Democratic platform had played a significant role in influencing the Republican platform, Kennedy thought, conceding that both parties were committed to great goals. The issue for voters to decide was "which party's record has fulfilled such promises in the past."

Answering Governor Dewey's charges that he had suggested that Eisenhower "apologize" to the Russians for the U-2 spy-plane incident, Kennedy said: "I didn't say that. I said at the time that the President should express regret. However, I don't really mind what Dewey said," Kennedy smiled, in reference to the speech in which the former New York governor had scored "smart-aleck Kennedy talk."

"Possibly some worse things have been said about me by some Democrats."

His campaign would terminate in Massachusetts, Kennedy said, and his chances of carrying Vermont and Maine were "pretty good," although the outcome would be close in those states. After a pause, Kennedy added, "It will be close in *every* state."

He would accept an invitation for a series of four television debates with Nixon, extended to him in a telegram from Robert Sarnoff, head of the National Broadcasting Company.

What he planned to give Jacqueline for her 31st birthday—to be celebrated with a party attended by Caroline and all the younger members of the Kennedy family—was not revealed. Smiling, Kennedy said only, "I'm drawing it." [9]

Senator Henry "Scoop" Jackson, Chairman of the Democratic National Committee, landed at Barnstable County Municipal Airport shortly before 10:00 A.M. and was brought immediately to the Kennedy house to take a small part in the nominee's press conference. He offered his view that Nixon's nomination had been a "forgone conclusion."

Later that day Jackson starred at his own press conference: "We agreed every state is vulnerable and exposed to the Democratic Party," Jackson said, referring to his meeting with Kennedy. "I don't say we have all fifty, but our plans are predicated on the assumption that we can take them. This is not true of the Republicans."

"We will even win in Maine and Vermont," Jackson predicted, citing the inroads Democrats had made in states with long Republican histories.

With the weekend at hand, Hyannis Port was steeling itself for another major and untoward invasion of tourists—expected to be the largest influx of sightseers so far—who congregated so close to the candidate's house that one portion of Kennedy's uncompleted stockade fence was knocked over.

Barnstable town policemen, aided by state troopers, were sealing off Irving Avenue to automobile traffic, to the vigorously expressed indignation of those whose access to adjacent summer homes was hampered by police inspection. There were rumors of a "protest" meeting being organized under the auspices of the Hyannis Port Civic Association.

Kennedy accepted the second network invitation to debate Nixon from Dr. Frank Stanton, President of the Columbia Broadcasting System, whose telegraphed offer of eight hours of prime evening time for such public-service appearances was predicated on the expectation that Congress would give approval to a measure revising "equal time" provisions.

Kennedy was involved in making short television clips and conferring with Frank Reeves, a campaign assistant, when Adlai Stevenson arrived at Hyannis Airport, accompanied by his law partner William Blair.

Met by Eunice, Stevenson, who was to be a guest of David K. Bruce, former Ambassador to West Germany and France, told reporters massed to greet him that he considered the proceedings at the Republican national convention in Chicago "appropriate for a stockyard." He was particularly distressed, Stevenson said, that Republicans apparently regarded "any criticism of Eisenhower's administration as either improper or disloyal."

Stevenson was not scheduled to confer with Kennedy until Saturday (the meeting was later postponed until Sunday morning), as the candidate was planning to spend much of Friday meeting with Lyndon Johnson, who was expected late that afternoon on a special Northeast Airlines flight, accompanied by his wife and a party of forty staff members and thirty Texas newsmen. Although Johnson and Stevenson were both in the vicinity of Hyannis Port at one time, plans did not call for a tripartite conference.

Johnson's arrival was delayed by bad weather, however. He landed at Otis Air Force Base in Falmouth around 9:00 P.M. "I have come to see my leader," Johnson said, coming off the plane in fog as thick as his Texas drawl.

Taken to the Kennedy house by car, Johnson and Lady Bird were overnight house guests of the nominee following a conference that lasted past 2:30 in the morning.

"I spent a very delightful evening with Mr. Kennedy," Johnson said, beaming and exuberant at the following day's press conference, as the candidates posed for photographs. "Nothing happened here in the last ten hours which will be of aid or comfort to Republicans," Johnson said, predicting victory in the elections. "November 8 will be a glorious day when the Democrats are returned to executive leadership in the White House."

At the same time Kennedy rejected Nixon's proposal for "weekend truces" that would permit campaigning prior to the projected September end of Congress. Johnson quipped, "I haven't noticed that Mr. Nixon's presence or non-presence in the Senate during the last eight years has made much difference."

Nixon's avowal that religion would not be injected into the campaign was, however, applauded by Kennedy. "I'm sure he won't and I take him at his word."

The religious issue was dead, according to Johnson: "Any attempt to bring it up will hurt the Republicans far more than it will hurt us," Johnson said, "and certainly, any discussion of it will hurt America."

"I heard a fellow observe that the last time he voted when religion was an issue, he voted Republican and we immediately had a Depression," Johnson said, grinning. "He thought that since things have been so good after Democrats returned to power that he wouldn't vote Republican again."

Disposing of the "youth" issue, along with the religious issue, Johnson—who would play "a role more influential, more significant than any vice president in recent times," according to Kennedy— admitted that he and Kennedy had "compared gray hairs" during their evening and early-morning conference disclosing plans for campaign tours that would take them to all fifty states.

"Will you campaign in places where you are not popular?" a reporter asked.

"Where are those places?" Kennedy snapped back, as Johnson contained his admiration with a just barely suppressed smile.

Posing with their wives for pictures with Texas newspapermen who had flown with Johnson from Kansas City, where he had attended a luncheon meeting with Harry Truman, the candidates offered an arresting contrast: Johnson's folksy guile, mellow and misleadingly prosy, juxtaposed with Kennedy's restrained matinee-idol boyishness.

Asked if he had a message for his thousands of admirers, Johnson drew a roar of delighted laughter from newsmen and a wide tolerant grin from his running mate when he drawled: "Bless them! Stand fast, and do just as I tell you." Then Johnson's entourage left for Otis and a flight to Nashville, where Johnson was scheduled to deliver a political speech.

The most affecting of the continuing list of visits by dignitaries making their postconvention *hadj* to Hyannis Port at the behest of the Democratic nominee, was the once-postponed appearance of Adlai Stevenson, twice a candidate himself and the only man, some said, who would have stood a chance against Kennedy at the convention, had he only chosen not to wait so long to declare his candidacy.

Balding and paunchy, Stevenson made the greatest effort to manage the meeting with grace and a light touch, radiating goodwill as well as an indefinable aura of pathos. The two met first at Kennedy's house, then later on board the *Marlin* cruising Nantucket Sound. Stevenson was presented at a news conference at Kennedy's back lawn on a warm Sunday afternoon.

"How we can live in this world without surrendering to the communist world, and how we can survive with freedom and justice

without war," was the issue Stevenson articulated with ringing elo-
quence. "Our country has been put to sleep. It has been made to
ignore the perils of these times."

Kennedy, standing silently close by nodded agreement when
Stevenson said, "What we must insist upon is a powerful military
establishment with greater consolidation and cohesion of the Western Alliance."

He had not been "pressured" to support Kennedy, Stevenson said.
"I have asked for nothing. I expect nothing," he announced in his
musical and lilting voice. "I shall serve if asked and shall do what I
am asked to do with all the energy I can give Senator Kennedy and
Senator Johnson," Stevenson added, promising that he would campaign on the West Coast and East Coast "and probably elsewhere in
between."

Of his own following, Stevenson said, "I haven't much doubt that
they will support the ticket."

Had he given Kennedy any advice on how to run his campaign? a
reporter asked. Stevenson sent the reporter a look of reproach.

"I think Jack knows enough to run his own campaign," he said
dryly.

"I like this notion of campaigning from a boat," he observed close
to the end of the press conference. "I'm the most relaxed man in the
North."

But it was all too evident, however, that Stevenson was not relaxed.
Next to Kennedy, so confident and coolly self-possessed, there was
something breakable and vulnerable about Stevenson that made
reporters somewhat uneasy in his presence and prone to treat him
with a gentleness due an elder statesman whose political sun was
being eclipsed by a more powerful light.

The reporters' ill ease was not entirely lost on Stevenson. When
the mild, somewhat perfunctory questions petered out, Stevenson
took note somewhat wistfully that "Senator Kennedy has softened
you all up." When he smiled it was a soft, hurt smile as he stood
alongside his host, who had with impeccable manners and consideration directed the afternoon's spotlight to be trained on Stevenson, an
attractive exhibition of modesty.

Kennedy was silent most of the half-hour, making only one brief
contribution:

Of his conference with Stevenson Kennedy said, "We discussed mostly foreign affairs, and where and how Stevenson could work for the victory in the fall." Stevenson would continue on the foreign-policy advisory committee chaired by Archibald Cox of Harvard, but Kennedy pointed out that "Stevenson will report directly to me."

After the news conference Kennedy led his guest to a huge crowd waiting at the front fence, where both went on a hand-shaking tour over the railing. "They pick one of his lilacs and you know he will get their vote," Stevenson observed, paying a pretty, if botanically impossible, compliment, for lilacs do not bloom on Cape Cod in midsummer.

Life in Hyannis, according to the Barnstable *Patriot*, had "calmed down somewhat, a week after the triumphant return of Jack Kennedy." The bunting that bedecked the Hyannis Inn Motel, streaked by rain and almost in tatters from high winds, was removed. The huge "Welcome Home" banner across Main Street (a loosened corner had been temporarily anchored to a parking meter in front of Woolworth's to prevent its whipping about too violently) had been torn from end to end and was finally taken down. The smaller welcoming signs distributed by the Hyannis Board of Trade, much in demand among souvenir hunters, had long disappeared from shop windows.

As Hyannis was returning to normal after a record-breaking influx of tourists, Hyannis Port was preparing to mount the first assault in its battle to preserve its way of life, which had been completely overturned by an unprecedented invasion of outsiders.

Jack Kennedy took time out from briefings on international affairs, conferences with distinguished guests, press confrontations and campaign planning to discuss by telephone the Hyannis Port Civic Association's intention of submitting to the Barnstable selectmen a petition protesting the tourist traffic that had overwhelmed the summer village since his return. Kennedy pledged his full cooperation in any action the Association recommended that would solve the problem, "short of moving out of Hyannis Port."

At the meeting held that Saturday under the Association's auspices at the primly circumspect New England-style Union Chapel and attended by more than three hundred residents, members and their guests, Hyannis Port made known its disapproval of "an intrusion of tourists and curious persons." The visitors accounted for a flow of traffic estimated by police at up to three thousand cars a day and, in the Association's view, were endangering the lives of children.

Drafting an appeal to selectmen of the Town of Barnstable to establish police-manned barricades at both entrances to Hyannis Port and to keep out unnecessary traffic—only residents, their guests and necessary tradesmen could gain entrance—the Association's chairman pointed out that, "In the not unlikely event Jack is elected President we're going to have the same problems for four or eight years, and I think it's not too soon to decide how we're going to handle it."

The "protest meeting," however, was in the circumspect pattern of Hyannis Port. There was no impassioned oratory—that was reserved for private discussion. Members of the audience exhibited a laudably restrained attitude, in marked contrast to some earlier meetings on less important subjects. "No one wanted to knock a presidential candidate," an observer remembered. "So after all the hullaballoo, what the protest meeting came down to was: 'Isn't the traffic awful?'"

Anti-Kennedy feelings, not uncommon in the Port since the days when Joseph P. Kennedy had written *I'm for Roosevelt* and read proofs in the midst of F.D.R.-hating Republicans, was kept at a subliminal level. The target for the members' potshots was the tourist: a frequently heedless, rude and aggressive type, who scattered his orange peels over impeccable privet and trampled beds of portulaca, stridently insistent on his prerogatives as a sightseer to take the full tour which now, dismayingly, included Hyannis Port on his itinerary.

Not all Hyannis Port, however, reflected the Association's view. One resident noted of the tourists: "Sure they're a nuisance; but the circumstances are pretty extraordinary after all. Everything'll calm down after a while. I can't see what the big fuss is all about."

Although resentment simmered—the most glaring evidence was a significant and obvious blossoming of Nixon-Lodge bumper stickers —widely circulated reports that his neighbors could be expected to repudiate Jack Kennedy's candidacy were not borne out by the results of an amateur but thorough opinion-sampling of the village undertaken by a Hyannis Port college boy whom "everybody talked to." The survey virtually paralleled the close percentages that were tallied throughout the country on Election Day.

Meanwhile, the Barnstable selectmen were making short work of the Association's petition; they returned it with a blunt rejection of the barricades proposal. Such restricted travel, they pointed out, was illegal, and, even if it were not, enforcement would offer enormous problems.

While Hyannis Port residents were insisting that tourist turmoil did indeed exist, pointing to the need for continued rigid policing even after Kennedy's departure, the Association's chairman announced from his Boston office that a meeting of the directors of the Civic Association would be held the following weekend: "Even under normal conditions in summer, traffic at Hyannis Port is heavy, especially around the pier. The situation these past two weeks and more poses a trying and unprecedented problem."

For all its privately expressed militancy, the Association relinquished its crusade easily enough. ("What else could they do?" a resident observed. "Move out of Hyannis Port? Nobody wanted to do that.") At its meeting the board of directors, "satisfied that everything legally possible is being done to cope with the situation" by town officials and police and somewhat docilely accepting the selectmen's tart letter of dismissal as having "presented their position fairly," decided to take no further action.

Hyannis Port's copyright on exclusiveness and privacy lapsed. The Port had become, thanks to Jack Kennedy, part of the public domain.

The controversy swirling about the village had no effect whatever on the continuing procession of national dignitaries proceeding to Hyannis Port, including David J. McDonald, silver-haired president of United States Steel Workers of America.

McDonald not only would support Kennedy "with every bit of power I can possibly muster" but also predicted that the majority of the more than 1 million members of his union would endorse Kennedy at their September convention.

Requesting the conference with McDonald because "I was concerned with the fact that steel production at this time is only 53 percent of capacity," Kennedy followed it with a discussion of plans to win the northern New England states with Bernard Boutin, Mayor of Laconia and a candidate for Governor of New Hampshire. That afternoon Kennedy conferred aboard the *Marlin* with Chester Bowles, who spoke of what he called Eisenhower's "warmed-over foreign policy which had failed in Africa, Europe, Asia and the Caribbean."

At the following afternoon's press conference, Kennedy supplemented an earlier attack on the administration's farm program by five Midwestern governors and three senators. Reading from a prepared text, Kennedy charged that Nixon was trying to "disassociate himself from a disastrous farm program he himself had helped formulate," adding that "in February of this year, Nixon hailed Secretary of Agriculture Benson as the greatest Secretary in our country's history."

Telling of a five-minute telephone conversation during which former President Harry Truman had been "very generous, cordial and kind to me and anxious to work to get a Democratic administration back into the White House," Kennedy announced that he was sending Governor Abraham Ribicoff, who would "continue to work closely with me . . . as counselor, supporter and friend"—to Independence, Missouri, to confer with the former President. Kennedy hoped to visit Truman himself later in August when he was to attend a Midwestern farm conference in Des Moines.

G. Mennen Williams appeared next at Hyannis Port. Particularly unhappy at the choice of Johnson as running mate, the tall, good-looking Michigan governor, wearing the floppy polka-dotted bow tie that had become his trademark, had come close to bolting the Kennedy-Johnson camp. His Hyannis Port visit, expected not only to make clear his role in the campaign but also to heal any remaining postconvention scars, offered testimony to Kennedy's powers of persuasion. After their conference Williams, who had thought a Midwesterner—possibly himself—would have made a better running mate, announced himself "content with the Kennedy-Johnson ticket" and expressed his complete satisfaction that Johnson was committed to the platform articulated at the convention in Los Angeles.

Walter P. Reuther, President of the United Auto Workers, followed Williams to Hyannis Port. "Senator Kennedy hasn't had to buy labor's support, he has earned it," Reuther said, commenting on Nixon's charge that Kennedy was paying for his labor support by making pre-election promises. He would work enthusiastically to elect the Kennedy-Johnson ticket in November, Reuther said, certain that all American labor would support the ticket.

During their hour-long conference, Reuther somewhat ceremoniously presented Kennedy with a memorandum on unemployment and other labor problems, a memorandum Kennedy told newsmen at a later press conference he hoped Reuther had sent a copy of to Nixon. "Most of the information was contained in a letter I sent to Eisenhower on June 23rd," Reuther said, adding that little could be done "at this late date to convert Mr. Nixon."

Ohio's cherubic and baleful governor, Michael V. DiSalle came next. Named to head an informal steering committee whose function was not specified, DiSalle predicted that Ohio would support the Democratic ticket. At the same time, Kennedy announced that he was "extremely pleased" that Governor Robert Meyner of New Jersey had consented to direct his campaign in that state. Then the candidate revealed the formation of a civil-rights section for the campaign, in which "Negroes will be integrated into every phase of the campaign," rather than working only on the "Negro vote." The committee was to be headed by Washington attorney Mrs. Marjorie Lawson, general counsel for the National Council of Negro Women and a participant in the October 1959 "brain trust" meeting at Hyannis Port.

Governor Herschel Loveless' arrival at Hyannis Port—he was named chairman of a "Farmers for Kennedy and Johnson Committee"—prompted speculation that he would be named Secretary of Agriculture if Kennedy was elected.

"I am running for a seat in the Senate," Loveless said, "and I expect to be working hard at that post for the next six years." [10]

Early Friday morning Kennedy was driven to Barnstable Municipal Airport in Hyannis. Only a few spectators and the omnipresent working press were on hand in the lightly falling rain to see the candidate take off on the maiden voyage of his newly delivered private plane Caroline. A sleekly refurbished twin-engine Convair, its interior like an executive suite in beige and pale green with separate quarters where Kennedy could work in comfort behind a large desk or watch television, the plane cost $15,000 a month to operate and was staffed by two pilots and a secretary-stewardess previously employed by Kennedy's father, who had advanced him $270,000 to buy the plane from Frederick B. Ayer and Associates of New York.

He left for New York, where he was taken directly to a packed Overseas Press Club to address editors and publishers of foreign-language newspapers in the United States. Then Kennedy lunched at the new Time-Life Building with editors of the Luce publications and met privately with West Germany's Secretary of State.

At the Kennedy family's Park Avenue apartment, the candidate met with Michael H. Prendergast, Democratic State Chairman; Tammany Hall boss Carmine de Sapio, and Representative Charles A. Buckley, veteran Bronx Democratic leader. These three men were targets of a group of reform Democrats headed by Eleanor Roosevelt,* Thomas K. Finletter and former Senator Herbert H. Lehman, who spoke with Kennedy on the telephone during his hectic one-day trip to New York.

His takeoff from La Guardia was delayed nearly an hour, and the plane, carrying Mr. and Mrs. Morton Downey, Governor G. Mennen Williams, Pierre Salinger and a pool of newsmen who had made the New York trip with the candidate, landed at Hyannis shortly before 9:00 to be greeted by Jacqueline, Caroline and an overexcited crowd of more than one thousand people.

By now Kennedy's tour of the fence was a tradition eagerly anticipated by the crowd in back of the barrier. But the fascination was mutual, for Kennedy seemed as stirred and eager for such closeness as did those who cheered him. His "fence walks" never smacked of the kind of lord-of-the-manor gesture a "star" would have made, granting a few crumbs of proximity to his fans. Kennedy's tendency toward crowds appeared to be an impulse prompted by genuine curiosity and appreciation of those who shouted their support and approval of him. The crowd, on its part, sensed his identification in the way he always looked at individual faces as he passed, a significant departure from the usual politician's general, point-blank response, best exemplified by the famed "Irish switch" artfully performed by Honey Fitz. If Kennedy sometimes referred in private to his constituents as a "they" of puzzling ambiguity, his face-to-face confrontations with crowds at the airport fence were clearly occasions of mutual satisfaction.

The following morning a delegation of Mid-Cape Junior Chamber of Commerce members called at the Irving Avenue house to present Jack Kennedy with an honorary membership in the United States

* In mid-August, Kennedy went personally to Hyde Park to seek support from F.D.R.'s 75-year-old widow, who had made no secret of her preference for Stevenson and had offered at the same time considerable resistance to Kennedy's candidacy.
"I asked for her help," Kennedy reported, "and she said she would help."

Chamber of Commerce, the Massachusetts Junior Chamber of Commerce and the Mid-Cape Junior Chamber of Commerce "in recognition of his distinguished public service."

Thanking the delegation, Kennedy commended the work the organization was doing locally and throughout the country; he then greeted Senator Stuart Symington and his wife, who would accompany him to Washington late Sunday evening.

On Sunday morning Kennedy attended mass at St. Francis Xavier, then led a caravan of cameramen to his grandmother's small summer house on Lighthouse Lane in Hyannis, to keep an earlier promise that he would allow photographs to be taken during one of his weekly, after-mass visits with the 95-year-old widow of Honey Fitz.

In a flower-print dress, the old woman seemed a little flustered by the crowd of newsmen packed into her modest living room. "What shall I do?" she said to her grandson.

"Just look at me, grandma," Kennedy said gently, taking her hand.

"How many photographers are there?" she said, squinting behind thick glasses.

"Quite a few," Kennedy said, "some taking still pictures and some taking movies."

When a series of flashbulbs abruptly exploded, startling her, she said, "All right boys, that should be enough."

Consenting to pose for "just a few more," she turned her gaze upon her grandson, patted his arm and smiling sweetly at him said, "You're the next president."

Asked if she would walk outside for a moment so that movie men could take pictures because the light inside the house was too dim, the 95-year-old great-grandmother balked. "I don't want to go outside," she said firmly.

Kennedy turned to cameramen and asked, if his grandmother stood in the doorway with him, would there be enough light? When they agreed, Kennedy applied gentle and skillful persuasion until the old woman somewhat hesitantly granted his request. He led her to the front doorway and they posed together, Kennedy directing his grandmother to look at him and smile.

While the cameras ground, she turned to her grandson, kissed him on the cheek and said: "God bless you. I know you'll win."

At noon Kennedy held his last press conference before leaving for

Washington; he announced the appointment of Symington as chairman of a committee to prepare a report of recommendations for streamlining the Defense Department.

"I'm honored and happy to have been appointed to make the report for the next president of the United States," said Symington.

Arriving at the Hyannis airport enroute to Washington, Kennedy was greeted by a crowd of 2,500 people outside the fence. In a brief ceremony the Cape Cod Democratic regional committee and Barnstable's Democratic town committee presented Kennedy with a gold plaque whose inscription read: "Good luck and Godspeed to you, Senator John F. Kennedy—Barnstable Democratic Town Committee, August 7, 1960."

Kennedy thanked the committee and all those who had come to the airport to see him off: "Come what may in November, I'll always be a Cape Codder," he said, "and will come back here as often as possible."

He looked magnificently tanned and fit, although he was still suffering from a throat infection he had brought back from Los Angeles. (During the coming session of Congress, the ailment reduced him to passing notes to his colleagues, despite medication and the efforts of a speech therapist * to guarantee his voice during the miles of campaign oratory in the months ahead.)

Mounting the stairway toward the open portal of *Caroline*, Kennedy, as was his custom, turned for one last wave to the crowd before the big plane roared down the runway and disappeared in the night sky, ending a two-week "vacation" that had depleted the energies of a large force of reporters and photographers—as well as titillating the less professional sensibilities of the throngs attracted to Cape Cod by the nominee's presence there.

Hyannis Port gratefully relinquished its front-page position, although a flood of tourists continued to cram its narrow avenues after Jack Kennedy's departure.

Kennedy's press headquarters on Main Street shut down,[11] a "vacancy" sign temporarily appeared as the Hyannis Inn Motel returned

---

* The professor of voice and speech at Boston University's School of Fine and Applied Arts also would travel with the nominee on campaign trips, in hopes of preserving the candidate's voice. "It's all a matter of breathing," the voice coach, a lifelong Republican who had "switched," said, adding that Kennedy had to use his voice as a singer would, "breathing from the diaphragm and taking care with his timing."

to its previous tourist preoccupations and "Kennedy for President" headquarters, located in a small, crumbling bungalow close by the former press center, was besieged by volunteers willing to devote part of their summer vacations to Kennedy's cause.

"People automatically associate us with the Kennedy headquarters," Robert O'Neil, chairman of Kennedy's local committee, acknowledged. Requests for campaign literature and advice on policy were coming from all over the country, from people who preferred to accomplish their business through Kennedy's "home town" office. Kennedy's busy Cape Cod headquarters did a thriving business in PT-109 tie bars selling for $1; but it dispensed small Kennedy buttons free. Although its staff did not conduct an organized fund-raising drive as such, it announced that contributions "have been and will continue to be accepted."

Nine

Wearing the olive-drab overseas cap emblematic of a post commander, signifying his past leadership of the veterans of Foreign Wars post named in honor of his brother, Jack Kennedy made a triumphant, if belated,[1] entrance at the VFW national convention in Detroit, where delegates accorded him a standing ovation.

Challenging Nixon's claims of continued American leadership in military and other fields as "an appeal to voters' complacency," Kennedy branded his opponent's optimism as "the siren call of false contentment," and from the same rostrum where Nixon himself had earlier addressed the convention, called for a larger defense buildup in answer to Khrushchev's missile flexing.

After a short return visit to Hyannis Port for a "quiet weekend," Kennedy made a stop in Boston, where he canceled an appearance at a planned fund-raising luncheon in favor of an airport meeting with Massachusetts politicians supporting his candidacy. He then flew to Washington for the Senate roll call on his medicare bill, as the "shirttail" session of Congress came to an end. (An alliance of Republicans and Southern Democrats—plus the threat of a presidential veto—blocked the bill and also Kennedy's minimum-wage proposals.)

"Enough Kennedys are doing the talking," Joseph P. Kennedy said bluntly, arriving in Boston en route to Hyannis Port. Asked if he was keeping in touch with his son's campaign, the former Ambassador brought a smile to reporters' faces when he answered, "I read about it in the newspapers," flatly refusing other comment.

A week later Cape Cod withstood the assault of mid-September hurricane Donna, which set beach cottages awash in Falmouth and Woods Hole, put out electric power temporarily in Hyannis and caused minor flooding before its winds broke over the Atlantic.

Jacqueline Kennedy returned to Hyannis Port in October to hostess a "TV listening party" similar to those being held across the country, part of a program initiated by the Democratic National Committee on the occasion of the first of the televised Kennedy-Nixon debates.

Dressed in a salmon-pink maternity dress, Jacqueline sat on the edge of her chair directly in front of a seventeen-inch, leatherette-covered portable television set hired for the standard $10 weekly fee from a Hyannis rental service.

Despite her surface calm, Jacqueline was admittedly "terribly nervous." She smiled slightly when her husband appeared at the program's start.

The partisan crowd of about thirty New England Democratic Party officials, friends and selected members of the press gathered in her living room applauded whenever Jack Kennedy finished a portion of his debate but listened attentively when Nixon spoke.

"I think everybody who watched profited by the debate," Jacqueline said at the program's end. "It was a wonderful opportunity for some Americans to participate in politics." The issues had been brought out well, Jacqueline thought; and her husband had been "brilliant."

Then the telephone rang. The room quieted while Jacqueline took the long-distance call in an adjacent room. Pressed for details, she admitted only, "We were both concerned about each other," adding, "The rest is privileged between husband and wife."

Jacqueline spent the remainder of the week in a chilly Hyannis Port veiled with fog, awaiting the arrival of her husband, who followed a tour of upper New York State with a trip from Syracuse to Cape Cod for the weekend.

While a quarter-million Republicans were greeting Nixon prior to a huge fund-raising dinner in Boston's Armory, Chet Huntley and David Brinkley were in Hyannis Port taping a one-hour interview with Jack Kennedy.

Despite an intermittent drizzle and a raw wind heavy with dampness coming up from the fog-shrouded harbor, the candidate and his wife took long walks beside the deserted beach, observing a monochromatically beautiful seascape.

Hyannis Port was still and austere, the trees stripped of leaves by the hurricane. But the quiet was welcome. There were no tourists clamoring at the gate, no prowling souvenir seekers, no civic associations bristling as each out-of-state license plate hove into view. Only a few year-rounders were in residence, and they kept their curiosity, if they had any left, well disciplined.

Even the press left the Kennedys pretty much alone. They concentrated their attention on complaints at how cold the off-season Yachtsman Hotel was, an ungracious way to repay hospitality that the management had frantically arranged; it had provided eighty rooms for the Kennedy entourage on two days' notice. (An appeal to Barnstable High School for several ambitious students willing to earn after-school dollars had provided temporary bellhops.)

Only one incident marred Kennedy's last vacation before the election: Nixon-Lodge stickers appeared on the stockade fence and were distributed on press cars parked about Kennedy's house. Some automobiles had pictures of Nixon pasted on the insides of the windshields, where his face could stare at drivers.

Just before leaving for Chicago, Kennedy emerged from his private plane with a large rag doll that he had received as a gift from Syracuse supporters and a vivid multicolored Sioux headdress, which he had declined to try on during an earlier midwest tour; both items were intended for Caroline, who had accompanied her mother to the airport to see him off.

The news that Kennedy planned to spend election night at Hyannis Port was not received in a spirit of unanimous celebration: "Word now has it that Kennedy plans to spend Election Night at Hyannis Port," the Barnstable *Patriot* reported. "This will mean an invasion of about 500 reporters, photographers and television men. Whatever happened to our nice, quiet Indian Summer season when Cape Codders could relax and enjoy themselves?"

In early October the good intentions of Barnstable "Kennedy for President forces" to register voters created confusion, amusement and, in some instances, indignation. Some five hundred postcards were mailed to already-registered residents of the Village of Barnstable, some of whom, the town clerk learned by telephone, had been voting for more than fifty years.

While the committee was laying plans for the final weeks of the campaign (plans that included participation in the nation-wide "call to victory" drive slated for the last 24 hours before the polls opened) and assigning workers in the town's eight precincts to arrange transportation to voting places on Election Day, widespread speculation that Kennedy would make his Irving Avenue home unofficial headquarters during the formation of his government was verified by one of his campaign aides. The aide announced that, if elected, Kennedy was likely to spend almost all his time before inauguration on Cape Cod and not to go south as previously announced.

Then Hyannis braced for election night. The major pre-election activity focused on the Armory on South Street, which Kennedy advance men (reportedly allocated only $800 by an insolvent Democratic National Committee) had persuaded hesitant National Guard officials to make available as an election night press-communications center. Although officials agreed to remove a large antiaircraft gun customarily kept in the building's main hall and canceled regular drill schedules, they adamantly refused to allow anyone to drill holes or drive nails in the new building, where Western Union was already installing hundreds of special long-distance lines and fifty teletypewriters. Twenty-five circuits wired into the Armory were to be manned by more than a dozen operators. During Kennedy's two-week vacation eight Western Union transmitters had been able to carry the load: some 125,000 words per week. On election night, however, that figure was expected to triple.

Altogether 125 telephone lines were installed, providing two hundred special telephones for newsmen and the radio and television staff; one small room alone contained 68 telephones in myriad pastel colors scattered over three long tables. In the off-season, a force of twenty operators was normally on duty at Hyannis' exchange, but this complement was quadrupled during the time that the Armory press headquarters was operational—and additional telephone personnel were kept on standby.

United Press International set up two wirephoto transmitters, one at the Armory, another at the servants' bungalow directly behind the Kennedy houses in Hyannis Port. Associated Press planned to operate four such machines. All major television and radio networks were mounting elaborate facilities in the Armory for transmission of election-night coverage.

A local television dealer was persuaded to lend a dozen sets for use in the Armory (one Hyannis dealer had flatly refused, another had begged off because "his stock was low"); television sets for use in the Kennedy houses were rented.

Mid-Cape Ford, on Hyannis' West Main Street, agreed to lend a number of automobiles to Kennedy's staff; local resources were pre-

vailed upon to supply carpenters and lumber for the temporary platform that would receive the candidate, as well as press-booth partitions and other structures. Chalk indicators were drawn on the
Armory floor by advance men supervising the establishment of press
accommodations, which included a "sack-out" room in the Armory's
basement target range, where a row of cots was provided for reporters
who wanted to nap without leaving the premises.

Folding chairs and benches were borrowed from local Protestant
churches (none was available from St. Francis Xavier), as advance men
went about collecting whatever accommodations were available off-
season from Hyannis' inns and motels. They assigned rooms to more
than 250 correspondents, including those from *France Soir, Le
Monde,* London's *Daily Telegraph,* the Toronto *Globe and Mail* and
newspapers in Japan, Germany and the Union of South Africa, as
well as to members of the national press who had not had the fore-
sight to seek advance reservations. (By election morning, late arrivals
were forced to take accommodations up to ten miles from the
Armory, as motel owners hung out "no vacancy" signs for the first
time in November.) Most of Kennedy's staff and the press train that
had attended him during the campaign were put up at the Yachtsman
Hotel.

In the midst of furious pre-election night activity, Joseph P.
Kennedy arrived at Hyannis Port, where a complex communications
system rivaling that in the Armory was being installed at the home of
his son Bobby.

Maintaining a stubborn silence toward disappointed reporters who
had hoped for relaxation of his strict self-censorship, the former
Ambassador took Caroline horseback riding at an Osterville farm the
afternoon before Election Day, refusing to make any comment.

That same day a large advertisement, sponsored by "Independents
for Kennedy" appeared in the Cape Cod *Standard-Times:* "For
Dynamic Leadership in the 1960s Give Jack Kennedy Your Vote
(Cape Cod's Own Candidate)."

As Election Day grew close, preparations for the "biggest night in
the town of Barnstable's 321 years" were announced by Hyannis'
police chief, who was canceling all days off in anticipation of the
"biggest crowd this or any other Cape town has ever seen" on Election Day. "I expect people will be coming here by carloads and busses
as far away as Boston, Brockton and Fall River," he said. "My entire

force of 30 regulars and 40 auxiliary police will be on duty . . . and I have enlisted the help of some of our neighboring police departments and the State Police."

Security measures called for no parking on either side of South Street immediately adjacent to the Armory. The one-day closing off of both Scudder and Irving Avenues in Hyannis Port would not be absolute; year-round residents living within the area would be allowed to reach their homes, along with those people "with proper credentials" and emergency equipment. Police were to be stationed outside the candidate's house, polling places, the Armory, the airport and "other strategic points."

By Monday Hyannis' normally composed late-autumn air began to taste of a generally well-contained pre-election excitement. As bunting blossomed at isolated outposts in Hyannis—the Yachtsman Hotel hung a large "Welcome Jack" sign on its front door—a campaign launched to decorate the whole of Main Street in honor of Kennedy's homecoming ran into strong resistance.

Robert O'Neil, Chairman of Barnstable's Democratic town committee, unofficially ventured a prediction that as many as thirty thousand people would be at the airport to greet Jack Kennedy on election morning and the crowd could swell to 50,000 during that day and night. He confessed that "the number of people who will flock here . . . is anybody's guess. But the number could be a great deal larger than the estimated 20,000 who crowded Hyannis when Kennedy flew in July 17 following his nomination."

Although final plans were still incomplete, Kennedy was to be officially greeted at the airport by Cape Cod's Democratic regional committee. Then, it was expected, a motorcade would escort him through Main Street to his house in Hyannis Port.

Meanwhile, Jack Kennedy was ending his campaign with a rally in Boston that was "the warmest, and the most satisfying in all the miles and in all the states" that he had visited since the September beginning of his campaign tour. It was also the rowdiest and the most undisciplined.

Windows in the limousine in which Kennedy was riding were cracked by a crowd surging to get closer to him, preventing his entrance into Boston Garden for more than half an hour. Inside, the Garden was bedlam. The wheelchair bearing Boston's paralyzed Mayor John Collins was jerked from police hands, and, for a moment, it appeared that he would be hurtled into the center of the jostling mob and trampled by the impatient celebrants, many of whom who had taken seats in the Garden at 3:00 that afternoon. Despite a vast contingent of Boston police, the unruly chanting crowd was almost out of control by the time Kennedy appeared at 10:00, producing a clamorous and "near terrifying" demonstration and a fifteen-minute ovation.

Giving a précis of every issue that he had touched on during his campaign, Kennedy told his cheering Garden audience: "Of all the great issues whose ultimate resolution may depend on tomorrow's choice, none is more important, or more urgent than the issue of peace—whether in the '60s the world will move closer to a secure peace in which freedom can flourish, or whether we will drift."

Kennedy dialed the first telephone call inaugurating his "call to victory" drive, expected to reach more than 2.5 million voters before the polls opened, and spoke briefly with a 74-year-old woman in San Francisco.

Then he left the Garden to make the final speech of his campaign: a televised address from Boston's "cradle of American liberty," Faneuil Hall, which Kennedy said "reminds us of how far we have gone and what we must do in the future."

"I now cease to be a candidate," Kennedy announced. "I'm now a voter."

In Hyannis Port, Jacqueline rose very early on Election Day to be driven to Boston, where she met her husband.

A crowd of about three hundred people had gathered at the West End branch public library, a former Congregational church built in 1737, the polling place for Ward 3, Precinct 6, where in the building's basement, Jacqueline voted first. Her husband spoke briefly to her before she entered the booth. She took fifteen seconds to vote. Giving his address to the clerk as 122 Bowdoin Street, Kennedy followed his wife into the booth and took twice as long—sparking later speculation that he had split his vote.

As he emerged from the booth, Kennedy told reporters in attendance, "I am very hopeful." Then he was driven to Logan International Airport for the ten-minute flight to Hyannis.

Kennedy's mood aboard the plane was mercurial, alternating between ebullience—he teased Salinger about "being out of a job"—and taut, preoccupied silence. By the time the plane touched down, he was tense and edgy, anxious to reach his Hyannis Port house without further ceremonials. Although he was originally to arrive at Hyannis at 11:00 A.M. to be greeted by local Democrats, Kennedy's schedule was changed because, it was alleged, Jacqueline was not feeling well and the candidate was concerned and anxious to get her back to Hyannis Port.

Preceded by two planeloads of the press and about eighty members of his staff, Kennedy's *Caroline* rolled to a stop at approximately 8:30 A.M., to be cheered by a group nearly outnumbered by massive police protection: roughly 150 police to control a crowd of about 250 spectators.

Although it contained nowhere near the twenty thousand people that had been expected, the crowd was vocally enthusiastic nonetheless. A large banner reading "Welcome Home, President Jack" was borne by a dozen young ladies, students from Cape Cod Secretarial School.

If the local Democratic welcoming committee was dismayed and embarrassed at so poor a showing on such an historic occasion it was only because it had allowed partisanship to overrule good sense. It was no secret that many Cape Codders were finding it difficult to identify Jack Kennedy as a "home town" candidate on the basis of his seasonal residence. Prejudice against "summer people," coupled with the Cape's vintage Republicanism, was a formidable obstacle. And few members of Hyannis' winter population possessed either the leisure or the inclination to stand in the cold at the airport as crowds of idle summer vacationers were wont to do. The anticipated invasion of off-Cape traffic equal to Hyannis' seasonal population had not materialized.

The size of the crowd, however, hardly seemed to matter to the candidate. Kennedy's response to the welcome was perfunctory. His smile was half-hearted and strained. Posing with Jacqueline for photographers at the airport's apron, he looked tired, his face puffy with fatigue. Squinting against the bright cold sunlight seemed to deepen unsuspected lines in his perpetually young-looking face. And, though he walked with the same long brisk stride as always, advancing to say a few words into radio and sound-film microphones, some watchers detected a limp.

Drawn aside by Jacques Lowe, his official campaign photographer, to be reminded of a promise that he had made to pose with all the permanent cameramen who had accompanied him on the campaign and wanted a souvenir group of pictures of themselves with the candidate, Kennedy said, in a voice ragged with exasperation, "All right, let's do it right now."

Then he made his way toward the airport's double doors. Apprised of the Democratic town committee's motorcade plans, Kennedy turned the idea down flat and walked through the airport's lobby, hailing a car driven by his cousin, Ann Gargan, and asking her to drive Jacqueline and himself to Hyannis Port.

Preceded by two automobiles carrying news photographers and escorted by a dozen state troopers on motorcycles, Kennedy's car swept around the rotary onto Route 28, bypassing Main Street in Hyannis, only partly decorated in anticipation of his arrival.

En route, Kennedy snapped off an order to his police escort to separate the automobiles bearing the press from his car. Then, turning onto Bearse's Way and passing the Memorial Skating Center named for his brother, his car swung onto North Street and around the West End rotary to Scudder Avenue, rapidly making its way to Hyannis Port, where only a straggle of well-wishes watched for the candidate at his Irving Avenue house, which was surrounded by a cordon of police.

The Port was serene and nearly deserted, basking complacently in a cold bright sun. One sailboat flaunted its white canvas against the cold blue sky above Hyannis Port's harbor, and an indefatigable foursome plied the greens at the golf club on Sunset Hill.

After breakfasting at his father's house with nine members of his family—during the next hours all the others would be reunited at Hyannis Port—Kennedy walked across the lawn to his own house and emerged moments later in a heavy topcoat to take a place on his back porch, huddled against the sharp wind sweeping across Nantucket Sound.

Joined by an aide, Kennedy spoke of the long hours of waiting that lay ahead of him, bemused by the knowledge that, for the remainder of this day, he would have, for the first time in months, nothing to do.

A small chartered plane spluttered into view overhead, circling as it descended toward the house, slipping within two hundred feet of the porch before photographers trained their cameras on the closely wrapped and squinting candidate, who partly raised his hand in greeting.

Remembering a sack of toys that he had accumulated for Caroline during his campaign travels and then forgotten on the plane, Kennedy dispatched a messenger to retrieve them from the Convair parked at Hyannis' airport. One gift in particular, "a little stuffed pony," was certain to delight Caroline.

A horseshoe of red roses ten feet tall, with a looped red moiré ribbon on which elaborately scrolled gold letters spelled out "Good Luck," was delivered by a policeman. The card accompanying the tribute had been misplaced during its transfer at the police barrier. Kennedy's eyes flickered with startled amusement as the policeman held out the floral display for his examination; one thin wrought iron leg, part of a tripod arrangement allowing the bouquet to stand free, dangled in the wind.

"Just leave it," Kennedy said.

Then Joseph P. Kennedy approached from across the lawn. His son at once stood up and went to meet him halfway. Bent close together father and son spoke quietly but animatedly for a moment. Jack Kennedy received a reassuring squeeze on the arm before, exchanging smiles, they separated.

A little before noon, a delegation of photographers arrived at the candidate's house for a scheduled formal picture-taking session. Immediately Kennedy's change of humor was evident. No longer the easy, ever-cooperative model who performed before the camera with professional aplomb, he was restless, balky and tense during the quarter-hour he allowed.

Afterward, Kennedy appeared on his patio escorting Caroline by the hand for a walk. Finding his brothers tossing a football back and forth on his father's vast lawn, he signaled for the ball. Catching it gracefully, he cocked his arm back, sent off a pass to Ted, then retrieved the ball again and, as Caroline watched, repeated the maneuver several times before returning to his house. He entered through a warm kitchen redolent with the aromas of apple brown betty and baking ham, to lunch alone with Jacqueline.

After lunch, he crossed the lawn dressed in a sweater over a sport shirt, tan slacks and loafers for his first visit to the "command post" established at his brother Bobby's house.

Crossing the large living room, the candidate looked into the sun porch connected by glass-paneled doors with the dining room, where a telephone central had been established in a T-formation arrangement of long tables. Fourteen women were stationed at telephones linked with Democratic headquarters across the country; each headquarters had been given a special Hyannis Port telephone number in order to report directly how some ninety key districts were voting.

At the head of the table stood Kenneth O'Donnell, Larry O'Brien and, from time to time, Bobby Kennedy himself, evaluating telephoned information that had been immediately transferred to mimeographed blanks before processing and analysis by Lou Harris, an opinion-polltaker and statistician who had worked throughout Kennedy's campaign.

Harris was ensconced in a second-floor pink and white child's bedroom entirely cleared of furniture, except for tot-sized chairs stacked in one corner, poring over reports at a desk littered with telegrams, notes and dispatches taken from teletypes in the hallway outside by Peter Lawford. In an adjacent bedroom Ted Kennedy and Stephen Smith commanded a battery of telephones from a table untidy with election documentation and facing a portable television set. A paint-by-number clown was framed against the wall.

At midafternoon—after a quick visit to his father's house—Jack Kennedy returned home for a nap. The day's election-watch activity accelerated at Bobby's house with the arrival of additional staff members, campaign workers and other members of the Kennedy family. The servants' bungalow behind Joseph P. Kennedy's house was already occupied by a selected group of the press, including representatives from *Life*, gathered about a rented portable television and watching the first desultory returns from obscure villages. They ate dainty cream-cheese-and-olive sandwiches and fortified themselves periodically from a private liquor supply.

As darkness fell and chilling cold descended with the sun, Jack Kennedy rose from his nap to revisit the communications center in his brother's sun porch.

Looking in past Ethel Kennedy's dining room, where two electric typewriters and a calculator rested on the sideboard and four telephones and a large-screen television set created a further tangle of wires over the rug, the candidate startled two employees of the Mayflower Catering Service. They were already preparing a buffet consistent with the known Kennedy family penchant for "simple food," including tuna-, chicken-, lobster- and egg-salad sandwiches and an assortment of petit fours, éclairs and turnovers. A large urn of coffee was periodically replenished throughout the night by deliveries from the Mayflower Restaurant on Hyannis' Main Street.

Jack Kennedy spoke directly by telephone with John Bailey in Hartford, his close adviser and skilled political tactician, who asked, "Who's this?" Kennedy replied, "Who do you think it is?" Bailey had good news to report. Early Connecticut results, taken from malfunctioning voting machines prematurely opened for inspection and repair, indicated a Kennedy sweep.

After jubilantly stopping off at his father's house to relay the news of Bailey's prediction, Kennedy returned to his own house to watch the slow progress of the election on a rented portable television set in his own sitting room. Then, restlessly, he retraced his steps to Bobby's house, passing into the glare of floodlights from mobile television units posted outside his house. (Cameramen were admonished not to take any unauthorized pictures of the candidate's back-and-forth lawn crossings until specific permission was granted.)

When Kennedy returned to his brother's house shortly after 7:00 P.M., however, he found a tenser mood prevailing. First summary totals calculated by Associated Press showed Nixon leading 203,628 to 166,963.

Hunched over the communications center's head table reviewing data handed him by the girls manning telephones, Bobby Kennedy grimly took note: "We're being clobbered!" His brother mounted the stairs to the second floor bedroom to pay a call on Lou Harris, who informed him that Kansas was going for Nixon by a large margin. (As early as 4:00 P.M. Harris had been able to analyze more than 17 percent of the election's returns from that state, where Nixon was running as well or better than Eisenhower had in 1956. Other farm states, Kennedy was told, could be expected to follow Kansas' lead.

Then at 7:15 a bulletin flashed from CBS: The network's IBM console computer, after analyzing previous voting habits of some five hundred preselected precincts located throughout the country, was giving odds on Nixon's victory at 100 to 1, predicting that he would win the election by 450 electoral votes.

Kennedy absorbed the news calmly enough, flatly declaring that the computer was "nuts," a view his father shared when the candidate spoke with him a half-hour later. Then, with a grin, Kennedy challenged Harris to prove the IBM computer wrong.

Asked to comment on the progress of the voting that election night Joseph P. Kennedy continued to maintain his official silence. "I am home with my family and I think on this night I deserve to be with them alone," he scolded. "I want to watch the returns just like all Americans."

The expected good news from Connecticut was shouted up the stairs by Bobby's excited voice. Bailey had just telephoned with a prediction of a more than sixty thousand-vote majority, as results from that state poured in. A second telephone call a few moments later predicted a margin of one hundred thousand.

Gloom had pervaded the Armory in Hyannis after the news of Nixon's predicted victory flashed from CBS. More than two hundred members of the press, many of whom had accompanied Kennedy on his campaign and were unashamedly partisan, wandered aimlessly about the cluttered, smoky, crowded main hall. They sampled doughnuts and coffee at a snack bar that the National Guard had installed or sipped tonic water from the Mayflower Catering Service's more bountiful buffet, while a maze of television cameras, telephones and typewriters stood idle, awaiting more dramatic news than that provided by Pierre Salinger's infrequent bulletins on what Kennedy was doing at Hyannis Port.

Around 8:00 the Armory was electrified by CBS' announcement that its computer was switching sides and now predicted that Kennedy would win by a scant 51 percent of the ballots cast. As the tide of victory seemed to be turning in their favor, reporters covering Kennedy—luckier than those assigned to Nixon's election-night camp —were further cheered by a message from Eunice. "He thought the returns from Connecticut were fantastic," she said, reporting that her brother was smoking "a big cigar and was in a very good mood." She told the press in the servants' bungalow behind her father's house that "Jack jumped with joy when he heard" the Connecticut vote tallied.

While Kennedy's majority mounted, reporters followed with keen interest the arrival of a heavy-set man with a dour, disapproving expression. He mounted the bunting-draped platform and proceeded to jounce heavily on it, testing the unsteady-looking structure, apparently unconvinced that it could support the weight of a full president-elect's party made up of the populous Kennedy clan. Other plainclothesmen peered behind partitions, pennants and the drooping monk's cloth hung behind the platform.

A telephone call from Lyndon Johnson brought Jack Kennedy to an upstairs bedroom at his brother's house for a private dialogue with his running mate, who reported, "I heard *you're* losing Ohio, but *we're* doing fine in Pennsylvania." Johnson's "joker" hit a nerve, for Ohio was the source of the only bitterness that Kennedy was to express during the night's long election watch. Rolling up a shirt sleeve, he bared a right hand and lower arm swollen, scratched and callused from handshaking.

"Ohio did this to me," Kennedy said, recalling the six campaign trips he'd made through Ohio. Then, replacing the sleeve, Kennedy turned his attention back to the television set, switching channels whenever local results interrupted national coverage.

The mood of growing elation in Bobby Kennedy's living room was further enhanced by the appearance there of Mrs. Rose Kennedy. Morton Downey, a guest of Joseph P. Kennedy, passed trays of sandwiches and pastries from the buffet among the crowd of casually dressed men and women happily and avidly following the returns on the large television set in a corner. Peter Lawford, in black stocking feet, thirsty from running up and down the stairs to tear sheets from news tickers, asked a waitress from the caterers if she had anything "stronger" than coffee.

Kennedy returned to his own house to bid Caroline goodnight, holding her on his lap before sending her upstairs. He then settled down in his own living room for a preprandial daiquiri with Jacqueline and their guest, artist William Walton, who had relinquished his atelier for the campaign trails on Jack Kennedy's behalf during the Wisconsin, West Virginia and California primary fights.

In the large formal white dining room furnished with antiques— where no radio or television marred the quiet—dinner was served promptly at eight. The merit of the nautical painting on the wall beside a Riviera landscape Kennedy himself had painted was the major topic of dinner conversation. Then Kennedy returned to his living room and turned on the portable television set for further election results. While he watched, members of his campaign team arrived periodically to bring information from the communications center across the lawn.

Around 10:30, when a landslide seemed inevitable, Jacqueline turned to her husband, who was pensively watching the screen, and said, "Oh, Bunny, you're president now."

"No," Kennedy replied firmly. Without taking his eyes from the set, he added, "It's too early yet."

But reporters at the Armory shared Jacqueline's certainty that it was all over but the conceding. Television scoreboards showed Kennedy ahead by 1.5 million votes; he had 241 electoral votes out of 269 required for election. At 11:00 chairs were arranged on the platform in anticipation of the victorious arrival of a candidate, who, rumor had it, would arrive immediately following Nixon's imminent concession.

At 11:30 Jacqueline retired for the night. Then Kennedy crossed the lawn to await the final outcome of the election at the communications center itself, arriving at his brother's house to find that his majority had reached 2 million and was still climbing. Early returns from California suggested that Kennedy would carry Nixon's home state as well.

With victory in sight, an infectious spirit of gaiety gripped the command post. Ted's wife Joan was animatedly trying to collect an election bet from "a Republican friend" on the telephone, and even Bobby Kennedy, who had stubbornly resisted all premature optimism, looked happy and relaxed for the first time since returns had first been broadcast.

In an upstairs bedroom Ethel Kennedy, clad in brightly patterned wool slacks, was being greeted by members of the press brought over from the servant's quarters.

"Are you happy?" a reporter asked her.

"Sure I am," Ethel said. "It's terrific!"

As photographers focused their cameras on Eunice, she turned to her actor brother-in-law and teased, "Show me how to pose like they do in Hollywood, Peter." When Lawford pulled a face, everyone laughed.

As National Guard officials circulating amid the turmoil in the Armory's high-vaulted main hall fretted at the untidy floor, the mood was jubilant. Photographers were measuring the platform with light meters, choosing in advance the likeliest positions in the event that Salinger announced a Kennedy appearance. Reporters rolled copy paper into their typewriters, mentally composing lead paragraphs for the victory stories that they would shortly be dispatching to their newspapers.

"The state cops told me the motorcade's forming right this minute outside the house," a misinformed local reporter said, as news quickly circulated that advance men had already slipped away to bring Kennedy to the Armory to make a statement.

Having granted to Jack Kennedy better than a 2 million lead, the ballot counting began to show a new trend. Earlier results had been recorded from Kennedy strongholds in the Northeast, swelling the totals disproportionately. Now ballots were pouring in from the Midwest and the Far West, reflecting traditional Republican strength.

The gay party atmosphere at Hyannis Port's communications center faltered, quieted, then fled, as apprehensive glances were fixed on television sets. At the busy telephone central, Bobby, observing his brother's steadily dwindling lead said, "We aren't losing, but we aren't winning, either."

The candidate occasionally paced, holding a small white writing tablet and a paperback book; he seemed hardly ruffled by the reversal that was steadily diminishing his margin. Removing a tweed sportscoat lined with golden horseheads (the living room had grown very warm), Kennedy stood in neatly pressed white shirt, loosened tie and slacks, frequently escaping the televised returns for reassuring visits to Lou Harris' room upstairs.

At 1:00 A.M. a monitored message of congratulations emanating from Washington and signaled over the special Western Union wire sent Pierre Salinger to a telephone to verify the message with James Hagerty, Eisenhower's press secretary, who admitted that the premature release of the President's telegram had been a "mistake."

The incident, however, triggered a ripple of elation at the command post, for it was a possible indicator that Ike could have advance information that made him think Nixon would soon concede. At the same time Salinger petitioned Kennedy on behalf of the Armory press for at least a token appearance there. Despite the decline of his popular vote, Kennedy was adding to his total of electoral votes. With 262, he needed only 7 more to achieve the required 269.

As if to verify the speculation that Eisenhower's prematurely released telegram had precipitated, the television screen became a scene of uproar and confusion as cameras zeroed in on a clamorous press-room scene at the Ambassador Hotel in Los Angeles, where, it was announced, Nixon would be arriving at any moment to make a statement.

The living room grew quiet with expectancy. Kennedy, hunched forward in concentration before the television set, with a partly eaten chicken-salad sandwich in his hand, watched intently as the uproar temporarily subsided and a news commentator took over, suggesting that a concession by Nixon could be forthcoming. "Is there any milk in the house?" Kennedy asked. Before anyone could answer he had left the room and returned from the kitchen to report: "There's no milk left. Just beer."

A further delay followed as announcers stalled for time, awaiting Nixon's appearance. Then the screen switched back to a renewal of state-by-state election totals but was abruptly interrupted by a return to the Ambassador Hotel, where, at 3:30 A.M., Nixon appeared on camera accompanied by his wife Pat barely holding back her tears.

"I am sure that many are listening here who are his supporters . . . are supporting Mr . . . uh . . . Senator Kennedy," Nixon began over the noise of the crowd. "I know, too, that he probably is listening to his program," Nixon went on. "And while the . . . and I . . . please. *Please!* Just a minute!" Nixon was interrupted by shouts of "We Want Nixon," cheers and applause.

Although he struggled to smile, Nixon looked harried, rattled and on the verge of losing his temper. "Just a minute," he said. When the crowd subsided, he went on: "As I look at the board here . . . while there are still some results to come in, if the present trend continues, Mr . . . uh . . . Senator Kennedy will be . . . the next President of the United States . . ." the rest was lost in the engulfing sound of protesting voices crying out "No! No!" superseded by another defiantly fervent "We Want Nixon" as the cameras followed his retreat from the scene.

Those gathered in Bobby Kennedy's living room were stunned. After waiting for Nixon to concede, they felt a frustrating letdown. Nixon's maddeningly vague speech seemed to have been willfully calculated to tantalize, to withhold the expected victory needlessly.

Jack Kennedy was unruffled, however, almost light-hearted, at Nixon's announcement, in contrast to the bitterly expressed disappointment of his partisans.

"Why should he concede?" Kennedy said. "*I* wouldn't."

To Salinger's reiterated plea for a Kennedy appearance at the Armory to balance Nixon's, Kennedy replied, "You want me to go down into *that*." He gestured at the television set still lingering on the scene at Los Angeles and refused at the same time to comply with an out-of-town newspaper's request for a photograph of him holding a front page headlined "Kennedy!"

"Nothing doing," Kennedy said, recalling the Chicago *Tribune*'s disastrous gun-jumping in 1948. He was going to bed, Kennedy announced. They should all go home to bed, he added.

Salinger's announcement at 4:00 A.M. that Kennedy would not appear to make a statement "until a more definite victory is evident" was greeted by groans of disappointment from those who had waited for Kennedy outside the Armory through the cold night; some had stood near the Armory's double doors for more than nine hours.

Most newsmen packed up their equipment and left the Armory at once. Almost all the police chose to stay, after spending the evening and early morning with little to do.

"The job's only begun," one commented, "Wait until tomorrow."

Before leaving his brother's house, Jack Kennedy summoned all present to the living room: campaign workers, the girls who had manned telephones on the sun porch, newsmen and policemen stationed outside the Kennedy houses, who had called at Bobby's back door for periodically warming mugs of coffee. Kennedy tendered his thanks, then went about the room shaking hands.

One waitress said, "Congratulations, Mr. President," when Kennedy took her hand.

"It's a little early for that," Kennedy said, smiling tiredly. "But thank you anyway."

Kennedy stopped off at his father's house, then walked across the lawn to his own house, where a light had been left on at the back door. After waking Jacqueline to inform her that the election's results so far appeared to indicate that he had won—although he could not be certain until morning—Kennedy read quietly until 4:30.

At Bobby's house, newsmen and staff members filed into a waiting bus that would deliver them to the Yachtsman Hotel in Hyannis, leaving behind only Bobby, personally telephoning precincts for spot checks. The chattering teletypes continued their unsupervised clatter, and two employees from the Mayflower Catering Service in wrinkled white uniforms retrieved plates, cups and saucers; dismantled the coffee urn, and emptied heaped ashtrays in the shambles of a party's aftermath.

Shortly before six the first gray streaks of chill dawn broke over Nantucket Sound. The steady slap of water against the Hyannis Port breakwater was clearly audible when the caterer's station wagon was checked out at a cordon point manned by police, recently joined by secret service men.

At 5:30 A.M. Burrell Peterson, a guest at the Holiday Hearth Motel on West Yarmouth's garish Route 28, received instructions from Washington to establish security at Hyannis Port while television monitors were ceding Michigan's twenty electoral votes unofficially to Kennedy, giving him a tentative total of 285. A separate delegation was dispatched to secure the Armory.

Wednesday morning was cold but clear. Sunshine was pouring through the vacant sun porch's windows when Ethel Kennedy served ham, eggs, rolls and coffee to eleven guests—"The maids are all out," she explained. Breakfast was followed by a brisk walk in the bracing sea-charged air. Apparently indefatigable, Bobby carried a football during the walk, but no one else felt like playing.

At Jack Kennedy's house all was quiet. A temporary cook was bustling in the kitchen when Ted Sorensen arrived at 9:30, to be invited upstairs where the candidate was sitting sleepily on the edge of his bed in wrinkled white pajamas. Sorensen immediately reported that California had been won. Kennedy was President. Shortly afterward Pierre Salinger arrived, confirming Sorensen's news. During the brief conference that followed, however, all agreed that, even though the election was won, it was still too early for Kennedy to claim the victory publicly.

When they left, Kennedy went to a bedroom window, waving to an aide standing in his driveway and a knot of cameramen congregated on the lawn.

He had breakfast with Jacqueline and Caroline, who earlier had gone horseback riding on her Irish pony with her grandfather. Prompted by Jacqueline, the child greeted her father, "Good morning, Mr. President."

Life was stirring at the Armory. A straggle of returning newsmen arrived in time to receive word that Kennedy's scheduled 10:00 A.M. appearance had been canceled. Although he led a United Press

International compilation in both popular and electoral votes, Kennedy would have nothing to say, according to Salinger, until Nixon officially conceded the election. There was no Nixon statement until 9:00 A.M. Pacific Time—noon in Hyannis. At 10:00 EST the only word from Nixon's press secretary Herb Klein was that the GOP candidate was still "sizing up the situation."

An hour later the platform in the Armory was checked again. Then two carpenters appeared, to pound nails, in the hope of reinforcing the temporary structure's rickety stairway.

Outside, more than one hundred state and Barnstable police were keeping the ever-increasing crowd in check, a crowd that had been considerably swelled by school children released by the principal of Hyannis' Junior High School for the occasion. Other Cape schools remained open, however. Efforts by town Democrats to borrow Barnstable High School's marching band to provide a musical fanfare for Kennedy's expected Armory arrival had been dropped as "too complicated." (Although no morning ceremonials were planned by a Democratic town committee chastened by the previous day's aborted motorcade, a "victory parade" was held that evening. It was not well attended by local supporters and campaign workers, who were too exhausted from the election night's vigil to participate.)

After breakfast Kennedy brought Caroline out of doors and lifted her to his shoulders for a piggy-back ride on the lawn. Then, hand in hand, they headed for the beach for a walk, inviting Teddy to join them. Other members of the Kennedy family and Ted Sorensen appeared, taking places in a processional that crossed the dune grass adjacent to the sand to face a chilly wind blowing off the Sound, as secret servicemen followed at a discreet distance.

After the walk the group assembled on the steps of Joseph P. Kennedy's house, where a campaign aid tried to puzzle out Kennedy's defeat in Wisconsin before the group returned to Bobby's house. Pierre Salinger was waiting to inform the candidate that James Hagerty had advised him that congratulations were on their way from President Eisenhower. Nixon's formal concession could be expected at any moment.

The television set in Bobby's living room was turned on. It was expected that at any moment either Minnesota or Illinois would add the decisive margin to Kennedy's total, still officially short of the required electoral votes.

The election continued to hang fire.

At noon Kennedy returned home for lunch. At a little past 12:30 he officially won Minnesota, clinching his election. Twelve minutes later Nixon conceded in a statement read by his press secretary Herbert Klein:

> I want to repeat through this wire the congratulations and best wishes I extended to you on TV last night. I know that you will have the united support of all Americans as you lead the nation in the cause of peace and freedom in the next four years.

Afterward Kennedy crossed the lawn in the same sports clothes he had worn the previous evening for a meeting with his staff at Bobby's house. "When Jack came into the room he was no longer Jack," an aide said. "He was President of the United States. We all stood up—even his brother Bobby. It was just an instinctive thing."

"All right," Kennedy said. "Let's go."

Salinger finally had an announcement for the news reporters who had waited through the long previous night. Announcing that Jack Kennedy would meet the press at approximately 1:45 P.M., he gave out Kennedy's draft reply to Nixon's telegram:

> Your sincere good wishes are gratefully accepted. You are to be congratulated on a fine race. I know that the nation can continue to count on your unswerving loyalty in whatever efforts you undertake and that you and I can maintain our long-standing cordial relations in the years ahead.

At the Irving Avenue house, Jacqueline seemed somewhat dazed as congratulations were pressed upon her. Donning a raincoat and flat-heeled walking shoes and winding a scarf around her hair, she went for a solitary walk along the beach, while other members of the Kennedy family were urged to change clothes for a formal victory picture to be taken in Joseph P. Kennedy's living room, where Jack Kennedy had received the private congratulations of his parents.

Returning to his own house to change, Kennedy asked, "Where's Jackie?" He then went down to the beach to get her.

All members of the Kennedy family were in their places when Jacqueline arrived on the porch of her father-in-law's house. When the President-Elect escorted her inside, the assembled family burst into applause, a spontaneous expression of their own pent-up feelings.

After the picture-taking, the motorcade began to form outside Joseph P. Kennedy's big white house; all members of the family climbed into automobiles, except for the former Ambassador himself. He had, that morning, expressed his intention not to attend the ceremony at the Armory.

With the motorcade nearly under way and his son insistent on his presence, Joseph P. Kennedy at the last minute allowed himself to be persuaded. As he joined the motorcade, a further delay was caused by the Kennedy family's long-time chauffeur. He had expected to drive the next President of the United States on the historic trip to the Armory but was prevented from doing so by secret servicemen, who allowed only their own men to drive the President. Kennedy's intervention on behalf of the chauffeur was without avail. He was driven by a secret serviceman. The chauffeur followed in the next car, with Mr. and Mrs. Joseph P. Kennedy as his passengers.

Not until the procession neared the Armory was there any mass welcome. Beaming, Kennedy stepped from his limousine to acknowledge the cheers of a crowd of about three thousand standing outside the Armory and spilling across the street in front of the dark red brick of Hyannis' former normal school and maritime academy—now Cape Cod Community College.

Somewhat grim and pale, Joseph P. Kennedy made his first public appearance since before the announcement of his son's presidential candidacy, preceding the President-Elect into the Armory with his wife through a narrow passageway lined solidly on both sides by state and local police.

Then came Jacqueline, who seemed radiantly happy, followed by the President-Elect (accorded a deafening burst of applause by reporters), smiling broadly as he slowly made his way through the narrow aisle, shaking hands that reached out but favoring his swollen right hand. Bobby and Ethel were last in the entourage, stopping on their way to the platform to exchange greetings with well-wishers and friends in the audience.

After mounting the crude, squeaking stairs (Joseph P. Kennedy had taken care to grip the hand railing, mistrustful of the carpentry), the Kennedy family assembled in a row to face the audience, which responded with a renewed burst of applause. "I felt an emormous sense of pride," Robert O'Neil said. "Not only for Jack Kennedy, but for his family, too."

To the many year-rounders in that audience the sight of the Kennedy family arrayed on that platform brought to mind other associations that recalled afternoons when Jack Kennedy, a member of a barefoot and dungareed group, had lightheartedly roamed Hyannis' Main Street before taking his place with his brothers and sisters on the curbstone in front of a Hyannis jewelry shop to await the chauffeur-driven car that would take him back to Hyannis Port. There were also memories of a seventeen-year-old Jack Kennedy returning camera and film purchased the day before because he had forgotten his own camera in Florida and, according to his father, he could jolly well do without a camera all summer long if he were going to be so careless of his belongings.

Some in that audience had been dance partners at the Wianno Club. Others had handed him ice-cream cones across a marble-topped fountain or raced their boats in Hyannis Port's harbor against the *Victura* and *Flash II*.

When the applause subsided, Kennedy stepped to the microphone to read the text of Nixon's telegram and his own reply. Then he read President Eisenhower's telegram of congratulations:

> My congratulations to you for the victory you have won at the polls. I will be sending you promptly a more comprehensive telegram suggesting certain measures that may commend themselves to you as you prepare to take over the responsibility of the presidency next January.

"And I have sent him the following wire," Kennedy said:

> I am grateful for your warm and good wishes. I look forward to working with you in the near future. The whole country is hopeful that your long experience in the service of the country can be drawn upon in the years to come. With every good wish, signed John Kennedy

Then Kennedy addressed the Armory audience and a long row of grinding television cameras stationed on high ramps above the spectators.

> May I say in addition, to all citizens of this country, Democratic, independent, Republican, regardless of how they may have voted, that it is a satisfying moment to me and I want to express my appreciation to all of them and to Mr. Nixon personally.

I particularly want to thank all those who worked so long and so hard in my campaign and who were generous to me in my visits throughout the country and who were generous enough to support me in the election yesterday.

To all Americans I say that the next four years are going to be difficult and challenging years for us all. The election may have been a close one, but I think there is general agreement by all of our citizens that a supreme national effort will be needed in the years ahead to move this country safely through the 1960s.

I ask your help in this effort and I can assure you that every degree of mind and spirit that I possess will be devoted to the long-range interests of the United States and to the cause of freedom around the world.

So now, my wife and I prepare for a new Administration and for a new baby. Thank you.

There was a smile—hesitant and boyishly disarming—and a roar of applause amid the glare of popping flashbulbs, but the most affecting moment was to come when, presenting members of his family to the audience, Jack Kennedy introduced his father.

Stepping forward the old but still vigorous-looking man confronted his son. Then their arms went around one another.

"You could feel the strength they were deriving from personal contact," said an eyewitness. The President-Elect had chosen not to conceal his feelings of filial pride and devotion, a rare public demonstration of emotion.

Despite the political differences Jack Kennedy was at pains to point out periodically—of his divergent views, to reassure members of his liberal following—the emotional bonds between father and son were very strong. "You can't really separate Jack's personality from his father's," a Hyannis Port neighbor observed.

Then Joseph P. Kennedy—evidently deeply moved by the public gesture—moved back to his place in line, as his son introduced the other members of his family.

The party descended from the platform and began inching its way out of the Armory, where another burst of cheering and applause greeted Kennedy before his motorcade made its way back to Hyannis Port for a bantering, boisterous luncheon celebration of victory, during which, with the full family Sorensen and William Walton present, "everyone got kind of choked up."

In the afternoon a rough touch-football game on the lawn, demonstrating the traditional family aggressiveness, was interrupted midway when Jack Kennedy trotted across the lawn to take part, quarter-backing a team opposing Bobby's. Secret servicemen on the dunes watched horrified as flailing players tangled and fell on the hard ground.

As he watched, from his veranda, such ritual exercises must have been cause for deep satisfaction to Joseph P. Kennedy, under whose direction the playing fields of Hyannis Port had been as instructive as those at Eton.

That evening the President-Elect and the future First Lady dined with William Walton and the Benjamin Bradlees, who, mostly in jest prompted by the celebratory occasion, suggested, "There's just one thing you should do—fire J. Edgar Hoover!" It was "much more important that you get Allen Dulles out of the CIA," Kennedy was told, because "he would be trying to carry on his dead brother's policies in your administration." *

Toward the dinner's end, Joseph P. Kennedy appeared, to invite his son and guests to a private screening of a double feature: *North to Alaska*, starring John Wayne and Fabian, and *Butterfield 8* with Elizabeth Taylor. Although Jack Kennedy was not in the mood he obliged his father nonetheless. *North to Alaska* was interrupted after twenty minutes; the start of *Butterfield 8* was observed briefly before Kennedy slipped out of his father's basement projection room and went home.

The next morning Kennedy and four of his top staff members conferred at Bobby's house, preparing a reply to Eisenhower's offer of a cooperative transition from one administration to the other.[2]

At that morning's press briefing, Salinger announced that he hoped to have Kennedy's reply to Eisenhower's wire later in the day, as well as an answer to a congratulatory cablegram from Nikita Khrushchev, which had been delivered to Hyannis Port in Russian and in which the Soviet Premier had expressed the hope that "relations between our countries will again follow the line along which they were developing in Franklin Roosevelt's time."

Referring to disarmament and a peace treaty with Germany as

---

* The next morning's newspapers announced that Kennedy "had requested that the directors of the FBI and the CIA remain in their posts.

"I, of course, am highly honored that President-Elect Kennedy has asked me to remain as director of the FBI," Hoover said.

"I am gratified," Dulles said, "that the President-Elect desires me to continue to serve."

major unresolved questions, Khrushchev pledged that his country was "ready to continue efforts to solve such pressing problems," stressing his conviction that "world peace depends largely on the state of Soviet-American relations." [3]

Canceling a press briefing scheduled for later that afternoon, Salinger announced that Jack Kennedy would hold his first press conference as President-Elect at the Armory the following day.

Looking rested and happy, Kennedy arrived at the Armory, shaking hands with the reporters he recognized before taking his place on the platform for a twenty-minute press conference.

"Mr. President, if you please, sir," a voice called out when Kennedy's opening remarks could not be heard by a reporter at the edge of the crowd gathered in the Armory. Kennedy flashed a pleased smile, then moved closer to the microphone.

Commenting on the narrowness of his victory—he had attained the White House by a majority of 112,881 votes—Kennedy admitted that such close election results might handicap the legislative programs he had outlined during his campaign:

> It was a close election, which I always thought it would be. I didn't know it was going to be quite as close as it turned out to be. But I knew from the beginning it would be a close, hard fight. There were many problems which were present for us during the campaign, but we finally emerged successful.

Kennedy then read the text of a telegram that he was sending to President Eisenhower,[4] before announcing the appointments of Kenneth O'Donnell of Worcester and Theodore Sorensen to serve him as special assistant and as special counsel respectively. At the same time, Kennedy announced that Pierre Salinger would be his press secretary —amid a burst of reporters' applause. For the first time in history a Negro, Andrew P. Hatcher of San Francisco, was named to serve as associate press secretary.

Kennedy was not ready, however, to announce his choices for Secretary of State or other Cabinet posts.

> I think it will be some time in the future after I have come back from a short rest. I will then be able to give you a definite time schedule, but I would make a general judgment that not before Thanksgiving will I have any public statement to make on appointments.

Asked if he planned to give Adlai Stevenson a major role in his administration, Kennedy answered, "I talked to Governor Stevenson Wednesday on the matter, and I would prefer to postpone until I come back the whole question of appointments and responsibilities."

To the suggestion advanced by Senator Mike Mansfield that Kennedy use Nixon's abilities in some assignment, Kennedy said: "I have not had a chance to talk to Nixon and I don't know what Senator Mansfield suggested. I hope to have a chance to see Nixon between now and January 20." He remarked that he would rather talk with Nixon before saying anything. "I don't know what he is planning to do," Kennedy added with a slight smile.

Asked what part, if any, his two brothers would play in his administration, Kennedy hedged. "I have not discussed it with either one of them," he said. "I have no idea what they're going to do. They're going to take vacations separate from me for a while," he said, smiling. "They are all going in different directions. I haven't talked to them about what they are going to do."

Kennedy had already tentatively broached the idea of the Cabinet post of Attorney General to his campaign manager, and Bobby had flatly refused. His inclination after the election, friends were told, was to separate himself from government service altogether, perhaps travel around the world and even write a book about what he saw. When Joseph P. Kennedy's powerful influence had finally convinced Bobby that he should accept the job, Jack Kennedy said, "We'll announce it at midnight so no one will notice."

Asked where he was going to establish his summer White House, Kennedy replied: "My summer home is here in Hyannis Port. We are going to stay here for a few days and then we are going away for a vacation. I am going to come back here with my family, if possible, for Thanksgiving."

Announcing his intention to resign his Senate seat some time before the end of the year, Kennedy stressed that the responsibility for filling the job was Governor Foster Furcolo's. "I hope to have a chance to talk with him about the matter," Kennedy said.[5]

Then a reporter asked Kennedy for a frank evaluation of his health, asking how much of a burden his back condition and his rumored case of Addison's disease would impose upon him in performing his duties as president. The question seemed the height of incongruity, for Kennedy looked remarkably fit and completely recovered from the stress and sleeplessness of the long election watch, whereas reporters gathered below the platform were haggard and red-eyed, their pallid indoor complexions testifying to their attendance at victory celebrations.

For the first time Kennedy reacted with something less than pleasure. Replying tartly that "I never had the matter to which you refer, Addison's disease," Kennedy pointed out that his back had cleared up in 1955, was no longer a problem and had not been one for some years.

Regarding his general health, he said: "It was fully explained in a press statement in the middle of July.[6] My health is excellent. I have been through a long campaign and my health is very good today."

He announced that he would fly with Jacqueline and Caroline to Palm Beach in two days and, the following week, would visit the Texas ranch of Vice President-Elect and Mrs. Johnson. Kennedy said that he would not be traveling much "because the job must be done in Washington, not on good will tours or conferences here and everywhere."

To United Press International's long-time White House correspondent, Merriman Smith, was given the honor of saying the traditional, "Thank you, Mr. President," signaling the end of the press conference.

Kennedy then walked across the stage, came down the steps and greeted reporters and photographers he recognized, to the dismay of secret servicemen attempting to escort him from the Armory for the return to Hyannis Port.

That evening at a reception for newsmen at his father's house (Joseph P. Kennedy absented himself), Kennedy agreed with his brother's observation that he could not have been elected without the help of the television debates. Asked how he preferred to be addressed, Kennedy said, "Maybe, until January, you should call me Senator." Then, he added, "Of course, those who know me call me Jack."

At Salinger's press briefing the next morning, a wide-ranging drive to recruit "the best brains in the country" for service in the United States government and a program designed to "prune out deadwood" were announced to be high on a list of Kennedy objectives. A concerted effort would be made to seek out only qualified people for specific offices, according to an aide, who said that Kennedy wanted "people who are willing to work all hours in order to get things done. He's not looking for 9 to 5 people."

The practice of "buying" ambassadorships or naming men to them for strictly political reasons—a practice some unkindly suggested had been responsible for F.D.R.'s appointment of Joseph P. Kennedy to an ambassadorship—was to be entirely dispensed with. Heavy campaign contributors had been warned that "they could contribute if they wanted to but that the money would not guarantee a job of any kind."

When he arrived at Barnstable Municipal Airport, attended by a large escort of police and directed by secret servicemen to drive directly onto the field, almost to the door of his plane, Kennedy reverted to his pre-election custom. He broke away from his protectors to stroll along the chain-link fence, shaking hands with a huge—by off-season standards—crowd of some 2,500 people, who had waited several hours in forty-degree weather to catch a glimpse of the departing President-Elect.

Bidding his son goodbye, Joseph P. Kennedy returned to Hyannis Port, as the other Kennedys scattered: Patricia and Eunice to New York on a Christmas-shopping trip, Jean and Stephen Smith to Washington, Ted and Joan to San Francisco and Peter Lawford to fulfill show business commitments in California. Only Bobby and Ethel remained at Hyannis Port with their parents, their vacation plans not revealed.

Hyannis Port's population dropped back to its normal early winter census of eighteen residents, although Barnstable police maintained surveillance, in anticipation of the heavy weekend traffic that near-perfect fall weather was expected to attract—visitors likely to drive through the summer home of the nation's President-Elect.

In Hyannis, where more than thirteen thousand telegrams of congratulations had been received in one 24-hour period, Victor Adams, Chairman of Barnstable's Board of Selectmen, issued a statement:

Senator Kennedy may vote in Boston, but his home is here.

He has brought great honor to the town of Barnstable and to Cape Cod in the just-concluded presidential campaign. His tremendous personality, his superior organization and his approach to world and domestic affairs, strongly reminiscent of FDR, proved a little too much for vice-president Nixon and the Republican Party.

Now in typical American fashion we must all close ranks behind the new president so that no one in the world may doubt that we are truly united.

President-elect Kennedy will shoulder responsibilities such as none save Eisenhower have ever assumed before. Only with the help of Almighty God and a united country can he lead humanity from the very threshold of self-destruction to peace and unprecedented prosperity which all the world can have if it is wise enough to choose the right road.

Television, radio and newspaper reporters deserted Hyannis, returning to big-city headquarters for other assignments. Communications experts and teams of workmen set about the task of dismantling installations at the National Guard armory, the Kennedy servants' bungalow and Bobby's house.

Most auxiliary policemen were released from duty. State troopers returned to their barracks, and Hyannis' chief of police praised as "orderly and well-mannered" a crowd that had admittedly been very much smaller than predicted.

Most year-round residents had watched Kennedy's acceptance speech at the Armory on television. Some had gathered at the television department of Sears Roebuck on North Street in Hyannis, just two blocks from the Armory itself. Many had followed returns into the early morning hours; the Tastee Tower of Pizza on Route 28 in West Yarmouth recorded an unprecedented demand for its wares during an election night in which Cape Cod had strongly resisted the lure of its "home town" candidate.

Although Kennedy carried Provincetown and lost Falmouth by fewer than one hundred votes, Nixon took all other Cape towns, most of them by lopsided margins.

The Town of Barnstable gave Kennedy 2,783 votes to Nixon's 4,515; Kennedy won only one Hyannis precinct, by a vote of 857 to 783. Hyannis South Precinct, including Hyannis Port, went for Nixon by 1,124 to 733 for Kennedy.

Cape-wide, the vote was 20,402 for Nixon compared with 12,423 for Kennedy, a poor showing considering Kennedy's senatorial triumph of 1958.

In its postelection editorial, "Comes the Dawn," the Barnstable *Patriot* best expressed the natives' view of Kennedy's election:

Despite the razor-thin popular majority vote, we expect to see young Mr. Kennedy inaugurated as the 35th president of the United States.

And we applaud the fine sportsmanship of the vice-president in combining his acknowledgment of defeat with congratulations to his opponent and his reminder to the rest of us that the election is over and that we must now close ranks. We note, too, the generous invitation of President Eisenhower to coach the replacement on what the score is at this writing.

President-elect Kennedy appears grateful for these considerations as well he ought to be. But for all the considerations that may be extended to him from any and all quarters, the clock ticks steadily on to the day when he will be on his own and will have to come up with some answers he failed to find in his campaign speeches.

It will soon be necessary, for example, for him to give serious thought to a method of financing his welfare projects for young and old, at home and abroad; of rebuilding the standing of the United States among its neighbors and restoring our ability to fill the hearts of potential enemies with terror, all within a balanced budget.

On better acquaintance with his new job, which President Eisenhower has made immediately possible, the president-elect is likely to discover that the United States is more highly regarded by its neighbors than he had thought, and definitely more feared by would-be obstreperous ones.

Even so, there are still his lavish pie in the sky promises to all and sundry and his pledges to labor of still greater freedom to whipsaw and hamstring the national economy and national defense. On these, the retiring administration cannot help him. The new president will have to decide for himself how far he can go and what he'd best forget . . .

Toward the end of November, Mr. and Mrs. Joseph P. Kennedy became grandparents for the eighteenth time. While horseback riding in Osterville, the former Ambassador said, "We're all very happy about it."

"I'm delighted," 95-year-old Mrs. John F. Fitzgerald said when she was told the news. "John Fitzgerald Kennedy, Jr., will be my thirtieth great-grandchild!"

As the year drew to a close, Hyannis Port's once-famed Gables Hotel fell victim to a wrecking crew's assault. Formerly the ultimate in summer swank, the resort was now considered "obsolete" by the village, which raised $75,000 by private subscription to buy the property.[7] The Swiss cottages annexed to the old hotel were to be remodeled and sold. Joseph P. Kennedy participated in the real-estate venture, in which he and his cosubscribers registered no profits: The subscription returned 78 cents for each dollar invested.

At a New Year's Eve party in Osterville, the suggestion that a champagne toast be dedicated to John F. Kennedy was dismissed as "ridiculous," precipitating a short-lived, but heated argument over the President-Elect's qualifications that came abruptly to an end just before the end of 1960, when all present were asked to join hands and sing "Auld Lang Syne."

Afterword

THREE PRESIDENTIAL SUMMERS

*"President Kennedy giving his acceptance speech
at the Armory in Hyannis constituted undoubtedly the most significant and dramatic historic
event ever to occur on Cape Cod. Nothing to
approach it is likely to happen again."*
        from Town of Barnstable Annual
        Reports for the Year 1960

Even as John F. Kennedy stepped from his plane at Barnstable
Airport on a rainy May evening in 1961—his first return to Cape Cod
since his inauguration as President—the ties that had bound him
since boyhood to Cape Cod were coming undone.

His election had brought "great honor and world-wide publicity"
to the place where his candidacy had been repudiated by a solid
margin. Those on Cape Cod who now sought belatedly to lay claim
to the success of a "local" had waited too long. The nation, succumb-
ing to the allure of a Kennedy style and deluged by publicity pouring
from newspapers and magazines, was already memorizing his growing
mythology.

As the site of the summer White House, Hyannis Port became
"internationally known." The thousands visiting the Port to view the
summer house of the candidate in 1960 had, in Barnstable selectmen's
view, "greatly disturbed the quiet tranquility of that little village.
We fear that last year's problems will be insignificant when compared to what will happen this summer when the President and his
family are in the Port."

While his blue presidential flag flew above them, Kennedy's neighbors were distributing amongst themselves small yellow windshield
stickers to facilitate passage to and from their own places of residence.

But those badges of identity were to prove pale shields against so overwhelming an invasion of outsiders.

The narrow shaded avenues, hospitable to the boy in dungarees, the young author of *Why England Slept* and later tolerant of the politician on-the-rise, could not accommodate the President of the United States. Even a security force made up of local and state police and secret service men stationed in small white clapboarded outposts at the compound's perimeter often seemed hard pressed to cope with the crush.

Kennedy's cruises on *Marlin* and the newly christened presidential yacht *Honey Fitz* were the occasions for conferences with advisers who shared chowder and hot-dog lunches on board and interrupted their councils for a swim or to watch the First Lady water-ski. The cruises were, as well, visited by a plague of water borne sightseers, held at bay only by Coast Guard and police patrol boats whose supervision of the busy waters of Nantucket Sound, if too zealous, brought sharp criticism of presidential bad manners.[1]

As early as October 1961, Kennedy was confessing that two successive weekends at Newport had provided "the best vacation I've had in a long time," providing more rest and relaxation than had been possible at Hyannis Port.

Spring 1962, saw the arrival of the first "reverse freedom rider," sent to Hyannis by white citizens councils of southern communities seeking to embarrass Kennedy's strong stand on civil rights. The long, 52-hour, one-way bus route had been traveled by more than 39 negro children and their parents who had been told that good jobs and housing awaited them on Cape Cod. The Barnstable *Patriot* protested that such a "fraudulent promotion" could be overcome at only one level, "from Washington itself."

> Until President Kennedy, who professes a deep and abiding love for Cape Cod, and his brother, the Attorney General who professes to be a champion of the Negro race, come out and make some effort in behalf of their professed loves, the Cape and its newest one-way guests are in the hapless position of being unable to solve the complex question of what to do next.

"To date," the *Patriot* concluded, "no word is forthcoming from either."

Accommodated temporarily in a vacant dormitory at Cape Cod

Community College, the refugees were removed to National Guard barracks at Otis Air Force Base until their relocation off-Cape.

That summer Kennedy moved to Morton Downey's house on more private and secluded Squaw Island. His growing restlessness was apparent from the frequent trips he took to Newport, and from such other excursions as his weekend spent on an island off the Maine Coast as the guest of former heavyweight champion Gene Tunney.

That autumn, Hyannis realtor James Woodward was requested to make an appraisal of the unpretentious, four bedroom, former summer White House on Irving Avenue and set its value at approximately $80,000. Rumors persisted that Kennedy intended selling the property to his sister Eunice.

By 1963, Kennedy's faithful summer presence at Hyannis Port had brought to Cape Cod "an influx of tourists which would be the answer to any Chamber of Commerce's dream." Yet, the Barnstable *Patriot* was more particularly concerned with what it believed to be the deterioration of Cape Cod's "image" during a time when it was "in the limelight as never before in its history."

The natural beauty of Cape Cod was being "marred and destroyed" in the wake of the boom attending Kennedy's well-advertised seasonal residency. After two summers of unprecedented prosperity, Cape Cod's commercial development had accelerated to a degree that promised to rejuvenate even Hyannis' run-down and traditionally rowdy West End. Here a new Queens Buyway was projected to rise from the debris of the old.*

John F. Kennedy passed his last summer on Cape Cod in a stranger's house, "Brambletyde," a rented weathered-shingle structure on Squaw Island with a spectacular view of Nantucket Sound. It was here Jacqueline awaited the birth of her baby while official arrangements for her confinement at Walter Reed Army Hospital in Washington were being made. A considerable controversy raged over the cost of renovating a former nurse's barracks at Otis Base Hospital to provide the First Lady a ten-room suite on an "if needed" emergency basis. Patrick Bouvier Kennedy was born five and a half weeks prematurely at these Otis facilities, developed a serious respiratory

---

* Renamed "Windmill Plaza," the new shopping area came nowhere near its former aspirations. Containing two beauty salons—one devoted exclusively to poodles—a real estate office, a "connoisseur" shop dealing in expensive knick-knackery, the plaza's major and most popular tenant was a branch of "Dunkin' Donuts" chain of franchised coffee and pastry shops.

ailment and died some 30 hours later at Children's Hospital in Boston.

Attending mass the morning after his son's burial in Brookline, Kennedy heard the pastor of St. Francis Xavier express the parish's sympathy. When Kennedy emerged from the church's side door, angry shouts of "Down in front" and a spatter of cheers and applause greeted him from a jostling crowd that insistently surged forward to get a better view.

Then came what for some of his local partisans was the inevitable Kennedy announcement: a 16-acre estate in Newport had been leased for the months of August and September of 1964. Despite assurances by Pierre Salinger that Kennedy would resume his summer weekends on Cape Cod in June, anything more than a summer transiency could not be expected. No house had been reserved for Kennedy's future tenancy at Hyannis Port.

In October, Kennedy returned to New England. He addressed a morning convocation at the University of Maine, watched the first half of the Harvard–Columbia football game at Cambridge, then visited his infant son's grave in Brookline.

That night Kennedy attended an "All New England Salute" held in his honor at Boston's Commonwealth Armory, the first of a projected series of fund-raising dinners designed to raise money to finance his 1964 campaign for re-election.

One member of that large audience who had paid $100 a plate to plead for Democratic unity in the forthcoming elections was Fred Caouette, a Hyannis painting contractor and paperhanger. Threading his way through the emptying tables at the evening's close, Caouette was stopped short of his goal and brusquely challenged by a secret service agent. Kennedy was at the head table autographing programs for the waitresses who had served the dinner.

Seeing Caouette, Kennedy called out, "Let the little guy through." Then, after Caouette was escorted to the platform, he said, "Freddy, it's awfully nice to see you," explaining to an aide that Caouette never failed to be on the corner of Oak Neck Road and Sea Street when Kennedy's motorcade passed en route to St. Francis Xavier. Then Kennedy added, before Caouette withdrew, "I'll see you next year."

The following morning Kennedy flew to Cape Cod, spending most of the afternoon with his father aboard the *Marlin* cruising the calm and nearly deserted waters of Lewis Bay.

When Kennedy's helicopter left the compound on Monday morning, his father was not at his customary place on the veranda to wave goodbye since the weather had turned sharply cold and rainy. But a small group of year-rounders, watching from a parking area atop Sunset Hill, had a clear view of Kennedy's craft as it lifted into the air above Hyannis Port. At Otis, Kennedy quickly mounted the stairway, sending an abbreviated backhanded wave to those few watching behind the barrier before ducking under the *Air Force One*'s open portal.

The plane's doors closed, the stairways marked "Welcome to Otis" were pulled aside, and the huge Boeing VC707 jet roared down the wet runway.

There was only a misty, fleeting glimpse of Cape Cod below, an island-like curve of land connected by two toy-like structures bridging the flat grey expanse of surrounding ocean.

It was a view of Cape Cod Kennedy had observed many times before—one he would never see again.

Plans for the Kennedy family's traditional Thanksgiving reunion at Hyannis Port were already well advanced—turkeys ordered from a local market, notice given that the President and members of his family would be arriving on Wednesday before the holiday. Arrangements for another family hockey game at the Joseph P. Kennedy, Jr., Memorial Skating Rink were being made on Friday, November 22. At 1:44 P.M. those tuned to radio station WOCB heard Wes Stidstone, program director, interrupt "Accent on Broadway" to read a bulletin just received from Dallas.

NOTES

PRELUDE: HYANNIS PORT

[1] This singularly inappropriate stucco and fieldstone structure of dim mock-Tudor inspiration was built in 1896 by wealthy Hyannis Port summer residents. Cape Codders regarded it at that time as an offense against the conglomerate, yet nicely consistent, New England village of white clapboard and gray weathered shingle—an apt example of the kind of alien culture that summer invaders could be expected to bring with them. The church weathered the severe hurricanes of 1938 and 1944, and time, together with natural elements, has contrived to erode much of the building's original exoticism. It now seems curiously indigenous and wedded to its setting as it rises on the crest of Sunset Hill, its streaked walls covered with twisted vines. Many distinguished clergymen have served the church in summer, notably the Reverend ZeBarney T. Philipps, former Chaplain of the U. S. Senate.

[2] The Indians believed that a crow had brought the first grain of corn to Cape Cod, and, although crows frequently robbed the fields, few Indians would kill them.

[3] Almost all the colonists were from the West of England and would have most likely sailed from Barnstaple, England, the most convenient port. They would have noticed the resemblance of the settlement's shore front and harbor to those of their port of origin. Historical records also show the name as "Barnestable" and "Bastable."

[4] Professions of Christian liberty and charity did not apparently extend to tolerance of the Quakers, who were much discriminated against in Massachusetts, including Cape Cod. The General Court ordered in 1655 that "no Quaker be entertained by any person or persons within this government under penalty of 5 pounds for every such default, or be whipped."

[5] It is from "Iyanough" that the names "Hyannis" and "Wianno" are derived. Early town records show such various spellings as "Yannos," "Iyanos," "Hyan-

nos," "Hyanus," "Yannis," "Hianna" and "Highannus." By the time of the Revolution, it had become "Hiannis." After 1800 all town records agree on "Hyannis."

PART ONE—CHAPTER 1

[1] By the fall of 1926, however, wholesale mortgage defaults and hurricanes had combined to drive land values in Florida to disastrous new lows. The boom had gone bust. A later editorial, "Keeping Cape Cod Cape Cod" in 1927 took a hastily reversed point of view: "Booms, like other abnormal things are rarely salutary, but steady growth is always reproductive.

"If fewer houses have been built this year on Cape Cod, those few are better than the houses of mushroom variety apt to spring up during a boom. The Cape's development during the past years has been sound and of such nature as to give the region increased prosperity without destroying its characteristic charm."

[2] For years, the sobriquet, "son-in-law of former Mayor of Boston," would invariably accompany Kennedy's name in New England newspapers until his own prominence in public life far outshone that of his father-in-law.

A consummate politician, whose frequent renditions of "Sweet Adeline" made him a nuisance and a legend of sorts in the gaudy, bare-knuckles political arenas of Boston's early 1900s, "Honey Fitz" could talk for hours on any subject, and "if he happened to know a little something about it, so much the better."

Said to have preferred another candidate for his daughter's hand—allegedly the engagement ring was presented to Rose Fitzgerald on a Boston sidewalk —"Honey Fitz" reluctantly blessed the marriage but during the early years made no secret of his disappointment.

Nonetheless, when his son-in-law's fortunes rose, he did not hesitate to take public credit for Kennedy's accomplishments. In 1926, when Kennedy purchased a film-producing company, the Boston *Post* headlined the story: "Fitzgerald a Film Magnate." Later paragraphs, although they correctly identified Kennedy as the actual owner, reported that his father-in-law was "actively interested" in film production.

[3] Joseph P. Kennedy was far more than a barkeeper's son in 1922. Graduated from Harvard in 1912 after attending Boston Latin School, one of the best preparatory schools in Massachusetts, he had succeeded, through borrowing and family connections, in gaining control of the Columbia Trust Company, a small independent neighborhood bank in East Boston. He had himself elected its president at the age of 25. By 1917 he was a trustee of the Massachusetts Electric Company, and during World War I, as assistant general manager of the huge Fore River Shipbuilding Corporation at Quincy, he supervised more than twenty thousand workers, coming into frequent contact—and conflict— with another young man on the rise, Assistant Secretary of the Navy Franklin Delano Roosevelt. After the war Kennedy joined the prestigious stock brokerage of Hayden, Stone, Inc., in Boston. Later, striking out on his own, he amassed the beginnings of a vast fortune by purchasing, with associates, a British-owned film-producing company, Film Book Office of America, Inc., and its distribution affiliate, Robertson-Cole Pictures Corporation, Inc.

[4] Kennedy was a good host. A teetotaler himself, he saw to it that the tenth reunion of his class at Harvard, held in Plymouth, wasn't a "dry" affair; he ar-

ranged to have liquor supplied for his classmates, as well as providing entertainment in the form of newsreel films of the Dempsey-Willard fight.

[5] *As We Remember Joe*, edited by John F. Kennedy, privately printed by the University Press, Cambridge, Massachusetts, in 1945. The volume contains tributes by Arthur Krock, Professor Harold J. Laski and Dr. Payson Wild, Jr., as well as by Honey Fitz, Kathleen Kennedy and Teddy Kennedy.

[6] Teddy recalled in *As We Remember Joe*: "We had our sails up just as the gun went for the start. This was the first race I had ever been in. We were going along very nicely until suddenly he told me to pull in the jib. I had no idea what he was talking about. He repeated the command again a little louder . . . Joe suddenly leaped up and grabbed the jib . . . and seized me by the pants and threw me into the cold water . . . then I felt his hand grab my shirt and he lifted me into the boat. On the way home from the pier he told me to be quiet about what had happened that afternoon."

CHAPTER 2

[1] Such residents as Judge Louis Brandeis at his summer home at Stage Harbor in Chatham resisted electrification for many more years. It was not until the late 1930s that the Supreme Court Justice could be convinced modern convenience would not interfere with his enjoyment of the simple joys of a rustic summer on unspoiled Cape Cod.

[2] The Town of Barnstable consists of Hyannis, Hyannis Port, Centerville, Osterville, Cotuit, Santuit, Marston Mills, West Barnstable, Cummaquid, Wianno and the Village of Barnstable. All of Cape Cod is encompassed by Barnstable County.

[3] Thomas E. Murphy was appointed Hyannis postmaster by Grover Cleveland in 1894 and served until 1898. He was to achieve local celebrity by becoming the first Democrat ever appointed to that post. Rigidly Republican Cape Codders were so outraged that some would not set foot in the Hyannis post office to transact such normal business as buying a postage stamp as long as Murphy held the job. "My father had three strikes against him in those days," the younger Murphy said. "He was a Democrat, he was a Catholic and he was Irish."

[4] During the summer of 1931, however, Honey Fitz played host to his "bitterest enemy" at a house he had rented on Hawthorne Avenue in Hyannis Port for the summer. Mayor Curley of Boston arrived at Lewis Bay aboard the yacht *Magician* and spent 24 hours as Honey Fitz's guest. Quite possibly politics was discussed.

[5] Both Wianno Junior and Wianno Senior boats were originated by the well-known Crosby Yacht Building and Storage Company of Osterville and were commissioned by the Wianno yacht club. Fourteen boats were built in 1913 alone. The boats are numbered from 1 to 137 (now being built); *Victura's* 94 was plainly visible on its mainsail. None of the Senior boats had ever been known to capsize. The cost today of a Wianno Senior is $5,400 without sails. A set of sails costs approximately $600. By 1933 *Tenovus*, a Wianno Junior, had been added to the Kennedy fleet, followed by *Onemore* in 1935. Two star-class boats, *Flash* and *Flash II* and a motor launch *Davilis* completed the inventory of Kennedy boats. The yacht *Marlin*, built in 1930 for Edsel Ford, was added many years later.

[6] The most famous among many stories involving Casa Madrid involves the

first and most notorious raid that occurred there on the evening of the day Massachusetts State troopers received their new uniforms. The club was known for its clever floor shows and entertainment, and the patrons at the club that evening, never having seen the new uniforms before thought that the troopers unannounced arrival, prefaced by the usual "this is a raid" warning, was part of the show and wildly applauded their entrance, to the momentary astonishment of the troopers. Regaining their aplomb, the troopers scooped up gambling implements and more than $7,400 from the gaming tables. It is alleged that Governor James Michael Curley was present that evening and was boosted over the wall by an understanding and obliging trooper.

[7] Kennedy, chosen at first for a seat on the SEC, refused to consider anything less than the chairmanship and finally won out. Although it was the commission's privilege to elect a chairman, Kennedy was appointed with the understanding that he would get the job. He had cherished the hope of being named Secretary of the Treasury. Instead, the Cabinet post went first to William Woodin and then to Henry Morgenthau, Jr. Deeply disappointed and never friendly with Morgenthau afterward, Kennedy nevertheless arranged for Morenthau to stay at the exclusive Wianno club during a vacation in June 1936. When Morgenthau applied for membership, he was refused, and Kennedy resigned his own membership, saying later: "I haven't been in the place since."

[8] When his summer neighbors in Hyannis Port decided to build a new beach house, Kennedy was approached and unhesitatingly wrote out a sizable donation. Later, when he was being shown blueprints of the proposed building's locker room, one of the project's organizers said, "Of course we won't allow children in there; it'll be strictly for adults."

"In that case," Kennedy said, angrily, "you'd better return my check. I don't want to put my money into a place where my kids or any kids aren't welcome." Plans were hastily revised so that children—Kennedy's and others—could use the locker room.

[9] James Roosevelt and his wife, the former Betsy Cushing of Boston, had been frequent guests at the Kennedy house in Hyannis Port in 1932, the year he purchased from the Crosby Boat Yards in Osterville, a Wianno-type sailing yacht christened *Half Moon*.

In the summer of 1933 Joseph P. Kennedy and his wife accompanied the younger Roosevelts to England. When he returned, Kennedy owned the United States franchise for Haig & Haig, Ltd., John Dewar and Sons, and Gordon's Dry Gin Company Ltd.

There were reports that Jimmy had hoped for a 25 percent partnership in the business and was dissuaded by Kennedy, who told him, "You can't do that, it would embarrass your father." The reports were dismissed later by Kennedy.

When Prohibition ended, Kennedy's newly formed Somerset Importers was able to meet the supply from already well-stocked warehouses. In 1946 Kennedy sold Somerset for a reported $8 million after an original investment of about $100,000.

[10] Kennedy had not lived in Boston since 1926, when he moved his family to Riverdale, New York, asserting that Boston was "no place to bring up Catholic children."

Chapter 3

[1] An attack of terns at the Kennedy estate that summer prompted Honey Fitz to lodge a vigorous protest with the Barnstable police. It had become necessary for him to don a peach basket before going to the beach adjoining the Kennedy house.

Because terns are protected by law, the police informed him that they had no authority and referred him to the Board of Selectmen, who, having no jurisdiction over the birds, suggested that a conservation officer be summoned. He in turn decided that the birds, protected by Federal law, fell more properly in the jurisdiction of the Federal Game warden in Boston.

Explaining that the birds' tendency to dart at human heads was "characteristic of their customs in mating season," the Warden was able to disperse the terns by firing a round of blank cartridges.

[2] Jack wrote from Harvard that, "while the speech seemed unpopular with Jews, etc. [it] was considered to be very good by everyone who wasn't bitterly anti-fascist."

[3] Chamberlain showed an advance copy of the speech with which he would declare war in the House of Commons to his good friend Ambassador Kennedy, who was moved to tears by the words, "Everything that I have worked for, everything I have hoped for, everything I have believed in during my public life has crashed into ruins."

[4] Although his father supported Roosevelt, Joe, Jr., was unalterably opposed to a third term. At the convention he cast one of the 12½ votes Massachusetts gave to James A. Farley. When the delegation was polled on the floor, Joe told the convention, "I am pledged to Farley and I am voting for Farley." Despite enormous pressure, Joe refused to change his vote. When his father was approached to use his influence on his son, Kennedy, Sr., said, "I wouldn't think of telling him what to do."

Chapter 4

[1] Roosevelt never saw Kennedy's telegram. When House Majority Leader John W. McCormack informed him that Roosevelt had expressed surprise that he had not volunteered, Kennedy immediately wrote a letter to the President. It was not until March 7 that an answer was forthcoming suggesting a connection with the huge wartime shipbuilding program then being launched. Kennedy's past experience with the Maritime Commission and, particularly with the Fore Shipbuilding Yard at Quincy, gave him superb credentials for such a post, and Roosevelt suggested that he get in touch with Rear Admiral Emory S. Land, a former colleague on the Commission.

But no specific job offer was forthcoming. There was bitter opposition to any Kennedy appointment within Roosevelt's administration. The Boston *Herald* blamed a "New Deal clique" among the President's advisers for opposition to any Kennedy appointment.

[2] In *As We Remember Joe*, Kathleen said of her brother: "Never did anyone have such a pillar of strength as I had in Joe during those difficult days before my marriage. From the beginning he gave me wise, helpful advice. When he felt I had made up my mind, he stood by me always. He constantly reassured me and gave me renewed confidence in my own decision . . . He could not have been more helpful and in every way he was the perfect brother doing, ac-

cording to his own light, the best for his sister with the hope that in the end it would be the best for the family. How right he was!"

PART TWO–CHAPTER 5

[1] In 1950 a meeting of Cape Cod realtors was addressed by the owner of the Yankee Traveler, a new motel in neighboring Plymouth, who extolled the advantages of motel operation, pointing out to the members of his unconvinced audience that the motel's success in the West and Southwest could be duplicated in the Northeast as well. Although the realtors listened politely, the consensus was doubt that the "fad" would "ever catch on in New England."

[2] Downey had his own fifteen-minute television show in the early network days when *Studio One* and *Roller Derby* dominated the 12½-inch screen. Once, when vacationing at Squaw Island in 1951, he admitted that he spent most of his time swimming, walking on the beach and "going down to talk to Jack Kennedy."

"Now there's a bright boy! We spend a lot of time talking together. Most of the time I just listen to the kid."

As a participant in the election watch at Bobby Kennedy's communication center in November of 1960, Downey saw his early estimate proved correct. His Squaw Island home would later provide a temporary haven for the "kid," who would occupy it as President of the United States.

[3] Curley did not endorse his secretary's candidacy, however. In a clever use of the Chinese-checkers rules by which the old pros played Boston politics, Honey Fitz successfully blocked any potential opposition to his grandson's candidacy by coming out in support of Curley's campaign for mayor. It was the only contribution the old man was allowed to make to his grandson's campaign. Joseph P. Kennedy prevented him from taking an active part in the campaign and told Jack, "You wouldn't last three hours with Honey calling the signals."

[4] Although this statement may have reflected the contempt Jack Kennedy felt for the "old blarney" school in which most Boston "pols" had matriculated, the hosts of former schoolmates, navy colleagues and friends who had rallied to his support during the campaign were not the only factor contributing to his success. Joseph P. Kennedy, back in the Boston swing of things after self-imposed exile, "testifying at State House Ways and Means Committee hearings on behalf of a proposed state chamber of commerce and being mentioned as possible Undersecretary of the Navy," was, in effect, managing his son's campaign. He brought into it such practiced political hands as Dave Powers and Francis X. Morrissey, a former secretary to Governor Maurice Tobin, who was given the honorary title of "campaign manager." The first twelve signatures on Kennedy's nomination papers were those of Morrissey's family and relatives. There was also his father's cousin, hard-bitten Joe Kane, who had tutored Jack Kennedy in his own brand of political pragmatism and whose motto was: "Politics is like war: to win, three things are necessary. The first is money, the second is money and the third is money."

[5] That August, John F. Kennedy presented a check for $650,000 to Archbishop Richard Cushing in the name of the Kennedy family, the largest contribution in the history of the Boston Archdiocese. Given toward the cost of a $2 million Joseph P. Kennedy, Jr., Memorial Hospital in Brighton for underprivileged and mentally retarded children, the gift marked the start of annual

announcements of such bequests on the succeeding anniversaries of the death of Joseph P. Kennedy, Jr.

In 1947 Representative John F. Kennedy announced gifts totaling $250,000 at a Veterans of Foreign Wars breakfast in Boston: Catholic Auxiliary Bishop John J. Wright accepted for Archbishop Cushing $100,000 for a parochial school for retarded children and $50,000 for Christopher Columbus Catholic Center in Boston's North End. A check for $50,000 each went to Boston Children's Hospital and Associated Jewish Philanthropies.

In 1949 Cape Cod Hospital was listed among the recipients of bequests totaling $500,000 made by the Joseph P. Kennedy, Jr., Foundation, which brought to $1.5 million the amount the Foundation had disbursed since its establishment.

The check for $15,600 was presented to the Cape Cod Hospital building fund by Edward "Ted" Kennedy on the fifth anniversary of his brother's death. The gift had been made when Joseph P. Kennedy found the hospital's fund was only $15,600 short of its first million.

[6] There was a time when the "swallow" was a very rare bird on Cape Cod indeed, most particularly in winter. By 1850 the first small Catholic society had been organized in Hyannis, to the accompaniment of the headline "Horrors!" in a contemporary weekly journal.

By 1874 the first Catholic church had been built. Eight years later a new parish was established, encompassing Hyannis, Yarmouth, Falmouth, Woods Hole and Nantucket. The Reverend Cornelius McSwiney, the first parish pastor, labored hard in this large and sparsely settled vineyard for some twenty years in the face of "unpropitious elements."

By 1938 most of the "unpropitious elements" had been propitiated to the extent that the observances of Father Downing's 25th year as pastor in Hyannis and his 50th year in the priesthood, on his 75th birthday, were the occasion for a civic testimonial.

It was not until July 1949 that Cape Cod Jews were able to conduct their first services in a synagogue after more than fifteen years of ceremonies in private homes and rented halls. On that happy dedication day, a spokesman described the fortunate solution of a ticklish problem presented by the building's architecture: "It's Jewish, it's Cape Coddish, and it's beautiful!"

[7] On the wall above a small fount of holy water is a scratched brass plate that reads:

The Main Altar
presented by
Mr. and Mrs. Joseph P. Kennedy
in Memory of their Son
Lt. Joseph Patrick Kennedy, Jr. U.S.N.R.
Killed in Action
Aug. 12, 1944.

CHAPTER 6

[1] The following week the Cape Cod *Standard-Times* published an editorial entitled, "Talking Out of Turn":

Senator McCarthy of Wisconsin is not a man to yield the front pages easily. It will take more than a war in Korea to induce him to abandon the course he set out upon last February.

Although he has updated his charges by tying them into the Korean affair, he still is accusing the same persons of the same things. And he still has failed to produce proof.

No fair individual would proclaim flatly that there is no reason at all to inquire into the government's previous course of action in Asia. There may well be evidence of colossal error, if not outright subversion.

But when a war is being fought the time for such investigation is after a decision has been reached. Unity is the need of this hour, as some of McCarthy's GOP colleagues have recognized in announcing their intention to look into delays in South Korean arms shipments only when the fighting is over.

McCarthy's methods were reckless from the start. Both his methods and his purpose seem wholly out of key with the critical times we have now entered upon.

[2] Kennedy did, eventually, have that responsibility in 1961 while he was President. According to Theodore Sorensen's account: "Kennedy never made a final negative decision on troops. In typical Kennedy fashion, he made it difficult for any of the pro-intervention advocates to charge him privately with weakness. He ordered the departments to be prepared for the introduction of combat troops, should they prove to be necessary. He steadily expanded the size of the military assistance mission (2,000 at the end of 1961, 15,500 at the end of 1963) by sending in combat support units, air combat and helicopter teams, still more military advisers and instructors and 600 of the green-hatted Special Forces to train and lead the South Vietnamese in anti-Guerilla tactics."

[3] "If only candidates recognized how important good manners are," a Falmouth committeewoman said after a Republican candidate for Congress had lost the sympathy of his listeners by rudely dispensing with an inane question asked by a member of his audience. "Why Jack Kennedy wins more votes just because he's always polite and pleasant, whatever the circumstances, than by his position on issues."

[4] During his senatorial campaign in 1964, Bobby Kennedy and his mother very nearly duplicated this colloquy. Rose Kennedy admitted to the audience that she used to spank her son regularly with a ruler, and Bobby conceded that his mother's advocacy of his candidacy had convinced an initially laggard party official in Syracuse. Not so gallant as his brother, Bobby teased, "She used to campaign for Grover Cleveland." And, while his mother took evident umbrage, he added, as the audience roared: "Or was it Abraham Lincoln? I know it was sometime during the last half of the nineteenth century."

[5] In derogating the teas, Henry Cabot Lodge had overlooked their true focus: the most attractive exposure of a candidate possible, in surroundings that pretended to be social occasions. Lodge had, as well, seriously miscalculated their effects.

"My husband was a member of the local Democratic club," a participant in the New Bedford reception recalled. "But I was never very interested in politics and neither was he. The club gave him an excuse to play cards and drink beer. And once a year there was a clambake and a dance. I went to the reception," she said. "It was really wonderful and exciting. I signed one of those little cards. About a week later I got a call from Kennedy's headquarters. I could only work one night a week, but they seemed glad to have me. I stuffed envelopes mostly, but I enjoyed it. It was the first time I'd ever had anything to do with a political campaign. I even made a few telephone calls on Election Day," she added, laughing. "My husband didn't know what had come over me."

[6] Brewer later announced that his newspaper had not carried an advertisement sponsored by Lodge supporters because "there were a number of obvious misstatements which we asked to be corrected before it was run. We received a categorical order to run the ad as it was, so we refused it."

[7] Brewer did, of course, better than that. In 1958 former Boston publisher John Fox testified before a House Influencing Investigating Subcommittee that he had concluded that Lodge was "soft on Communism after talking with Basil Brewer" and, that, as Lodge had refused to discuss the matter when he raised it later, Fox had shifted his allegiance to Kennedy during the last weeks of the campaign.

"I did use my influence to get the *Post* to oppose Lodge and support Kennedy in 1952, not because of Lodge's being soft on Communism, though," Brewer admitted, commenting on Fox's testimony. "I had proof that he wasn't. My emphasis with Fox was that Lodge had no firm convictions which he was willing to support on any issue, that his approach was purely political based always on what he thought best for Lodge."

The major issue of controversy and investigation in 1958, however, was a $500,000 loan made by Joseph P. Kennedy to Fox after his newspaper endorsement. Fox testified that the former ambassador was in his office having a drink when he broke the news of his paper's support for his son. "After that we talked about a loan," Fox said, admitting that he had obtained the money in December 1952.

Joseph P. Kennedy rebutted Fox's story in a statement from his New York office:

> It should be clear from Mr. Fox's testimony that no loan was ever discussed or contemplated at the time the Boston *Post* endorsed the Democratic nominee for the Senate in 1952. That this endorsement which followed a long *Post* history of endorsing Democratic candidates was made without the prior knowledge of any members of the Kennedy family.
>
> The loan as mentioned was made after the election as a purely commercial transaction for 60 days only, with full collateral, at full interest and was repaid on time, and was simply one of the many commercial transactions in which this office has participated.

[8] Soon after the war, when he had recovered from his injuries, Kennedy toured the war zones, including Japan, where he tried unsuccessfully to find the man who had commanded the destroyer that had rammed his PT boat.

"I regret very much that I missed the opportunity of meeting you during your last visit to Japan," said the Japanese commander's letter, which had been prompted by an article in *Time* that August dealing with Kennedy's campaign and mentioning his naval experiences. "As I was living in Fukushima Prefecture, northern part of Japan, I could not make contact with you during your brief stay in Tokyo."

The letter concluded, "I take this opportunity to pay my profound respect to your daring and courageous action in this battle and also to congratulate you upon your miraculous escape under the circumstances."

CHAPTER 7

[1] Ironically enough, the "eased blue-law bill" was signed into law by Lieutenant Governor Edward F. McLaughlin, Jr. (in the absence of Governor Volpe), at his summer home in West Hyannis Port, a modest, middle-class cluster of nondescript but pleasant cottages that bore no similarity to *the* Hyannis Port.

The bill, bitterly disputed in both houses of the legislature during long weeks of debate, repealed laws that went back to the Revolution.

Of most interest to Cape businessmen were provisions that permitted owners of gift shops and antique dealers to be open for business on Sundays and holidays and allowed the showing on Sunday of real estate for sale or rental.

[2] In June 1954, buyers of real estate were admonished by a local practitioner that "big business is seldom wrong." In a pitch reminiscent of the 1920s boom, the broker added, "Prices may seem high today, but in a few short years, real estate—the backbone of the nation—will be much higher."

Under a banner headline reading: "Don't Sell America Short—She Will Always Be Triumphant," a waterfront cottage of six rooms, with all modern improvements and a two-car garage was offered for $14,000, with "easy terms." (It was exactly what was meant by an editorial in *Cape Cod Magazine* of June 1920, headed "Don't Profiteer": "The temptation to take advantage of an opportunity to obtain excessive prices is great at the present time. There seems to be no end to the upward trend of prices and nothing but a man's conscience stands in the way of his becoming a 'profiteer.' ")

[3] Vacationing at Wellfleet that August, Welsh went into seclusion after a reported threat against his life resulted in a search by Cape police of all incoming buses and trains for a man described on interstate police teletypes as being en route from Washington to kill him. Several years later Welsh purchased a house on Wychmere Harbor in Harwich Port and converted a fishbarn on the property into a studio for his series of television appearances.

[4] Joseph P. Kennedy was received by Pope Pius XII in one of the longest private audiences granted since the Pope's critical illness the previous December. Kennedy later described the audience:

I had not seen the holy father for three or four years and I was much impressed by his physical condition. He looked terrifically well. We talked about conditions in the United States. He expressed his great love for America and talked with pleasure of the trip he made there before he became Pope.

Kennedy was accorded a distinction usually reserved for leading prelates and heads of state when the Pope permitted photographs to be taken of them together—before Kennedy conferred with the Vatican's secretary of state for extraordinary ecclesiastical affairs.

[5] Alas, this plan did not work. Through some inexplicable and rare lapse in Kennedy public relations, neither representatives of the *Patriot* nor Cape correspondents of Boston newspapers were notified when the check was passed to the Barnstable selectmen's hands at 5:00 P.M. on a quiet Sunday afternoon in early October.

It was, in the *Patriot*'s words, "a new high—or low—in our journalistic experience. Consequently the *Patriot*, picture-wise, was 'scooped' on an event which we had known about for a year. And the representatives of the Boston morning papers likewise were beaten . . . in releasing news they had known about for months."

The Cape Cod *Standard-Times* had a cameraman and a reporter on hand.
[6] Committeewoman Monica Murphy of Fall River defended Kennedy from such charges: "Senator Kennedy did interview me, but there was never any mention or implication of gifts. These are very harsh words from Mr. Burke. Kennedy is the very highest type person and a credit to the Democratic party in Massachusetts." In 1958 John F. Kennedy ran unopposed in the Democratic primary.
[7] Ribicoff further advanced Kennedy's vice-presidential candidacy three weeks later at the annual Governors' Conference in Atlantic City. Disclosing that he had discussed the matter with James Finnegan, Stevenson's campaign manager, but had obtained no commitment, Ribicoff pointed out, however, that both Finnegan and Adlai Stevenson "had reacted favorably. Both have a high regard for Senator Kennedy," Ribicoff said at a press conference. "Kennedy would be a definite asset to Stevenson. Like Stevenson he is a middle of the road man and that type reflects the basic temper of the country at this time."

At the same conference, Governor Christian A. Herter of Massachusetts conceded that Kennedy "might possibly" carry the state for the Democratic ticket in November if he were the vice-presidential candidate. "Kennedy certainly would strengthen the Democratic ticket in Massachusetts," Herter said, and was likely to help the ticket in Rhode Island as well. A dissenting voice, however, was that of Raymond Carr of Oklahoma, chairman of New York Governor Averell Harriman's campaign, who said that Kennedy would attract few Midwestern voters "because he voted for Eisenhower's farm program."
[8] At the death of Marie Daly, widow of J. J. Daly, a close friend of the Kennedy family and President of the Regal Shoe Company of Abington, the house had been appraised by James Woodward at "around $50,000." An agent representing Jack Kennedy inspected the house prior to the purchase. During the winter of 1962, Woodward again appraised the house, this time for "around $80,000," as rumors spread that the property would be sold to Eunice and Sargent Shriver.
[9] *Mayflower II* soon left Provincetown's harbor for Plymouth, following the route of the original *Mayflower*, but the new ship had the benefit of a tow around Long Point by a coast-guard motorized lifeboat. Rounding the point, the ship hoisted sails in a favorable wind and was escorted by the tug *Yankton* across Cape Cod Bay to Plymouth's harbor and celebration festivities there led by Vice-President Richard Nixon.
[10] Robert Kennedy, who had served in this capacity under the watchful eyes of his father in the first campaign of 1952, was occupied with the Hoffa hearings in Washington; the Senate Investigations Committee, of which he was chief counsel, had called the leader of the Teamsters' Union to testify about alleged gangland extortion schemes involving the union.
[11] Editorially the *Patriot* said: "The Kennedy-Ives Bill and its fate are now history. It is not, of course, proper to speak ill of the dead, but the most fitting epitaph we have seen on this subject has come from the pen of Steven B. Derounian, a Republican Congressman from Long Island. Said he:
'I want to make sure, as one who voted against the bill, that people know

what little protection the Kennedy bill gave the working man. Supposedly a civil rights bill—it contained no prohibition against racketeer picketing; did not provide for an honest count of the ballots . . . did not deal with secondary boycotts; subjected employers to a $10,000 fine and one year's imprisonment if they spent over $5,000 on their employees; and made it a crime for employers to give employees a raise in pay or other benefits when such action coincided with union attempts to organize; did not require that union members be allowed to see financial or other records of the union; did not impose fiduciary responsibilities on union officials with regard to the funds and property of the membership; did not empower union members to go to court to sue for violation of trust by union officials charged with the care, custody and use of union funds and property; did not carry out the recommendations of the McClellan committee and did not carry out the recommendations of the President and Secretary of Labor (both opposed the bill).'

"The fact that the Kennedy-Ives bill was defeated shows that a majority of legislators felt the same way as Mr. Derounian. Next year, they'll have a chance to show us what they mean by a real labor reform bill. We'll be looking forward to it."

[12] The Editor

Barnstable *Patriot*

Hyannis, Mass.

Dear Sir:

An editorial on labor reform legislation which appears in your newspaper recently has been called to my attention. In order that you and your readers may be fully informed about the facts concerning this legislation, I am taking the liberty of addressing this letter to you so that there may be no misconceptions about the matter.

First of all I should like to remind you that it was a Democratically-controlled Senate which established the McClellan Investigating Committee whose work has been conducted under the leadership of the able senior Senator from Arkansas, Mr. McClellan. In March of 1957, the Committee made its first interim report which included five legislative recommendations. Two days before this report was made a Subcommittee of the Senate Committee on Labor and Public Welfare, under my chairmanship, began hearings on labor reform legislation having already reported a bill to regulate pension and welfare plans. This legislative Subcommittee continued its hearings through the month of May and reported a bill to the Senate which covered each of the recommendations by the McClellan Committee. The bill was finally passed with only one dissenting vote on June 17th. The bill had the support of interested and informed members of both sides of the aisle including Senator McClellan and Senator Knowland, who, as the Senate debate closed said: ". . . the workers will be the ones who will suffer if Congress does not finally act on legislation of this sort at this session." After passage by the Senate, the bill was referred to the House where it was taken up and defeated in the closing days of the session. Despite the fact that both Democratic and Republican House members recognized in the bill a major step forward in labor reform, over four fifths of the Republican members of that body rejected the bill, while more than two thirds of the Democrats voted for it.

Under the circumstances outlined above, it is difficult indeed to understand how you could ascribe the failure of labor reform legislation in the 85th Congress to the lack of activity by the Democratic members of Congress.

With respect to the merits of the bill itself, I can only conclude that you have not had an opportunity to examine the text of the bill. If passed, the bill would have required detailed reporting of all union financial transactions to the government, the public, and union members; it required full reports by union officers on personal conflict of interest transactions; it gave the Secretary of Labor broad investigatory powers; it provided criminal sanctions for embezzling of union funds, failure to make reports, false entry in books or destruction of union records; it prohibited loans by employees to unions or union officers and established the right of union members to sue for recovery of embezzled or misappropriated funds.

The bill covered all but two of the recommendations made by the President in his labor message to congress last February. It went beyond the Administration's recommendations by providing effective means to regular trusteeships which have been a notorious means for maintaining control of trade unions by racketeers. The bill also provided for a secret ballot of all union elections and a real opportunity to nominate candidates for union office; it forbade the use of union funds to finance the campaign of any union officers; it provided the machinery by which the Secretary of Labor through the courts, could correct any impropriety in union elections.

Other provisions of the bill prohibited extortion, picketing and made applicable to such picketing the mandatory injunction provisions of the Taft-Hartley Act. The bill also forbade fictitious payment for unloading cargo from interstate carriers. The Senate-passed bill provided stiff criminal penalties for the extension or acceptances of bribes to influence the right of workers in collective bargaining situations.

This brief enumeration of some of the provisions of the bill which I had the honor to co-sponsor with my Republican colleague from New York, Senator Ives, should give a clear indication that the measure rejected by the House Republicans was a major step forward in correcting some of the abuses disclosed in the course of the McClellan hearings. Many respected Republican members of the House voted for the measure recognizing in it a solid piece of legislation. Senator Ives, commenting on the House action said, ". . . my party played blind, partisan politics with the bill." I trust that this discussion of the labor reform bill will serve to clarify any questions which may have arisen in the minds of your readers as a result of your editorial.

Sincerely,

John F. Kennedy

[13] Kennedy ran far ahead of the Democratic ticket in all Cape towns. He carried Falmouth, Bourne, Mashpee, Sandwich, Truro, Wellfleet, Yarmouth and Provincetown; Celeste took Brewster, Chatham, Dennis, Eastham, Harwich and Orleans.

Most important, Kennedy carried Barnstable. In Precinct 3, which takes in Hyannis Port and Hyannis, Kennedy won 767 votes to Celeste's 314. Kennedy captured 59 percent of the votes cast, astonishing for a Democrat.

PART THREE—CHAPTER 8

[1] Advertised as a "working meeting" to which the press was not invited, it was attended by selectmen and other town officials to discuss the revised Kennedy-Saltonstall bill, which contained final modifications and maximums that the Park Service could take if the park was established: "If we must have a National Seashore Park," a spokesman announced, "here is the maximum

area each town can allow to be taken and still maintain the integrity of the town."

2 The Chamber's position appeared to be somewhat at odds with its usual philosophy, to paraphrase Honey Fitz, of "a busier, better Cape Cod." Not the least of the considerations contributing to the Chamber's anxiety about the park was its recreational aspects, facilities that could only mean "campers" —a notoriously thrifty group who bring not only their own accommodations with them but often their own food as well. Although Thoreau's values, the simpler outdoor life and uncluttered enjoyment of the beauties of nature, might have sufficed in the 1850s, they could hardly support the Cape's hard-driving summer economy. Natives shuddered at the prospect of an invasion of more than 2 million knapsacked "nonpaying" guests to clutter the highways and beaches and decried the advent of so large a number of "bohemians"—a word that, on Cape Cod, often meant nothing more than "tourists without money." The Chamber, having embarked on a signally successful campaign to persuade the retired to come to Cape Cod was, in 1960, less prone to put all its eggs in the summer-season basket, as it had done so eagerly in the past.

3 Expressing himself as "satisfied" to have Kennedy in full control of the Massachusetts Democratic State Committee—"although such committees normally were controlled by governors"—Furcolo pointed out the situation was different that year and had been for the past three years because of Jack Kennedy's presidential candidacy: "Under those conditions, the machinery of the party should be more responsive to the Senator, and that is done with my complete approval and satisfaction." Not all State politicians were as complaisant as Furcolo, however. The Jefferson-Jackson Committee, the state Democratic Party's major fund-raising branch, was under attack for devoting all its energies to Kennedy's campaign while largely ignoring recent state senate elections in which Democrats had been defeated. It was accused of being dominated by a "personality cult of Kennedyism."

4 Other members of the Kennedy family had already begun the cross-country trek. Bobby was already in Los Angeles; Patricia, married to actor Peter Lawford, lived in nearby Santa Monica; Ted and Sargent Shriver had left three days before, Joseph P. Kennedy was at Lake Tahoe, and the candidate's mother was expected the day before the candidate's arrival. Eunice and Jean planned to leave the day after Kennedy's departure, traveling with Ethel, Joan and a score of children.

5 Arriving in Paris on her way to the French Riviera with her husband and their neice, Ann Gargan, Rose Kennedy explained her husband's refusal to comment on his son's nomination by explaining in French, "My husband has been in politics himself, so he feels it is better not to comment." Asked if her son would win the election, she replied: "Certainly. I have no doubt about it. He will win."

Not even the New Bedford *Standard-Times* could wrest a comment from Joseph P. Kennedy during the convention, although a reporter was granted admittance through the big iron gates of the luxurious Marion Davies mansion, where police had relayed his name via a temporary intercom system to someone in the main house for clearance.

Dressed in shorts and sport shirt, Joseph P. Kennedy had warmly greeted the newsman but would make no comment for publication on his son's nomination, except to express his gratification that his son's first-ballot total had exceeded his own expectations.

6 One of the more spectacular and well-advertised attractions Provincetown had

provided in years was Norman Mailer's own trial for drunkenness and rude and disorderly conduct in June 1960, the aftermath of a melée that occurred when Mailer hailed a police car by shouting "Taxi! Taxi!" as he left a local bar.

A capacity audience—"the gaudiest and most bizarre assemblage ever gathered," according to local accounts—included men in flowered bathing trunks, chic society women and a disheveled artist sketching the proceedings from a second-row seat.

Mailer, appearing "disarmingly conventional" in a neatly pressed blue suit, acted as his own counsel and provided good copy cross-examining the unintellectual police officers who had arrested him.

He was charged with creating a minor skirmish on Commercial Street when police escorted him to a squad car on a drunk charge; Mailer had received a gash across the back of his head that required thirteen stitches while "resisting arrest."

Protesting that four drinks were not enough to make a man of his capacity intoxicated, Mailer readily admitted: "I was a bit coy when baiting the police, but those officers have seen too much television. They thought I was a dangerous beatnik."

The Court proceedings were frequently interrupted by applause on Mailer's behalf; one spectator was ejected for smoking. "This is not a circus," the presiding judge said after listening to arguments from both sides. He found Mailer guilty of the drunk charge but filed it and dismissed the disorderly complaint, blaming police for being too "thin-skinned"; he announced that positive corrective action would need to be taken if police misused their powers in the future. Mailer left the courtroom in triumph and made the front page of the New York *Post*.

[7] In August 1961, Jacqueline Kennedy made her first visit to Provincetown, appearing at a number of art galleries in a whirlwind tour that included dinner at the Flagship Restaurant and a visit to the Walter P. Chrysler Art Museum. She attended a production of *Mrs. Warren's Profession* at Provincetown's famed playhouse on the wharf and left, assisted by the company, by way of the stage to a waiting car, in order to avoid a large crowd assembled in front of the theater to glimpse her exit.

[8] Mayor Robert Wagner arrived at Hyannis Airport somewhat earlier than expected the following Monday morning and had to wait for Bobby to pick him up for a two-hour conference that Jack Kennedy announced was "extremely helpful."

"I have always considered New York and California as anchors to our success in the November election," Kennedy said.

Wagner was accompanied back to New York by Bobby Kennedy, dispatched to weld warring Democratic factions into a machine to support his brother's candidacy.

("It's time the junior Senator from Massachusetts got off his yacht at Hyannis Port and spoke for himself," Republican National Chairman Thruston Morton announced in Washington. "Kennedy should carry the presidential campaign ball himself instead of letting his brother do all the work.")

[9] During Kennedy's long postoperation convalescence, his wife had encouraged him to try his hand at painting. One of his pictures, a Riviera waterfront scene, hung in the dining room of his Hyannis Port house. The picture Kennedy referred to at his press conference was a water color done of the village's News Store. Jacqueline also received a wristwatch.

[10] Although he was defeated at the polls in the November election, Loveless was not offered the Cabinet post of Secretary of Agriculture; it was given instead to Minnesota's Governor Orville Freeman, who, during the 1956 Democratic convention, had found Kennedy's vice-presidential candidacy "unacceptable" because he had frequently supported Eisenhower's farm legislation.

[11] Noticeably missing from the thousands of words that Kennedy's press headquarters had released for the nation's newspapers was the name of Foster Furcolo, candidate for the Democratic senatorial nomination to oppose Leverett Saltonstall in the November election.

After losing the nomination to Springfield's Mayor Thomas J. O'Connor, Jr., in the September primary, Furcolo accurately guessed that his political career was over. Asked if he would accept an appointment if Kennedy was elected, Furcolo said: "I don't want to jinx Kennedy by saying what I will or will not do if he is elected." He remarked, however, that he didn't expect Kennedy to appoint many from Massachusetts if he were elected president.

CHAPTER 9

[1] Kennedy had sent his regrets, citing the press of Senate business and the expected vote on his medical-care-for-the-aged bill, offering instead to address the convention by special telephone hookup, an arrangement that was "wholly unacceptable" to officials angered that Kennedy had "kept them on the hook so long before saying if he would or would not show up." Kennedy did two days later.

[2] Eisenhower's telegram referred

to my initial telegram to you sent a few hours ago. I would like you to know that I stand ready to meet with you at any mutually convenient time to consider problems of continuity of government and orderly transfer of executive responsibility on January 20 from my administration to yours.

In the meantime or even in lieu thereof, in order to facilitate and prepare for this transfer, I would be happy to have one of your assistants meet with my principal staff assistant, Wilton B. Persons, to whom I am assigning coordinating responsibility. He will be prepared to make arrangements by which representatives designated by you could meet with present heads of executive departments.

Meetings of this kind over the coming weeks with the director of the Bureau of the Budget, might for example, be important in providing information to you concerning the budget now in preparation. In addition, the Secretary of State will be prepared for meetings to provide information on foreign policy activities on which there will be a special need for continuity until you shall have opportunity, after inauguration, to arrange these matters to your satisfaction.

Signed, Dwight D. Eisenhower.

[3] Kennedy addressed his reply to Khrushchev, Chairman of the Council of Ministers of the USSR: "I am most appreciative of your courtesy in sending me a message of congratulations. The achievement of a just and lasting peace will remain a fundamental goal of this nation, and a major task of its president. I am most pleased to have your good wishes at this time."

[4] I am grateful for your most recent wire and your willingness to meet and work with me in order to effect an orderly transfer of executive responsibility. I am asking Mr. Clark Clifford of Washington to meet with

General Wilton B. Persons regarding all meetings between present heads
of executive departments and representatives of the next administration.
I look forward to meeting with you and again express my appreciation
for your co-operation.

5 If Furcolo was entertaining any ideas of appointing himself to the Senate
seat that had twice eluded him, he was bound for disappointment; after his
"conference" with Kennedy, the unexpired term was given to Benjamin Smith,
an old Kennedy friend and campaign aide, to be kept "warm," it was said, for
either Bobby or Ted.

6 Denying statements made at the convention by supporters of Lyndon Johnson's candidacy, who had reported that Kennedy suffered from Addison's disease and "owed his life to cortisone," Robert Kennedy claimed: "These are
desperation tactics employed by those who are trying unsuccessfully to stop
my brother's nomination. These charges," he said, "show how really desperate
they are."

The charges had grown out of Truman's suggestion that Kennedy wasn't
"mature" enough for the presidency. In responding, Kennedy had stressed
the need for a young man of "strength, health and vigor" in the White House.
Then Johnson's partisans had countered with their attack, interpreting Kennedy's statement as an indirect allusion to Johnson's heart attack in 1955.

Doctors had reported Kennedy's health excellent. Salinger, issuing the statement quoting the doctors, said that the adrenal condition "might well have
arisen out of his war-time experience of shock and continued malaria." As few
prudent politicians would care to criticize a disabled veteran, the controversy
abruptly came to an end.

7 Remarking on the motives that had prompted such a subscription, a resident
admitted, "We wanted to be sure that the place didn't fall into the hands of
the wrong people, and the only way we had of guaranteeing that some motel-
builder or other undesirables wouldn't take over the Gables was to buy the
property ourselves."

AFTERWORD

1 PLEASE MR. PRESIDENT

While the Kennedys frolic each weekend in Lewis Bay and other waters,
and the press have a heydey, any of the public who also enjoy their water
sports are making sputtering noises not unlike that of a badly-tuned motor.
Every precaution has been taken to protect the President and his relatives
and friends from the public, but what precautions have been taken to
protect John Doe and his friends and relatives from the zestful Kennedys?
There are laws pertaining to water sports—motor boat speeds in certain
areas, etc.—and there are gentlemen's agreements about not cutting into
the course of a boat race or crossing the bow of another boat.

During a cruise to the Islands on a recent weekend the *Patrick J.* was
reported to be most "ungentlemanly" about "those little courtesies" and
irked one young sailor to the point of yelling "Damn you!" before he
realized whom he was addressing.

While the Kennedys are certainly entitled to their fun, we feel that the
laws of safety and courtesy should apply to everyone. Being President doesn't
make one an exception to this."

—Editorial, Barnstable *Patriot*
July 26, 1962